P.R.I.S.M

P.R.I.S.M

PRIMAL

RELIGIOUS

INSTRUCTION

SERVING

MANKIND

M.B.O OWOLOWO

SCOPE MEDIA GROUP

SCOPE MEDIA GROUP

ISBN-978-1-8384790-0-8

GRATITUDE
GOD and Family

I am grateful to ALLAH – The Creator, for creating me, and granting me the worthiness of being one of His creations.

Family:

My mother F.A Owolowo (FAO)

And

My father M.B.O Owolowo (MBO)

[March 24, 1931 – June 25, 1996]

My wife and children

My brothers and their families

My friends who have become family

Dedicated to Humanity

CONTENTS

PREFACE

Allah is the Light of the heavens and the earth. His light is like a niche in which there is a lamp, the lamp is in a crystal, the crystal is like a shining star, lit from ˹the oil of˺ a blessed olive tree, ˹located˺ neither to the east nor the west, whose oil would almost glow, even without being touched by fire. Light upon light! Allah guides whoever He wills to His light. And Allah sets forth parables for humanity. For Allah has ˹perfect˺ knowledge of all things– Quran 24:35

PRISM can be appreciated as divine light that permeates the soul and manifests as resplendent enlightenment – spiritual and intellectual. The purpose of this book is to shed some light – enlightenment via critical cerebral engagement, with rationalism at the core of postulations. This is a compendious narrative not encumbered by distractive problemitization, intellectual convolution or entanglement in academic jargon. A research-based explication of concepts; deconstructed for intelligible consumption. This discourse employs a multidisciplinary and rational approach to God, religion and a culmination in the message of Islam.

My personal journey involved a ratiocinative preoccupation with trying to comprehend human existence. By logical deduction, if basic things produced by human beings can have some sort of manual, guideline or set of instructions on operability, then what about something as advanced as man living in an extraordinarily complex world. Also, I pondered on the origin of morality and how human beings initially determined the difference between right and wrong – surely, there must be a criterion. How can man make such decisions without divine guidance?

Citing mankind's earliest documented murder – fratricide, as an example, how did Cain know Abel's murder was a wrong act? Or how did Cain know he had to bury his brother's corpse? Some may argue that it was instinctive and certain scientists may attempt to explain the situation as nature, but that is just an excuse to avoid confronting matters of God.

In confronting such matters, the question should concentrate on, who put that instinct there? I consider such a proclivity as divinely inspired – the God instinct and consider such divine guidance as religious instruction. For instance, the Quran states Cain was guided: "God sent a raven to scratch up the ground and show him how to cover his brother's corpse".

Such expositions ignited curiosity and spurred my interest in God. In my attempt to decipher the concept of God, I was exposed to many religions making similar claims and this led me to comparative religious studies about three decades ago. I had been fascinated by the existence of various religious texts, and I made it a duty to study and acquire some sacred texts. In my quest for enlightenment, I committed decades of my life to analysing scriptural texts critically and contextually, via historical, scientific and linguistic perspectives. Though my initial inquisition was to increase my knowledge base, it eventually became a passionate quest of conviction. During my enlightenment quest, I had fortuitous encounters with dedicated savants who had gone through the rigorous processes of religious sciences, particularly the selection criteria for religious universality. My inquisitive nature propelled me to do further individual research and analysis of world religions. Beyond the inquisition, my propulsion was necessitated by the need for a strong foundational conviction in whatever religion is eventually substantiated, through logical conclusion, as the primal belief system.

Due to my didactical approach to such matters, I have had decades of debates with people of various backgrounds – Christians, Jews, Muslims, atheists, agnostics, free-thinkers, and the irreligious.

Through my personal experience, I came to the realisation that logic, in all situations, supersedes illogicality and 'Truth' consistently evinces to defeat falsehood, in whatever manner or manifestation. Following a few inefficacious encounters and excogitative episodes, I decided, there is no point wasting my precious time, contending with people who were not ready to research, or unlearn and relearn. The primary objective of a debate should be knowledge acquisition or the discovery of truth, rather than the vacuity of eristical gusto. Consequently, I concluded, that it is an effort in futility, engaging people with preconceived notions, who are generally unwilling to accept facts, or ready to be imbued by the truths of any specific subject.

In view of these epiphanic realities, I decided to reserve my intellectual energies for productive causes and prefer channelling my zeal towards engaging those humble enough to admit some level of unknowing or nescience on the subject and were genuinely interested in being guided towards the assimilation of unbeknownst knowledge.

Erudition is crucial in having a full understanding of any subject matter. And, just as any subject matter, those who have done extensive research in a particular field are most qualified to instruct on the matter. For instance, if it is stated that not everyone is qualified to discuss certain matters, such a statement emanates from a pedagogical position. However, such a statement does not diminish the intellect or intellectual capacity of those not vast in that particular subject in any way, rather, the statement is underpinning that in a particular field, certain people have limitations. Citing my personal experience as an example, such instances of lacking the expertise, are applicable to me; as there are fields I am not professionally or academically qualified to extemporise or speak on extensively. In attempting to, I may end up ridiculing myself, because my knowledge may be pedestrian or even non-existent in that area. Howbeit, my limitation in a subject matter does not undermine my intellectual capabilities. The essence of the point is to establish that religion is a science and specialization, so when those knowledgeable in the subject edify, I pay attention and learn – I do not assume I know and miss an edification opportunity. Importantly, it must be emphasized that being interested in the study of religion, does not automatically translate to being religious. I have come across people who study religion and do not necessarily exude religiosity, but they are however, diligent in their research. There are people in academia who study religion as a science. Furthermore, it is pertinent to clarify that being religious and being interested in the study of religion does not necessarily equate to being religiously superior. This clarification is vital because the irreligious often present arguments of religious superiority, and attack people involved in religious matters on this basis. Using myself as an example, I am not better than anybody, not to mention being superior. I am just a knowledge seeker. However, my position is not generical, and does not discount the possibility of certain people, who, for reasons best known to them, feel superior to others because of their religious affinity or inclination. In such instances, the attitudes of those exhibiting a delusional superiority complex must not be generalized, but individually identified – possibly for their enlightenment in matters of religious discourse.

Certainly, scholarship is paramount, and I cannot overstate its importance. However, one does not need to be a scholar to be kind to others, and to enjoin good and forbid evil. Nonetheless, on certain matters, deference to highly trained scholars is pivotal. In this regard, I must categorically state, I am by no means whatsoever an 'Islamic scholar', neither would I refer to myself as such; for that would be hubristic and self-detrimental. Rather, I am but a humble student of scholarship – a researcher and constant seeker of knowledge and truth. And on that note, I apologise for any possible errors in my dissemination of knowledge. Admittedly, I am driven by my passion for knowledge and general love of humanity. I believe knowledge is a continuous stream and I intend to tap from that stream throughout my earthly existence.

Ideally, as our dynamic world evolves, so should our knowledge base, and by extension, our views about the world. I believe the pinnacle of knowledge-seeking should be preoccupied with the realities associated with the provenance and purpose of life.

> *The man who views the world at 50 the same as he did at 20 has wasted 30 years of his life.* – Muhammad Ali

PHILOSOPHICAL OUTLOOK

Knowing is a lifelong quest of learning and relearning, and there are many things known and unknown in our ever-evolving and dynamic world. The world is riddled with supernatural phenomena, unexplained mysteries, and uncertainties, and mankind has been grappling with issues such as, origin of life, purpose of life, death, and of course, the matter of God.

Over many centuries, philosophical perspectives about the existence of God have persisted. For instance, philosophy has been influenced by the works of various Western philosophers. In ancient Greek cosmology, the pre- Socratic Greek philosopher, Parmenides, argued the philosophical dictum – Nothing comes from nothing (*ex nihilo nihil fit*). After the post-Socratic era emerged Aristotle's Prime Mover, Neo-Platonic thoughts, theism and deism. Subsequent efforts include the ontological arguments of St. Anslem, Thomas Aquinas and Descartes. There were philosophers such as Al-Farabi, Avicenna (Ibn Sina), Al-Ghazali, Averroes (Ibn Rushd), Anslem –Archbishop of Canterbury, Maimonides, and others, whose arguments for the existence of God were intertwined theologically and cut across the philosophical spectrum. There have been various intellectual discourses emanating from ontological, cosmological and teleological arguments, about the existence of God. Some arguments have centred on natural theology, infinitude and the existence of a unique being, god or demiurge, and logical deduction and causation – including Kalam cosmological argument (modern version of *Ilm al-Kalām* – science of discourse). In addition, some arguments have focused on the intelligent designer or grand designer. For example, Thomas Aquinas was influenced by various philosophers – Socrates, Aristotle, Avicenna, Al-Ghazali, Averroes, et al. These philosophical influences were evident in his works, particularly the treatises of Summa Theologica; which included the logical arguments for the existence of God – 'Five Ways'. Another widely influenced philosopher was René Descartes, and his published works include, Discourse on Method (1637), Meditations on First Philosophy (1641) and Principles of Philosophy (1644). The statement *"Je pense, donc je suis"* was made by René Descartes circa 1637, and has been popularised in Latin as *"Cogito, ergo sum"* and in English as "I think, therefore I am".[1]

"I think, therefore I am" is an intellectually stimulating statement that should, ideally, evoke deeper pondering. Inversely, the statement is implying, 'I am, therefore I think'. Furthermore, 'I am, because of whom?' And 'Why I am'. The logical deduction from the initial statement –"I think, therefore I am" – 'I am, therefore I think'. Then taking the logic further, 'I am, because of whom?' The extrapolation must culminate in wanting to discover, 'Why I am'.

Based on this logical premise, the ideal intellectual trajectory ought to be – though I have come into existence, who created me and why? Essentially, 'I am, therefore I think'– meaning, since I exist, I can think. Further ratiocinative analysis should propound: 'I am, because of whom?' – What created me? And crucially, 'Why I am' – what is the purpose of my existence?

Though unravelling the purpose of human existence is a valid endeavour, unbridled philosophical pursuits may lead to an intellectual cul-de-sac, or even worse –an insuperable rabbit hole.

Contemporary intellectual pursuits must stretch apodictic philosophical boundaries beyond indubitability, through the utilisation of analytical frameworks and analogical deduction.

Ideally, extrapolations via paradigmatic methodologies should form the basis of prismatic arguments propounding the concept of God as The Creator.

I remember a teacher of mine stated that once God is eliminated from human discourse, the consequence is catastrophic.

> *The elimination of divinity in the epistemological pursuit of humanity is tantamount to stupidity and would result in catastrophe.*
>
> – Dr. Abdul-Hakeem Abayomi

PART ONE
GOD

CHAPTER 1

THE GOD CONCEPTUALIZATION

The conceptualization of God is probably as old as time and has challenged mankind from inception. The God concept cuts across all geographical and socio-cultural boundaries. God means different things to various people and has numerous attributes and names. Certainly, the discussions about God, particularly the existence of God, will continue to generate debates for a very long time. In discussing matters about God, especially from the existentiality viewpoint, it must be categorically stated, that in accepting the reality of our dynamic world, it is not possible to force anyone to believe in God, just as it is not possible to force anyone to believe in anything. There are those who believe there is no 'god' and often lament about the problems in the world as a justification for their position.

Those in this category are entitled to such opinions, even though I believe there are ratiocinative limitations associated with such views. As Carl Sagan contended, that there is no "compelling evidence" to support the atheist's position of the nonexistence of God.[2] Furthermore, there are those who believe in a 'god', and those who do not believe in anything god-like, including those who claim to believe exclusively in science – scientism. For centuries, science has been preoccupied with the origin of life, species and the existence of the entire universe. The real questions ought to concentrate on the initial cause of the existence of the universe that has existed for billions of years – 13.8 billion years according to latest research.

The main question that should preoccupy mankind ought to be: what exactly is the force behind the existence of the universe?

THE GOD CRITERION

No vision can grasp Him, but His grasp is over all vision: He is above all comprehension, yet is acquainted with all things.– Quran 6:103

There are various concepts of God across the globe, and processes of elimination can be employed to establish, or at least appreciate, God and all related attributes. In exploring the concept of God, the unique role of God as the Creator is crucial, because being a sole-creator cannot be replicated. Furthermore, it must be appreciated that all other aspects of our reality are a creation. For instance, the discourse of time often emanates during debates on creationism. Based on worldly realities, the existence of earthly time is prevalent; however, there are other realms that exist. For example, Carl Sagan popularised the Cosmic Calendar. Following cosmological research, cosmic time emerged. In view of these developments, there is the existence of earthly time and cosmic time, and a phase I would refer to as timelessness. Also, in the explication of some scientific phenomena relating to time, ad infinitum or infinity manifest as elements. In fact, what some scientists often refer to as infinity is highlighting the limitations of man's intellectual capabilities. It must be stated that infinity actually has its boundaries, when analysed from a creationist perspective. The association of infinitude with God comes up during discussions about the concept of God. Infinity is time-dependent, naturally, because of its association with time.

In other words, infinity is a consequence of time. In view of this, infinity is a creation of God The Creator. God is timeless because He exists outside of time, time realms and time zones, because He is the creator of time.

In view of this, the use of the term 'infinity' in attempting to explain God, inherently underpins human incapabilities, and further highlights complex comprehensive limitations.

Essentially, at the end of infinity is The Creator of all times and time zones. The One who began everything: The One without a beginning or end –The Creator –The Initiator.

Intellectual limitations which arise from misconceptions about God include theological and religious dogmas. For instance, in ascribing human attributes to God, the concept of God is primarily limited. A good example is the association of a begotten son with God, as is the case with some theologies. The Quran mentions that the owner of the heavens and earth has no partner and is not in need of partnership, neither does He have a begotten son.

> *He to whom belongs the dominion of the heavens and the earth: no son has He begotten, nor has He a partner in His dominion: it is He who created all things, and ordered them in due proportions.* – Quran 25:2

As such, approaching the subject matter of God from a human quality premise is problematic *ab initio* – primarily because of its flawed premise and potentially deleterious manifestation. For instance, perfection as an entity can be analysed as a consequence of a comparison to certain criteria, such as imperfection – perfection versus imperfection. Perfection can be perceived as a creative manifestation or attribute of The Creator, and not necessarily the nature of The Creator. As such, perfection as an entity is also a creation of The Creator. In this regard, The Creator is beyond the parameters of what perfection means or what perfection represents.

Perfection is based on human measurability and comparative standards. In view of these foregoing points, to fully understand the magnitude of the concept of God, the creation must appreciate that God is God and there is absolutely nothing like God! Anything that can be related to physically or be thought of mentally is not God, because what God is, is beyond the most innovative of human imaginations, and beyond human comprehension.

Importantly, it must be emphasized that the God in focus is the ultimate God that creates, and not the gods human beings have imagined mentally or conveniently created for personal and collective objectives. The primary focus is on God The Creator. So, if whatever anyone freely chooses to believe in, does not have the power to create, such an entity is not worthy of being referred to as God The Creator.

In this regard, that particular God is none other than God The Creator – the creator of everything that exists and was not created. By extrapolation, human beings were created and put within another creation (earth) and surrounded by other creations (nature). This can be understood as creation within creation and surrounded by creation – so everything that exists was created. As complex as that may seem, a not so complex process of elimination can be utilised to establish what God is not, or what is not God.

The use of logic and reason can be employed to establish factual realities and decipher the concept of God. I often apply logic when dealing with issues, especially epistemological topics, as I tend to use analogies that challenge the intellect. So, when certain people deny the existence of The Creator, it raises questions about their ratiocinative capabilities. Similarly, there are those who say that life ends here in this ephemeral world, claiming that once you die, that is it! However, this group of people still cannot give a cogent explanation for the existence of the soul. Also, this group still cannot give a valid reason for man's inability to create another man.

Having established the relationship between creation and The Creator, it behoves to elucidate on The Creator via certain criteria – The God Test.

On a lighter note, an adumbration of a considerably basic God Test will be highlighted, via the thought processes of the aborigines of South Australia. The aborigines call God *"Atnatu"*. Atnatu is a characteristic that signifies the one without impurity. Atnatu basically means "one without an anus", in other words, one that is free of the need to defecate. Anyone who does not need to eat does not need to excrete waste – via the digestive tract, colon, rectum, anal canal, and anus. Basically, if your god eats, then your god must defecate, which implies that your god is obviously not worthy of being God and is most definitely not God The Creator.

> *Say, "Is it other than Allah I should take as a protector, Creator of the heavens and earth, while it is He who feeds and is not fed?" ...*– Quran 6:14

Whilst on the faecal matter, I will narrate a rendition of a related sidesplitter I came across some years ago.

During a flight, an atheist seated next to an adolescent boy on an airplane turned to the boy and said: "Do you want to have a conversation? I have discovered conversations sometimes make flights less wearisome." And the boy then replied, "So what would you want to discuss?""Anything", said the atheist. "How about why there is no such thing as God, or there is or no Heaven or Hell, or no life after death?", as he smiled smugly. Then the boy said, "As interesting as those topics may seem, I would like to ask you a question first", "Go ahead," said the atheist. The boy then asks the question: "A horse, a cow, and a sheep all ingest grass, but a horse excretes clumps, a cow excretes cowpats, and a sheep excretes pellets, why do you suppose that is?" The atheist, visibly surprised by the little boy's level of reasoning, thinks about the question and replies, "Well, I have no idea!"

Then the boy looks straight at the atheist and says: "Do you really feel qualified to discuss God, Heaven and Hell, or life after death, when you really don't know s**t?"

The boy's epic response wiped the smirk off the atheist's face. This analogy certainly proves not everyone is qualified to speak on matters of God. Whilst this narrated encounter is just an example, such an approach becomes necessary for those who refuse to reason.

> ...*Then will you not use reason?* – Quran 37: 138

The instruction to reason is repeated in numerous verses of the Quran: Quran 2:44, Quran 2:76, Quran 3:65, Quran 3:118, Quran 5:58, Quran 6:151, Quran 11:51, Quran 29:63, etc.

Ideally, the pinnacle of science should culminate in identifying God The Creator. However, for some scientists, the peak of science often culminates in the Big Bang! Some genuine scientists may concede that an enormously powerful entity must have kick-started life in its entirety into being. Essentially, the 'Big Bang' process was highlighted in the Quran (21:30), fourteen centuries ago, even though this was relatively a recent scientific discovery.

> *Have those who disbelieved not considered that the heavens and the earth were a joined entity, and We separated them and made from water every living thing? Then will they not believe?* – Quran 21:30

Evidently, nothing happened by chance – everything that exists was intelligently planned by an intelligent designer – God The Creator. The concept of God as the sole Creator of everything that exists as creation is not only extraordinary, but challenges intellectual manifestations and the culmination of human thought about God. Furthermore, The Creator is an enormously powerful being that cannot be bound by matter, space and time. The Creator is an incomparable force that not only transcends time but is the very creator of time itself. Time, with all its manifestations – prehistoric and futuristic, is a creation operating within limits.

There are quite a few criteria for identifying The Creator, but the primary criterion is the absolute incomparability of The Creator with anything.

The criterion to determine, what God is and what God is not, is actually not so complicated. The God Test is universally applicable and can be conducted by anyone, particularly those seeking God or trying to understand the concept of God. The basis of The God Test is derived from Chapter 112 of the Quran – Surah Ikhlas (Oneness of God).

> *Say: He is Allah, the One and Only;*
> *Allah, the Eternal, Absolute;*
> *He begetteth not, nor is He begotten;*
> *And there is none comparable unto Him.*
> – Quran 112: 1-4

THE GOD TEST

Historically and contemporarily, the world has witnessed a diversity of supposed 'gods', either through attribution or declaration, though, in reality there can only be One God. A situation of many divinity-claimants makes it necessary to put all forms of 'god's to the test. The God Test is exceptional because it is a divinely inspired test to determine the divinity of any supposed contender for the position of the one true God.

The God Test is universally applicable anywhere, anytime and in any situation. Whatever the culture, tradition or religious inclination across the globe, the God Test can be utilized to determine the authenticity of all divinity-claimants; whether from the past, the present or the future.

The God Test is based on the following four distinctive criterions:

Criterion 1: He is God, the One:

Meaning there is only One of Him.

Criterion 2: God, the Eternal, Absolute:

Meaning He has no beginning or end, totality of power; all-encompassing.

Criterion 3: He begetteth not nor was begotten:

Meaning He does not have, need or require offspring, neither was He born.
Such attributes of His creation are far beneath Him.

Criterion 4: And there is none comparable unto Him:

Meaning, there is absolutely nothing you can compare to Him, because there is
nothing like Him. Whatever the human mind can fathom, imagine, think or
dream of, is not God, because whatever that thing is, can never be God, and
only be a creation of God.

Based on the above-mentioned enumerated criterions, any proclaimed or
acclaimed deity or god that does not fulfil the above prerequisites has failed
the God Test. Essentially, whatever that proclaimed or acclaimed thing is, it is
just an ordinary creation and obviously is not God – at least not God The
Creator. To fully grasp this fundamentality, it must be established that The
Creator is not, and never will be, the creation – and vice versa. The Creator, as
an entity, exists outside the realm of the creation. And more importantly, The
Creator, unlike the creation, is absolutely boundless and timeless.

Allah fulfils all the aforementioned criterions and passes The God Test.
Furthermore, Allah is inimitable and cannot be pluralized or genderized – He
is "The God" and The Creator.

CHAPTER 2

DEMYSTIFICATION OF DEITIES

ALL DEITIES MYTHICAL AND AUTOCHTHONAL

Deity comes from the Latin word for God – *Deus*, then in French it is *Deité*, and in the English it is 'Deity'. Deification is to deify – treat something or someone god-like. Deify can be appreciated as a cognate of deity. From an etymological perspective, Augustine of Hippo derived the term deity from "divine nature" – which is translated as *Deitas* in Latin.[3]

Deity is often associated with the supernatural or the divine and the identifiers can be pluralized or genderized as gods or goddesses – which are common terms in polytheism.

From history to date, all deities, regardless of their geographical situation, emanation or manifestation, are either mythological or autochthonous. There are many examples of autochthonous deities named after aspects of nature, natural phenomenon, cosmology and astronomy. For instance, sun and moon deities are revered across various cultural traditions and were at times given indigenous names or titles associated with a particular geographical location. According to Greek mythology, their sun deity was called Helios and sometimes Apollo. To the Aztecs, the sun deity was Tonatiuh, and for the Hindu, it was named Surya. As for the Arabs, the sun deity was named Shams, and to ancient Egyptian religion it was known as Ra.

Though, some of these deities had various references in different civilizations, nations and ethnic groups, their meanings and what they portrayed were very much similar across different geographical regions across the world. Generally, deities are meant to be totemic.

The African continent had many ancient civilizations with vast empires such as Oyo, Benin, Nubia, Egypt, Carthage, Songhai, Mali, Aksum, Kongo, and Zulu. Most of Africa's historic empires or kingdoms now exist as various nation-states and had autochthonous deities unique to their respective cultures. For example, the Yoruba of modern-day Nigeria have autochthonous deities revered in West Africa and Brazil, and some of them include, Obatala, Ogun, Sango, Esu, Yewa, Olokun, and Osun. Some deities according to ancient Egyptian traditions include Anubis, Bastet, Set, Horus, Isis, Osiris, Thoth, Ptah, Ra, and Hathor.

Mesoamerican beliefs such as the Olmec, Maya, Zapotec, and Aztec had hundreds of gods. A few examples of their gods include, Huitzilopochtli, Quetzalcoatl, Tezcatlipoca, Xiuhtecuhtli and Tlaloc, which were Aztec, and Itzamna, Ix Chel, Kinich Ahau, and Chaac for the Mayans.

Autochthonous deities existed across Europe, from east to west. Slavic traditions had deities such as Perun, Lada, Zorya, Veles, Dzbog, Belobog, and Czernobog. Greek traditions had deities such as Zeus, Athena, Hera, Poseidon, Demeter, Ares, and Apollo. Actually, Apollo was also revered among the Romans, and some of their other deities include Jupiter, Neptune, Pluto, Mars, Cupid, and Saturn.

Across Asia, cultures were also polytheistic with numerous autochthonous deities. The Hindu tradition comprises millions of gods, some of which include, Ardhanarishvara, Brahma, Durga, Ganesha, Harihara, Lakshmi, Parvati, Sati, Shiva, Saraswati, and Vishnu.

Some deities according to Chinese traditions include, Pangu, Fuxi Mazu, Xihe, and Ba Xian – which is translated as Eight Immortals or Eight Genies. According to Arabian traditions, Arabs literally had deities for each day of the year, at least 360 gods! Some of the Arab deities include, Abgal, Al-Lat, Al-Uzza, Manat, Anbay, 'Amm, Baal, Sa'd, Basamum, Dhul-Khalasa, Hubal, Quzah, Wadd, Suwa', Yaghuth, Ya'uq, and Nasr.

The Quran mentions the three aforementioned Arab deities as a trilogy:

> *Have you then considered Al-Lat, and Al-'Uzza (two idols of the pagan Arabs).*
> *And Manat (another idol of the pagan Arabs), the other third?*
> *Is it for you the males and for Him the females?*
> *That indeed is a division most unfair!*
> *They are not but [mere] names you have named them - you and your forefathers - for which Allah has sent down no authority. They follow not except assumption and what [their] souls desire, and there has already come to them from their Lord guidance.* – Quran 53:19-23

The aforementioned deities are just a few examples across some world cultures. Deliberately, not all deities of the world are enumerated, but based on extensive research, the summation is that the deity pattern is similar across all cultures and culturally-oriented religions globally. Autochthonous deities are usually part of a pantheon – often with hierarchical venerative attributions. Some ethnic groups, nations or civilizations had, and still have, their pantheon of gods, in the hundreds, thousands or even millions.

FOREFATHERISM AND ANCESTRAL WORSHIP

> *And when it is said to them, "Follow what Allah has revealed," they say, "Rather, we will follow that which we found our forefathers doing." Even though their fathers understood nothing, nor were they guided?*
> – Quran 2:170

Forefatherism occurs when the veneration of forefathers manifests as ancestral worship in any society. The institutionalization of forefatherism has impacted all world cultures. The honorific mantra of 'following our forefathers' is actually antediluvian, which has been the foundational basis of forefatherism. Based on historicity and exegesis of the Islamic tradition, idolatry foundations were inadvertently laid around the time of Prophet Idris (Enoch), and manifested during the era of Prophet Nuh (Noah). Forefatherism, in the form of ancestral worship, manifested in prevalence, and Nuh was faced with eradicating the embodiment of venerated men as statues, instituted during the era of his predecessor – Idris. According to some narrations, including The Book of Idols by Arab historian Hisham Ibn al-Kalbi, documented oral traditions elucidated the events that led to the establishment of idol worship in earlier times.

The pith of the narration is about the death of five men, who were deemed righteous by the community. Following the deaths, some of their relatives were grief-stricken, and people of that community decided to build five honorific statues to venerate these dead men.

As time went by, the veneration of these five men metamorphosed into forefatherism-oriented ancestral worship. From an exegetical analysis of Islamic historicity, that metamorphosis was a satanic plot that was seeded centuries before its manifestation. In the Islamic context, Satan means 'the accursed' – whose primary goal is to mislead mankind in totality.

The satanic modus operandi is to play the long game – the long con (borrowing from the confidence trickster's parlance).

This particular plot was crucial, so the long game had to be deployed stealthily. If the satanic advice of building idols for the primary purpose of deification and deity worship had been presented initially, it would have been summarily rejected, because that particular generation in history, were somewhat preoccupied with the worship of God. However, the satanic plot of deity worship was not intended for that earlier generation that erected the statues, rather, the targeted plot was actually intended for later generations.

Notably, one of the stories about Nuh in the Quran mentions five deities – Wadd, Suwa', Yaghuth, Ya'uq, and Nasr:

> *Noah said, "My Lord, indeed they have disobeyed me and followed him whose*
> *wealth and children will not increase him except in loss.*
> *And they conspired an immense conspiracy.*
> *And said, 'Never leave your gods and never leave Wadd or Suwa' or Yaghuth*
> *and Ya'uq and Nasr'.* – Quran 71:21-23

Through these series of narrated historical events, the aforementioned forefathers were transmogrified into deities. Consequently, Nuh became the first prophet to conspicuously deal with idolaters who had totally abandoned the worship of God. Furthermore, it must be emphasized that the idolatry issue laid its roots at that particular time in early history and has existed with mankind ever since. From that point onward, every culture gradually developed with its autochthonal peculiarities, which often includes mythological figures and deities firmly rooted in forefatherism.

A classic example of a society rooted in forefatherism with various idolatry manifestations, is the story of Prophet Ibrahim (Abraham) and his people. Whilst growing up, Ibrahim was surrounded by idols, primarily because his father was a sculptor and trader of idols. Ibrahim sometimes argued with his father about the idols. His father, like all the idolaters, endorsed their idolatry practices, based on the archetypal justification of continuing the legacy of their ancestors. For Ibrahim, it did not make any sense to him that people would call upon and worship idols that were man-made. So, Ibrahim often mocked the idols and by extension the people who believed in and worshipped the idols.

And recite to them the story of Ibrahim (Abraham).

When he said to his father and his people, "What do you worship?"

They said: "We worship idols, and to them we are ever devoted."

He said: "Do they hear you, when you call (on them)?

"Or do they benefit you or do they harm (you)?"

They said: "Nay, but we found our fathers doing so."

– Quran 26:69-74

One of the spectacular incidents that brought Ibrahim to prominence was when he publicly ridiculed the idolaters, during one of their pagan festivals. Ibrahim devised a plan to avoid attending the idolatry ceremony and waited at the temple that housed their gods. Whilst alone in the temple, Ibrahim mockingly asked the idols if they would not eat the offerings before them and why they did not speak. Obviously not expecting a response, Ibrahim defaced all idols, but one in particular – the biggest idol. When the idolaters came to discover what had happened to their pantheon, they were apoplectic with rage. Completely infuriated by the act, the people wondered who would be so daring to commit an unprecedented sacrilege.

Unsurprisingly, Ibrahim was summoned because of his antecedents of mocking the idols. After Ibrahim was confronted about the sacrilegious crime against the idols, he displayed not just courage, but uncommon wisdom. Ibrahim told the people to ask the biggest of their self-manufactured idols what happened to the other idols, since it was the only one left unscathed. Knowing full well it was impossible to question an idol, the folly of the idolaters became apparent, and they felt really slighted. Ibrahim's deft action with the idols exposed their compounded inanity, self-inflicted complicity and the futility of idol worship in general. The story of Ibrahim is well-documented in the Quran: The Prophets (Quran 21:51-67).

Ibrahim triumphed over many challenges in his lifetime and his experience became an epitome of rectitude – a unique person and prophet emulated and extolled globally.

Historically, all civilizations, without exception, had their beliefs and traditions built around some revered autochthonous ancestry, mythology, deities or pantheon. Whilst legends based on legendary figures exist across all cultural spectrums, certain beliefs and traditions that manifest as cultural mores can be appreciated as euhemeristic oriented veneration, deification or ancestral worship. In certain instances, some autochthonous beliefs still exist, whilst others have been infused through syncretization. For instance, the deity named Baal was common amongst Semitic traditions, particularly in Canaan, Phoenicia, Mesopotamia – Babylonia, with variations that included Ba'al, Ba'l, Baalim and Bel. Baal, like many other autochthonous deities, had, as part of their traditions, human sacrificial practices. Interestingly, Baal was notably mentioned in the Quran:

> *And indeed, Elias was from among the messengers,*
> *When he said to his people, "Will you not fear Allah ?*
> *Do you call upon Ba'l and leave the best of creators -*
> *Allah, your Lord and the Lord of your first forefathers?"*
> – Quran 37:123-126

The specificity of Baal symbolises all autochthonic deities that have been justified through forefatherism across the globe. Critically, a thought-provoking question was asked in the above verse of the Quran that ought to make a discerning mind ponder on its profound meaning – "Allah, your Lord and the Lord of your first forefathers?"

Fundamentally, were your first forefathers lords unto themselves or they had a Lord? If your first forefathers existed, then how did they come into existence, and who created them? Furthermore, what is the point of worshipping these forefathers incapable of creating themselves? Essentially, if any group of people or society, choose to take their ancestor as lords and worship their forefathers, then what about the forefathers before them, and the forefathers before them? Continuing this precursory pattern will surely terminate at an initial forefather, who was certainly created by The Creator.

Respecting cultural traditions is one thing; however, such practices should not elevate ancestral reverence to the level of worship, especially not as a substitute for The Creator.

CHAPTER 3

CREATIONISM: COSMOLOGICAL EXEGESIS

The Creator created the universe and all the existing planets. Interestingly, more planets are being discovered. At least 500 solar systems have been discovered and there are thousands of planets operating within thousands of planetary systems. There have been various extragalactic discoveries, including exoplanetary systems and exoplanets. An exoplanet is an extrasolar planet outside of the solar system that orbits a star.

The Sun is the largest object in our solar system and contains more than 99.8% of the total mass. Planet Earth operates with the Sun within the solar system. The distance between the Earth and the Sun is about 93 million miles or 150 million kilometres. There are stars millions of times bigger than the Sun and there are billions of stars in a galaxy and trillions of galaxies within the universe. There are billions of human beings on planet earth alone, not to mention the millions of other species. Despite our supposed size, the summation of collective insignificance is underpinned by the depth of our nothingness. The insignificance of the inhabitants of planet earth can be appreciated via 7 dimensional levels:

(1) Earth (2) Solar System (3) Milky Way Galaxy (4) Local Group (5) Virgo Supercluster (6) Observable Universe (7) Unobservable Universe.

(1) Earth: Planet Earth is estimated to be at least 4.5 billion years old. The entire planet has a total surface area of about 197 million square miles (510 million square kilometres). There are about 7.8 billion human beings on earth.

(2) Solar System: The entire Solar System is about 36 billion times larger than Earth. The Solar System comprises the Sun and all the objects that orbit it, particularly the 8 planets: Mercury, Venus, Earth, Mars, Jupiter, Saturn, Uranus, and Neptune. In terms of size, Earth is the fifth largest, coming after Jupiter, Saturn, Uranus and Neptune, and ahead of Venus, Mars, and Mercury.

Planet Earth can fit into Jupiter 1,300 times and fit into Saturn 764 times. All the planets can fit into Jupiter, and Jupiter can fit into the Sun, 1,000 times. About 1.3 million planet earths can be contained in the Sun. The Sun, which is just one out of billions of stars, has seven layers in total. The inner layers are the Core, Radiative Zone and Convection Zone and the outer layers are the Photosphere, the Chromosphere, the Transition Region, and the Corona.

Each layer of the Sun has varying levels of heat. The heat from the Sun causes solar granulation and the surface appears like boiling large hot bubbles. This boiling process allows heat from the core, where the temperature can exceed 27 million degrees Fahrenheit or 15 million degrees Celsius, suffuse through the convection zone, where the temperature is about 3.5 million degrees Fahrenheit or 2 million degrees Celsius, and into the photosphere, where the temperature is about 10,000 degrees Fahrenheit or 5,500 degrees Celsius.

(3) Milky Way Galaxy: The corrugated Milky Way Galaxy has at least 200 billion stars. It is estimated that about 40 billion Earth-sized planets are orbiting in the habitable zones of stars within the Milky Way galaxy.

(4) Local Group: The Local Group comprises at least 54 types of galaxies. Three of the largest galaxies in that category include the Andromeda Galaxy, Milky Way Galaxy, and Triangulum Galaxy.

(5) Virgo Supercluster: The Virgo Supercluster is a mass concentration of galaxies containing the Virgo Cluster and Local Group. The Virgo Supercluster contains at least 100 galaxy groups and clusters, and possibly 2,000 member galaxies.

(6) Observable Universe: The Observable Universe contains about 10 million superclusters, and the Virgo Supercluster is just one of them. There could be a conglomerate of at least 2 trillion galaxies within the Observable Universe. The Observable Universe is a summation of all possible observability, based on the attainable limits of human technological capabilities – the cosmic horizon.

(7) Unobservable Universe: The Unobservable Universe is anything beyond the Observable Universe. Basically, it is anything beyond technology-aided human observability. This realm is sometimes referred to as the boundless or unbounded universe.

In reality, what some scientists consider the unobservable or unbounded universe actually has bounds. The cosmos is not as infinite as science would want us to believe. What some aspects of science refer to as ad infinitum actually has its confines. Beyond those confines is The Creator - The Initiator - Allah. Allah transcends matter, space and time, because He is The Creator of everything that exists, which includes matter, space and time.

> *Do you not consider how Allah has created seven heavens in layers*
> *And made the moon therein a [reflected] light and made the sun a burning*
> *lamp?* – Quran 71:15 -16

Based on Islamic exegesis, the Throne of Allah is several levels above everything humans know as the unobservable universe – the cosmos. The cosmos does not even scratch the bottom surface of The Throne, because the Throne of Allah is above the 7th heaven (space) and what is oft-referred to as the cosmos, is at the lowest level of all the 7 heavens.

Indeed, We have adorned the nearest heaven with an adornment of stars
– Quran 37:6

To further buttress the insignificance of mankind as a mere creation within many levels of creation, all created by The Creator, more details about the Sun will be expounded. As previously stated, 1.3 million planet earths can conveniently fit into the Sun. Though the Sun is 93 million miles away from Earth, it can cause skin damage – via Ultraviolet (UV) radiation, and visual impairment. When humans see the Sun, it is actually rays from the Photosphere that are visible. Looking directly at the Sun, especially during a solar eclipse can cause permanent eye damage or blindness. Imagine a creator created the Sun, and then further ruminate on the absurdity of looking upon such a creator, when just one creation – the Sun – cannot be looked upon with the naked eyes. The impact of the heat penetrating the layers of earth could pulverize the entire planet earth. Imagine a scenario where the heat of the Sun is allowed to penetrate all the atmospheric layers on the Earth – Exosphere, Ionosphere, Thermosphere, Mesosphere, Ozone Layer, Stratosphere, Troposphere and Earth's Surface. The imagined Sun heating up the earth scenario further emphasizes our vulnerabilities. The Sun generates energy through a process called nuclear fusion. Through the process of nuclear fusion, Helium is created from the compression and fusion of hydrogen atoms. The Sun fuses 620 million metric tons of Hydrogen every second.

However, when all the Hydrogen is exhausted, heavier elements like Carbon are created and exhausted until it manifests as Iron: the point where fusion to heavier elements is impossible – this is the Iron Peak.

Presently, the Sun has used up about half of its hydrogen but still has enough to last another 5 billion years. The Sun is about 4.5 billion years old, which is about half of its estimated lifespan of about 10 billion years.[4]

Certainly, the Sun has as a terminal point, meaning it also had a beginning. This establishes that something created the Sun and kick-started the entire processes of nuclear fusion until its peak.

As unique as the composition of the Sun is, it is still a creation created by The Creator. Furthermore, as mesmerising as the Sun, Moon, stars and planets may seem, what is even more mind-blowing is that all aforementioned creations of the universe exist within just one heaven – the first heaven, and there are meant to be seven layers of heaven.

> *[And] who created seven heavens in layers. You do not see in the creation of the Most Merciful any inconsistency. So return [your] vision [to the sky]; do you see any breaks?* – Quran 67: 3

The seven layers can be interpreted as seven spatial dimensions, or multiple universes – a multiverse in the science fiction parlance, and String Theory in theoretical physics. The Quran mentions the multidimensional characteristics of the heavens with a word *Hubuk* – which can be described as paths, pathways, tracks, orbits or layers, including complex combinations.

> *By the heaven full of paths* – Quran 51:7

To further appreciate the vastness of creation and the insignificance of man within creation, I will cite the similitude of a ring in the desert. If a ring is dropped in the Sahara desert, all the 7 heavens are smaller than the likeness of the ring, and the Throne of The Creator is the Sahara desert.

Imagine how minute a ring is compared to the entirety of the Sahara desert.

Interestingly, Islamic esotericism, theological analysis and scriptural exegesis, have revealed that the distance between the first heaven and the next is about 500 years (light years) – which can be appreciated as symbolic representations of exceptionally long periods. To appreciate the distance, 500 years is multiplied by each of the seven heavens, including each level above.

In addendum, further scriptural research reveals that after the topmost part of the 7th heaven is the *Kursi* – The Footstool, and after that is *Almai* – the water, which is at bottom of the *Arsh* – The Throne of The Creator.

His Kursi extends over the heavens and the earth... – Quran 2:255.

CHAPTER 4

THE CREATION CALLED MAN

Indeed, We created humans in the best form. – Quran 95:4

For a certainty, human beings are a special creation created by God The Creator; unique beings created with a sophisticated physiological composition and advanced intellectual capabilities. Man is one out of at least 8.7 million known species – a wonderful creation with billions of atoms: about 7,000,000,000,000,000,000,000,000,000 (7octillion).[56]Nonetheless, no matter how sophisticated or advanced a creation is, it was still created by a Creator. Based on the existentiality of the Creator and creation relationship, the logical prerequisite is to humbly accept the reality of man being a mere creation and that a Creator exists. The Quran highlights the infinitesimality of man with a comparison to the creation of the heavens and earth.

> *The creation of the heavens and the earth is indeed greater than the creation of mankind, yet most of mankind know not.* – Quran 40:57

In view of this, man is one of many other creations, same as the sun and the moon. Creations exist within other creations, and so forth. As an example, it would be rather ludicrous to claim that because the sun is so unique in its composition compared to the other objects in the solar system that The Creator of the universe must have given birth to the sun!

Citing the moon as another example, if a blue moon coincides with a lunar eclipse, this creates a Super Blue Blood Moon eclipse – Supermoon.

Now, imagine a scenario where some people decide to state that because of the emergence of a special moon, like the Supermoon, then it implies that The Creator has given birth to the Supermoon. Progressing on a similar trajectory, imagine a scenario where a set of people decide to worship the unique moon. That is the similitude of worshipping the creation instead of The Creator. These analogies can be applied to any creation, including human beings. The act of giving birth in any manner or form is reserved for creatures with reproductive capabilities and cannot be associated with The Creator. For instance, the Quran gives a critical response to all forms of ideologies and concomitant manifestations that claim The Creator has a son.

> *And they say, "The Most Merciful has taken [for Himself] a son."*
> *Indeed you have done an atrocious thing.*
> *The heavens almost rupture therefrom and the earth splits open and the*
> *mountains collapse in devastation* –Quran 19:88-90

The inquisitive nature of man leads to conjecture, often warped in religious dogmatism. Generally, except for curiosity purposes, there is no functional significance in knowing the actual physical composition of The Creator, because such matters are beyond the scope of the creation. It can be argued that the exotericism or possession of such knowledge does not in any way assist the creation in its functional objectives. It is like computer software wanting to know the physical composition of the computer maker responsible for its design or creation.

Mankind often goes off in a tangent and gets preoccupied with convoluted otiosity, which does not assist human existentiality. The most critical fact remains; there are two separate entities, where one is reliant on the other to come into existence –Creator created creation.

Following the many centuries of continuous research, mankind is gradually attaining more knowledge about the conception of the creation within another creation (Man on Earth), related ontological revelations and coming to terms with the ever-present concept of God The Creator. Often, when the concept of a creator is discussed, the creationism discourse literally takes a new dimension. The limitation of the creation's (human) thought processes becomes evident and usually manifests as an impediment. A common challenge that confronts those who fail to fully grasp or acknowledge the existence of God The Creator, is due to the misplaced requirement or tangential prerequisite of physical evidence, particularly in science. Those in this category are primarily scepticism-oriented and observer-dependent, and openly professing the 'seeing is believing' mantra, often without deeper ratiocination. The fact of the matter is, not all observations are scientific, because science can only attempt, but not explain everything in our dynamic world. There are certain phenomena that are confined to the acceptance of our reality – social environment. For example, what would be the scientific objective of trying to prove the human nose can be used to see or be a suitable alternative for sight function, when the human eyes have been established for that purpose! A scientific endeavour to prove death is another example, because such an experiment will not only be an exercise in futility but result in irreversible death – which will be the only certainty.

Supposed scientific facts have inherent limitations, even though certain impediments may not be revealed at the time of discovery. In view of such developments, fluctuating facts and inconstant truths can be appreciated as inherent limitations to the eternality of science. There are no absolute truths in science; scientific facts are not set in stone and evolve from time to time. An established scenario in the field of science is when scientific theories are superseded, and a few examples include the Caloric Theory, Phlogiston Theory and Emission Theory. It is quite possible some people believed and died believing in such theories because those theories coincided with their own existence, and those theories may have been rendered obsolete after their demise. For example, Isaac Newton's work on universal gravitation – Theory of Gravity – held sway for two centuries, until it was upended by Albert Einstein's work on special and general relativity – Theory of Relativity.

Based on this premise, any aspect of science claiming the nonexistence of God, for example, should not be taken as fact, because of inherent flaws and potential falsifiability. For instance, a thorough dissection of the evolutionist view will reveal the entire process of evolution must have started after the initial creation. To a certain extent, the theory of evolution has been somewhat stultified by its inherent limitation. These often-inherent impediments manifest from the pivotal refusal to accept that creation evolved after a creator kick-started the entire process. As the centrality of Charles Darwin's Theory of Natural Selection (Evolution) is deconstructed, the initial natural process of existence is highlighted, and this ought to raise the question of the first natural selection process. What initiated the first process of natural selection? Did the first organism select itself?

The trajectory of this idea culminates in insinuating that the initial organism self-created. This is highly improbable and an impracticable scenario.

The same argument applies to self-replication theories, because to replicate is to copy. In other words, to be able to replicate something, that thing must exist. Without the existence of the thing to be replicated, then replication is impossible. Based on this premise, the entire replication process terminates at an initial thing – molecule, polymer, organism, etc. Whatever that initial thing to be replicated is, it does not possess self-creation abilities, and was a creation created by a creator. Fundamentally, an extremely powerful force must have initiated everything; something that existed as a sole, incomparable and resoundingly unique entity. In analysing the scientific viewpoint, even scientists – at least the sincere ones – accept, the undisputable certainty that one thing in particular, kick-started all this matter.

A critical aspect of the limitations of science is brought to fore when the matter of creation is explicated. Science may succeed in replicating creation, particularly in human form, but cannot give life to anything. Furthermore, the existence of the soul becomes problematic to scientists who doubt the existence of a creator. Personally, I am of the opinion that if science cannot create human beings, then I am inclining towards accepting the belief in the existence of a creator. Despite so called scientific achievements of mankind, human beings did not even create themselves. To put it succinctly, humans are a creation incapable of creation. To be clear, the creation in focus is not referring to replicative science – in layman's terms, copy and paste science – but actually creating something from nothing. The inabilities of man to replicate man as a creation are enough reasons for those who ruminate to accept the existence of a creator. If human beings cannot create (*creatioex nihilo*), then what exactly is the basis for arrogance?

Over fourteen centuries ago, a fundamental question on creation was asked in the Quran:

> *Or were they created by nothing, or were they the creators [of themselves]?*
> – Quran 52:35

Obviously, human beings were not created by nothing, neither did human beings self-create! In essence, all the billions of people that have existed in our collective histories, civilizations, including advancements in knowledge, sciences and technologies, are literally an insignificant tiny dot in the bigger scheme of universal affairs. Mankind sometimes gets consumed by its scientific achievements, and egotistical tendencies make humans forget they were once a drop of fluid (sperm).

Essentially, human beings were once nothing and would have remained nonexistent without the creative capabilities of The Creator.

> *Has there not been over Man a long period of Time, when he was nothing -*
> *(not even) mentioned? –* Quran 76:1

A deeper analysis of the creation phenomenon should ideally lead to a starting point. Historically, there have been debates between scientists, for and against, biogenesis and abiogenesis, respectively. Also, there are scientific theories that propose aquatic origins of life, including the Vent theory – hydrothermal vents. Cosmic scientists accept there must be one thing in particular that kick-started all this matter called life – a cosmic cataclysm! Also, there are scientific theories that attempt to explain the cosmological dynamics that led to the birthing of the universe, such as the Big Bang. Ironically, the Big Bang process was described in the Quran, over fourteen centuries ago, though it is a relatively recent scientific discovery.

> *Have those who disbelieved not considered that the heavens and the earth were a*
> *joined entity, and We separated them and made from water every living thing?*
> *Then will they not believe? –* Quran 21:30

Science often associates water with life. The possibility of water on other planets within our solar system fascinates scientists, as it is an indication of the habitability of various life forms – often referred to as 'extraterrestrials' or 'aliens'. So far, science with all its paraphernalia has not been able to convincingly prove the existence of other life forms, particularly from a humanoid prism. Although, it must be stated that, Islamic exegesis affirms that humankind is not the only life form and that other creations may have existed before. Also, the Quran states there are things Allah has created that are unknown: "And He creates (other) things of which you have no knowledge." (Quran 16:8), and everything was created from water.

Allah has created every [living] creature from water. And of them are those
that move on their bellies, and of them are those that walk on two legs, and of
them are those that walk on four. Allah creates what He wills. Indeed, Allah
is over all things competent.— Quran 24:45

Earth consists of at least seventy percent of water, which coincidentally is the
same composition of water in the human body. The Quran contains many
verses that mention man was created from the earth – clay, some of them
include, "He is the One Who created you from clay" (Quran 6:2), "He has
produced you from the earth" (Quran 11:61), "Man We did create from a
quintessence of clay" (Quran 23:12), "And He originated the creation of
humankind from clay (Quran 32:7)" and "He created man from clay like [that
of] pottery" (Quran 55:14).

> *And We did certainly create man out of clay from an altered black mud.*
> – Quran 15:26

Man is a creation within creation – Man within Earth. Naturally, there is a
unique affinity between the earth and man. They both have similar elements
such as oxygen, carbon, nitrogen and hydrogen, and have a water composition
of at least seventy percent (70%). Man's process of creation is rather
fascinating when compared with the earth. Man is created from black mud,
similar to loamy soil where various produce grow. From the dark soil emerge a
variety of foods, from cash crops to exotic and resplendent fruits. Beautiful
flowers with radiant colours bloom from the black mud – earth.

> *He it is Who spread the earth for you; and made in it paths for you, and sent*
> *down water from the sky, and then through it We brought forth many species*
> *of diverse plants.* – Quran 20:53

Poisonous and innocuous plants, edible foods of various shapes, sizes and colours emanate from the black soil, just as mankind emanated from black mud, with all its diversity – different skin tones, personalities and characters – "the good, the bad and the ugly".

> *And Allah has caused you to grow as a growth from the earth*
> – Quran 71:17

Another notable similarity between humans and plants is dioecy – having one distinctive male or female reproductive organ per specie. Human beings have male and female species that are required for reproduction.

> *And He is the One Who spread out the earth and placed firm mountains and rivers upon it, and created fruits of every kind in pairs.He covers the day with night. Surely in this are signs for those who reflect.*– Quran 13:3

The creationist viewpoint that mankind originated from Adam and Eve is in accordance with the Islamic position. The Quran mentions mankind were created from a single pair:

> *He is the One Who created you from a single soul, then from it made its spouse so he may find comfort in her. After he had been united with her, she carried a light burden that developed gradually. When it grew heavy, they prayed to Allah, their Lord, "If you grant us good offspring, we will certainly be grateful."* –Quran 7:189

> *O mankind! We created you from a single (pair) of a male and a female, and made you into nations and tribes, that ye may know each other not that ye may despise (each other). Verily the most honoured of you in the sight of Allah is*

(he who is) the most righteous of you. And Allah has full knowledge and is well acquainted (with all things). — Quran 49:13

Notably, there is no specificity in the Quran about the era Adam and Eve existed; the way it was specified by the scriptures of certain religions.

Furthermore, beyond the debates associated with radiocarbon (Carbon-14) dating, the various studies in human genetics, such as the patrilineal Y-Chromosomal Adam (Y-chromosomal most recent common ancestor –Y-MRCA) and matrilineal Mitochondrial Eve (matrilineal most recent common ancestor – mt-MRCA), are not exactly at variance with the Islamic viewpoint on creationism.

CHAPTER 5

TIMELESSISM THEORY

Beyond the arguments about time and the illusion of time, including positions on presentism and eternalism, I posit timelessism. Timelessism is the study of time as a creation. From a cosmological perspective, time emanated from the absence of time; meaning there must have been a period of existentiality that time did not exist. Time is primarily beneficial to the creation confined within creation – man within a spatial environment. Time is a continuous process that measures existence in the past, present and future. Universal time is calculated based on planet Earth's rotation in relation to distant celestial bodies crossing the meridian – a great circle on the surface of the earth passing through the poles (North and South).

Historically, time has been measured in units of seconds, minutes, hours, days, years, decades, centuries, millennia, and in certain cases, eras, epochs and aeons. Without the measurement of time, then time cannot be calculated and without the existence of creations – terrestrial and celestial, then there will be no time. Furthermore, the geological time scale, comprising the Hadean, Archean, Proterozoic and Phanerozoic, would be impossible to calculate without the existence of natural elements.

Essentially, time as an entity, is a creation dependent on the existence of other creations, created by The Creator.

> *He has ˹also˺ subjected for you the sun and the moon, both constantly orbiting, and has subjected the day and night for you.* – Quran 14:33

There are varying time zones existing concurrently within and without the universe. To buttress this point, a day to Allah is not the same as to humans –

earthly time. Time within the human realm is confined to the limitations of creation and rather different from time outside the realm of creation – The Creator's description of time. In certain situations, the Quran describes days for specific events, which can be understood as periods or phases outside the human realm of time. The specificity of the Quran on certain events is highlighted in some instances, where a day in the human realm is compared in the thousands.

> *It is Allah Who has created the heavens and the earth and everything in*
> *between in six Days, then established Himself on the Throne. You have no*
> *protector or intercessor besides Him. Will you not then be mindful?*
> *He conducts every affair from the heavens to the earth, then it all ascends to*
> *Him on a Day whose length is a thousand years by your counting.*
> –Quran 32:4-5

Evidently, the 'six days' mentioned in the above cited verse is beyond human comprehension and different from the daily twenty-four hours, by earthly standards. In the subsequent verse, a day is compared to one thousand days for ease of human decipherment. Also, in a related verse, a day is used analogously to describe another specific event that is fifty thousand years.

> *The angels and the Spirit [i.e., Gabriel] will ascend to Him during a Day the*
> *extent of which is fifty thousand years.* – Quran 70:4

The specificity with days in the Quran is intriguing. For instance, the analogy expressing a day as a thousand years primarily discusses the ascension of 'every affair', whilst the analogy that describes a day as fifty thousand years is specifically discussing the ascension of 'angels and the Spirit'.

An important point to highlight is that the similitude of a thousand or thousands of years to explain a day, may not be earthly time oriented as well; it may be a time zone mankind is yet to encounter or apprehend.

Another instance of specificity with days, involves the creation process.

The standard six days for the creation of the heavens and earth are equally portioned into two-day segments – two, four, and six. Two days for the heavens and four days for the earth and its sustenance: total six days.

Ask ⸢them, O Prophet⸣, "How can you disbelieve in the One Who created the earth in two Days? And how can you set up equals with Him? That is the Lord of all worlds.

He placed on the earth firm mountains, standing high, showered His blessings upon it, and ordained ⸢all⸣ its means of sustenance—totaling four Days exactly—for all who ask.

Then He turned towards the heaven when it was ⸢still like⸣ smoke, saying to it and to the earth, 'Submit, willingly or unwillingly.' They both responded, 'We submit willingly.'

So He formed the heaven into seven heavens in two Days, assigning to each its mandate. And We adorned the lowest heaven with ⸢stars like⸣ lamps ⸢for beauty⸣ and for protection. That is the design of the Almighty, All-Knowing."
–Quran 41:9-12

In another verse about the creation of the earth, the 'six days' duration is specifically delineated from the perspective of fatigue:

Indeed, We created the heavens and the earth and everything in between in six Days, and We were not ⸢even⸣ touched with fatigue. – Quran 50:38

The usage of 'days' must not be misconstrued as the typical human days that comprises 24 hours and could be a representation of eras or aeons.

The contextuality of days is a similitude based on limited human capacity and understanding of the divine. The matter had to be broken down to the human level of comprehension. Furthermore, the statement can be appreciated as an emphatic clarification of the Judeo-Christian position that God 'rested' on the 'seventh day' as stated in Genesis 2:2, Genesis 2:3 and Exodus 31:17, respectively. It must be emphasized that Allah does not need any rest; He only needs to say "Be" and whatever He wills is created.

Though the Quran mentions the process of creation using days as an analogy, the Quran does not however, reveal when exactly this creation event occurred – primarily because it is not contextually relevant. So, the creation event described may have occurred millions, billions or trillion of years ago. From a scientific prism, the latest research estimates that the universe is at least 13.8 billion years old, whilst the earth is at least 4.5 billion years old.

Islamic exegesis details events that defy human logic and underpin why humans are the creation and Allah is The Creator. The Quran mentions a few examples about these extraordinary events that defy earthly time.

There is an intriguing story mentioned in Quran 2:259 about a man who wandered through a derelict township and wondered how Allah resurrects things that were dilapidated or dead. It is noteworthy to highlight that exegetes, such as Ibn Kathir, have linked the story of the man in the story to Uzair; which is associated with Ezra in the Judeo-Christian tradition. However, as it is with many other Quranic stories, the Quran did not explicitly mention the man's name. The primary reason for not mentioning is because it is not as important as the crux of the message.

Or, (do you not know) the example of the one who passed through a town that had collapsed on its roofs. He said: "How shall Allah revive this after it is dead?" So, Allah made him dead for a hundred years, then raised him saying: "How long did you remain (in this state)?" He said: "I remained for a day or part of a day". Said He: "Rather, you remained (dead) for a hundred years. Just look at your food and your drink; it has not spoiled. Now look at your donkey. (We did) this to make you a sign for people! Look at the bones, how We raise them, then dress them with flesh." So, when it was clear to him, he said: "I know that Allah is Powerful over everything." – Quran 2:259*

This is a really fascinating story with many lessons. Basically, the man who wanted to understand resurrection got a practical lesson on the subject. He was made to die for a century and when he was resurrected intact, the man assumed he had been in that state for a day or less. Even more intriguing is that, whilst his food and drink were kept in a pristine condition, the man witnessed the resurrection of his decomposed donkey. This particular scenario had different realms operating concurrently – the earthly time of hundred years continued unaffected, the man's edibles were imperishable for that period, the decomposed donkey and the man's intact resurrection to witness the entire phenomena. The Quran addresses the matter of resurrection in many other instances, such as Surah Qiyamah – The Resurrection (Quran75), Abraham and the four birds (Quran 2:260), Jesus' resurrection miracle (Quran 3:49), and the slain man resurrected during Moses' era in the story of The Cow (Quran 2:73).

In a detailed response to doubters of the possibility of resurrection, the Quran reveals the process of creation with mesmerizing references. The scientific world is still trying to comprehend some of these resurrection phenomena many centuries later.

O humanity! If you are in doubt about the Resurrection, then ⸢know that⸣ We did create you from dust, then from a sperm-drop, then ⸢developed you into⸣ a clinging clot ⸢of blood⸣, then a lump of flesh—fully formed or unformed—in order to demonstrate ⸢Our power⸣ to you. ⸢Then⸣ We settle whatever ⸢embryo⸣ We will in the womb for an appointed term, then bring you forth as infants, so that you may reach your prime. Some of you ⸢may⸣ die ⸢young⸣, while others are left to reach the most feeble stage of life so that they may know nothing after having known much. And you see the earth lifeless, but as soon as We send down rain upon it, it begins to stir ⸢to life⸣ and swell, producing every type of pleasant plant. – Quran 22:5*

In a related story – admittedly one of my best stories, resurrection is presented in a way that is not only mind-boggling, but in a manner that arouses the intellect about the concept of time.

The Companions of The Cave: The companions of the cave aka the sleepers of the cave, existed during the era of an idolatrous king, who subjected the people to idol worship. It was the official duty of the king and his minions to persecute anyone who refused idol worship. This persecution policy made a particular group of believing youth – believers in Allah who refused to be idolaters – escape to the outskirts of town. As they migrated beyond the clutches of their persecutors, the companions, accompanied by a dog, decided to take refuge in a particular cave. Whilst inside the cave, the companions prayed to Allah to protect them from their persecutors and prevalent disbelief. Following this, the companions fell asleep inside the cave, and so did their dog, by the cave's entrance. After the companions awakened, they were unsure if they had slept for a day or part of a day.

To relieve their famishment, they nominated one among them to recce the area for any persecutors and stealthily go into town to purchase edibles. As the chosen companion made his way, he noticed the environment was unusual.

At the marketplace, a commotion ensued after the nominated companion presented an ancient currency in exchange for food items. Then the wandering companion realised they were living in a completely different era and dispensation. As word spread, the companions became revered by the people. The township was under a new king, who was fortunately not an idolater, but a believer in the oneness of God.

The Quran describes the companions' paranormal sleep process and how they were turned on alternate sides, including their positioning in relation to orbital motions – Earth rotation around the Sun.

> *And [had you been present], you would see the sun when it rose, inclining away from their cave on the right, and when it set, passing away from them on the left, while they were [lying] within an open space thereof. That was from the signs of Allah. He whom Allah guides is the [rightly] guided, but he whom He sends astray - never will you find for him a protecting guide.*
> *And you would think them awake, while they were asleep. And We turned them to the right and to the left, while their dog stretched his forelegs at the entrance. If you had looked at them, you would have turned from them in flight and been filled by them with terror.*
> – Quran 18:17-18

Also, the Quran reveals the companions spent over three hundred years in the cave asleep (some miraculous form of sleep).

And they remained in their cave for three hundred years and exceeded by nine.
Say, "Allah is most knowing of how long they remained. He has [knowledge
of] the unseen [aspects] of the heavens and the earth. How Seeing is He and
how Hearing! They have not besides Him any protector, and He shares not
His legislation with anyone."
– Quran 18:25-26

The phenomenal incident of the cave sleepers can be described as time freeze in effect, or from a science fiction prism – time inversion meets time travel. A miraculous sleep lasting over three hundred years is beyond average human comprehension, but for the Creator of everything that exists – which includes time itself – anything is possible. This spectacular incident is one of many signs from The Creator – Allah.

The Quran contains many other extraordinary stories that seemingly leave science playing catch-up. A good example of the time manipulation sequences mentioned in the Quran is the transportation – quantum teleportation – of the Queen of Sheba's throne by one of the courtiers of Sulaiman (Solomon). The preface to this remarkable story starts with a missing bird (hoopoe) among the assembly of birds for formation during a routine parade.

Sulaiman was gifted with an army of human beings, jinn, and animals, and had the ability to communicate with various creatures. The Quran mentions how a particular individual gifted with a certain type of scriptural knowledge – esoteric – teleported the throne instantly.

He said: "O chiefs! Which of you can bring me her throne before they come to
me surrendering themselves in obedience?"
An Ifrit (strong) from the jinns said: "I will bring it to you before you rise from
your place (council). And verily, I am indeed strong, and trustworthy for such
work."

> *One with whom was knowledge of the Scripture said: "I will bring it to you*
> *within the twinkling of an eye!" then when [Sulaiman (Solomon)] saw it*
> *placed before him, he said: "This is by the Grace of my Lord to test me*
> *whether I am grateful or ungrateful! And whoever is grateful, truly, his*
> *gratitude is for (the good of) his ownself, and whoever is ungrateful, (he is*
> *ungrateful only for the loss of his ownself). Certainly! My Lord is Rich (Free*
> *of all wants), Bountiful."*
> – Quran 27:38-40

This extraordinary episode affirms certain creations, including humans, have special gifts, at least from an historical prism. More importantly, all exceptional feats are only made possible by The Creator – The Initiator and Owner of time.

> *By time, Indeed, mankind is in loss, Except for those who have believed and*
> *done righteous deeds and advised each other to truth and advised each other to*
> *patience.* – Quran 103:1-3

CHAPTER 6

RATIONAL ANALOGIES

THE COMPUTER MAKER ANALOGY

The Computer Maker Analogy is the anatomization of the inner-workings of the computer via the creationism context. To fully appreciate The Creator contextually, the dynamics of a computer's creation and operation will be adopted. The processes involved in a computer's operational lifecycle gives an insight into the process of creation. Typically, the computer has various interoperating units that make it function. Some of the main components include the Motherboard, Central Processing Unit (CPU), Random Access Memories (RAM), Hard Drive, Video/Graphics Card, Monitor and Processor.

The objective of mentioning these components is not to go into the academic depths of computer science. Rather, the crux of highlighting these units is to establish that, within a computer are various interoperable hardware and software components that assist with its functionality.

Following a design process, a computer manufacturer or maker, makes a computer. During the manufacturing process, the computer and programs are tested for operability and functionality. To achieve the desired functional objectives, the computer maker creates a procedure that involves numerous intricate processes that work in tandem for the computer to function properly. The computer is a platform that makes it possible for a program to be executable. Executable programs can run on any platform, i.e., Supercomputer, Mainframe, Server, PC, Laptop, Netbook, Tablet, Smartphone and Microcontrollers. These various computers and platforms make up a system, operate as a matrix and are interconnected through a primary source –

a maker. At this juncture, it must be emphasized that the computer maker is an entirely separate entity from the manufactured computers in whatever form. The essential objective is for the computer program to operate within the computer system, based on the computer maker's guidelines. Furthermore, the computer maker created the computer system; deals with any anomalous behaviour, and is aware of all the permissions, permutations and possibilities by all programs and processes operating within the system. Basically, the entire scope of all inputs or outputs, including source code, machine code or object code, and all specific outcomes are already known. The outcome of any choice of action is based on the available options, which are predetermined via a master flowchart or process map. As the computer program operates, many processes are initiated within the computer system. Also, the computer program permits certain developments, configurations and modifications within the limits of its environment – which is to the extent that the computer system allows. Due to these processes, so many other programs and sub-systems have been created within the existing computer system. The interoperability and interdependencies of hardware and software within the system ensures functionality. Expectedly, as these programs evolve within the computer system, at some point, some of the emanating software may be oblivious of the existence of a computer maker that made the first computer and computer program that initiated the entire system in which they currently operate. They are oblivious of the reality that their current operating process is a consequence of an initiated process by a special designer – maker - creator. Relating the computer analogy to mankind, man can be likened to a computer program operating within a computer system. Man has been given some permissibility to evolve within the boundaries of the world in which he exists. The evolution has somewhat disillusioned man to the extent of being oblivious to the existence of his creator and by extension damning his very own existence as a mere creation.

Crucially, what must be emphatically stated is the inherent distinction, that man is a creation and is totally separate from The Creator. Also, The Creator is tasked with dealing with anomalous behaviour within the system. The computer system has its limitations, particularly because all computer programs, and ultimately the system, have a lifespan. Intermittently, there appears a code of ethics and guidance that advises the programs about the consequences of running certain operations. The computer programs' advisory states that if programs can abide by certain code of ethics, there is actually a better platform than the current environment. In this situation, adhering codes will be rewritten for super-operability in a better, highly advanced and flawless platform. On the flip side, if the computer programs reject the counsel from the programs' advisory, the computer programs will be eventually expunged and dumped where anomalous computer programs are abandoned. The programs' abandonment zone is not a very conducive environment and has been described as extremely hostile!

Based on the above premise, some potential scenarios can be expounded. There are two groups of programs (codes or software), given permission to operate with guidelines within the computer system. The computer maker has set primary objectives and tests. The primary objective is to allow the system to evolve – run its course, and through assessment, test those who would still believe they are a creation created by a creator. Some of the tests include distractions designed to derail computer programs from primary their objectives. By default, there are assuredly computer programs that will abide by the guidelines for their operability. Certainly, there are programs that will dismiss this notion of any prerequisite test; reject the programs' advisory and refuse to accept there is a maker responsible for their operability. The wayward computer programs tend to be hypnotized by the sophisticated operability of the computer system, despite apparent inadequacies.

In the human context, the two programs can be likened to two groups of human beings, created and given permission to exist within the world. Similar to the computer, man is meant to operate with guidelines that are designed to assist with his worldly functionality.

The test is to live and evolve in the world, and ultimately acknowledge that man and the environment in which man functions, are creations created by The Creator. Belief in The Creator is the ultimate test of man. Basically, if certain prescribed guidelines are complied with, and the test is passed, there is an elevation to the next level, a much better world – paradise – a blissful afterlife is guaranteed forever. Also, for those who choose not to abide by the guidelines, there are adverse consequences as well. With so many worldly distractions, it could be a very tough process accepting such a stark reality. Seemingly, the easier option is to just go with the flow – live life without rules! Just as certain programs reject the computer maker's guidelines, some human beings deny the existence of The Creator. Some of those who deny the existence of a creator may even request The Creator appears before them, as a prerequisite for believing in the existence of a creator. Imagine the absurdity of computer software asking for the person who created the software and the computer to appear before it!

The thought of a man entering a computer system to reveal himself to computer software he created is ludicrous enough to appreciate the inanity. That is how absurd it is asking a creator to appear before its creation. The Creator can show various signs to his creation, but will definitely not appear physically, because of its illogicality and antitheticality to reason. It must be appreciated that God The Creator is completely different. A crucial part of the problem is the assumption that The Creator is a likening of the creation. Nothing could be farther from reality because the creator and creation are very separate entities. Just as the computer, including all of its components and the computer maker are two separate entities; man, and God are also separate entities – The Creator and the creation.

The main reason why some people find it difficult to understand the concept of God is because they cannot conceptualize God as The Creator. God The Creator is a sole entity without any equal or partnership; the Eternal and the only Absolute. The creator of everything that exists, including our overly complex world and all that is contained within it, and our planets and planetary systems and all that surrounds it; the universe and beyond – this life and the afterlife. Generally, those that fall into the denial category are not interested in an afterlife because they are too mesmerised by the trappings of the creation they currently abide, and the manifestations of that habitation. Ideally, those who deny the existence of The Creator need not worry about the consequences of rejection and the afterlife, but that is not always the case. Experience has established that the deniers are probably the most perturbed! Certainly, those in denial could be dismissive of the existence of The Creator, and question how it is possible to monitor the activities of everything – creation. The situation becomes more complicated for those who deny the existence of The Creator with the advent of technology – specifically recording technology.

RECORDING TECHNOLOGY ANALOGY

I am certain some centuries, or even just some decades ago, the concept of accountability must have seemed absurd or strange to previous generations. Some of those who existed in the generations past, would have laughed at the notion of accountability, and summarily dismissed the concept of human beings accounting for their actions. Imagine a scenario of some pious man telling people centuries ago that God The Creator is All-Seeing and All-Knowing, and every move we make is being documented. Some people would have scuffed and mocked at the idea of human beings being accountable for all their actions on earth. At the time, such an idea would have been totally incomprehensible! Those who may have heard such a story probably would not be able to visualize or conceptualize it at the time and would have erroneously concluded its impossibility.

Contemporarily, some people still deny the possibility of this constant recording feat happening. How is it possible for God The Creator to record everything we did since birth daily? Fortunately, with the advent of technology, later generations can conceptualize the recording of every action in its full context. In present-day, a man's entire life can be recorded from its beginning to its very end – cradle to grave. Unfortunately, for those who deny at least, these technological developments should ideally cause the deniers of accountability to have a ratiocinative reflection on these matters. The advent of technology should undoubtedly wipe the smile off the faces of many arrogant deniers who doubt the possibility of an afterlife. Technology has made many things that were thought impossible, possible in our generation. Personally, my background as an Information Technology professional, made me realise decades ago, that there is enough evidence that man – a creation – will undoubtedly face detailed evidential accountability. I worked on projects that required data capture, data processing and data storage. These are various types of data that could easily be made available via a central repository within seconds, with just a few button clicks. Characterised metadata such as images, videos and documents that have been stored for decades in a central repository could be seamlessly accessed. The millennium witnessed the emergence of online video-sharing platforms like YouTube and birthed new technological possibilities. For example, there are videos on YouTube of people who have been recording themselves daily for years. People's entire lives are being saved on YouTube. Decades earlier, an older type of technology such as the closed-circuit television – CCTV, was developed in 1927.

The 1998 Hollywood movie, Enemy of the State starring Will Smith, highlighted how the CCTV and other technologies could be synergised to monitor people's daily lives. There have been gradual technological improvements since then, especially in the area of satellite technology, i.e., nanosatellite. Coincidentally, another 1998 movie, The Truman Show, starring Jim Carrey, depicted the prospects of surveillance for purely entertainment purposes. The Truman Show movie was about the 24/7 camera recording of the main character (Truman Burbank), as he went about his daily activities, and he as the protagonist was unaware.

In the literary world, mass surveillance was thematic in George Orwell's dystopian 1949 novel, 1984, with an accurate prediction of a 'Big Brother' system. Decades later, the world was forced to endure Big Brother and other vacuous reality TV shows that promote constant human surveillance. The primary objective is the observation of the daily activities of select subjects as entertainment – guinea pigs for amusement!

Based on these examples and possibilities, if a mere creation (man) can do this, just imagine how easy it is for The Creator to store the data of our lives, with obviously more advanced capabilities.

Evidently, The Creator will have a more advance and sophisticated method of precision-based documentation, than the mere creation called man. The Quran mentions this recording process in precise detail over many verses, some of these verses include:

> And indeed, [appointed] over you are keepers
> Noble and recording
> They know whatever you do.
> – Quran 82:10-12

And We have already created man and know what his soul whispers to him,

and We are closer to him than [his] jugular vein

When the two receivers receive, seated on the right and the left.

Man does not utter any word except that with him is an observer prepared [to

record].

– Quran 50:16 -18

And the record [of deeds] will be placed [open], and you will see the criminals

fearful of that within it, and they will say, "Oh, woe to us! What is this book

that leaves nothing small or great except that it has enumerated it?" And they

will find what they did present [before them]. And your Lord does injustice to

no one. – Quran 18:49

And We place the scales of justice for the Day of Resurrection, so no soul will

be treated unjustly at all. And if there is [even] the weight of a mustard seed,

We will bring it forth. And sufficient are We as accountant. – Quran 21:47

That day, We will seal over their mouths, and their hands will speak to Us,

and their feet will testify about what they used to earn.– Quran 36:65

The above-mentioned verses are essentially stating that God The Creator is aware, is All-Seeing and All-Knowing, and is aware of absolutely everything His creation does. Apart from the established point of appointed keepers documenting all actions in individualised accounts, God The Creator is aware of all the thought-processes and innermost desires of His creation, without the uttering of words!

And conceal your speech or publicize it; indeed, He is Knowing of that within the breasts. – Quran 67:13

God The Creator is aware of the creation's moves before excogitation and execution. More importantly, these verses establish every man (creation) will account for actions, and there will be evidential proof.

Furthermore, what I find particularly intriguing is the aspect of man's mouth being sealed up and the hands will speak. There are a few ways to analyse this phenomenon. One possible explanation is that our hands could be made to speak up literally. Another explanation is to appreciate such a phenomenal feat through technology. Some decades ago, mobile phones were incomprehensible to a particular era. After mobile phones were invented, the use of buttons became commonplace on devices, later came the combination of computers and phones to create smartphones. Initially, smartphones with buttons were a novelty. Then touchscreen became a standard with smartphones. Nowadays, a lot of touchscreen gadgets exist, and people are recording their lives via mobile phones and other handheld devices. Also, there are handheld gadgets that can project images onto any platform, and there are gadgets that can project or reflect images onto the hand. Advancements in holography and holographic technology are highlighting the possibilities of better 3D Holographic User Interface (HUI), which can be projected and controlled by hand. Movies like Marvel's Iron Man have depicted the potential capabilities of hand-controlled holographic projections. Contemporary technological advancements and movies have definitely broadened our intellectual horizons and may assist our imaginative capabilities to have a glimpse into futuristic possibilities. There are things that were unfathomable to previous generations that make sense to human beings presently, just as there are things that may be strange to our understanding now but will make much sense to later generations. Essentially, the aforementioned Quranic verses about hands speaking up could mean hands acting as handheld devices or as part of a projector system that displays actions in detail. Until these events occur, we can only imagine and marvel at the possibilities.

What we would actually witness on the day of reckoning may be some advanced super technology that can only make sense at that moment in future. Ideally, these thought-provoking verses ought to trigger a ratiocinative inquisition in any discerning mind. The beauty of the mind is in its dynamism, and the application of thought can produce astonishing results at any level. Generally, there ought to be some level of contemplation about human technological advancements; if human beings can produce such sophisticated technologies, surely, the creator of human beings can create things that are even more sophisticated.

THE CORONAVIRUS ANALOGY

Around late 2019, the world was hit by the "severe acute respiratory syndrome coronavirus" (SARS-CoV-2) or Covid-19. The origin of the coronavirus was traced to Wuhan, China. As the pandemic unfolded, I thought about the irony of atheists insisting on seeing God as a prerequisite for accepting God's existence but running scared from what cannot be seen. Evidently, the "seeing is believing" mantra is not applicable in this coronavirus situation!

Though the coronavirus cannot be seen with normal human vision, there are some specialized equipment that can be utilised for this purpose. The human eye can see as small as 0.1 millimetres, and the coronavirus is not even detectable with the standard optical microscope. The coronavirus measures around 100 nanometres. To put the size in perspective, about 10,000 coronaviruses can fit into the millimetre of a standard ruler. In measurement; 1 million millimetres make 1 nanometre, so 10,000 millimetres makes 100 nanometres. So, at 100 nanometres, the size of the coronavirus is very small, and the smallest wavelengths of light that the human eye can see with a standard optical microscope measures around 400 nanometres. To be able to see something as small as the coronavirus, requires magnification or acceleration with a device that uses shorter wavelengths than visible light. This is where electron microscopy comes in handy. There are two types of electron microscopy techniques available: Scanning Electron Microscope (SEM) and Transmission Electron Microscope (TEM). The two electron microscopy techniques offer different views.

The SEM scans surfaces of sample viruses and processes the information that bounces back. Its information relay process can be compared to that of a satellite in orbit. The TEM operates by transmitting electrons of virus samples and projecting a cross-section of its internal structure. A combination of these two techniques gives adequate coverage and assists with monitoring how the virus operates. This process gives a clearer understanding of how the coronavirus penetrates host cells with its ribonucleic acid (RNA), its self-reproduction capabilities and potential chimerical manifestations. Essentially, the whole world was literally brought to a standstill by a virus not visible to the naked eye. Nonetheless, the coronavirus remains a creative manifestation or a consequence of creation, in its minutest form. Allah is The Creator and Observer of everything that exists, from the indefinitesimal to the indefinite and from the infinitesimal to the infinite.

> *And in His Providence are the keys of the Unseen; none knows them except He. And He knows whatever is in the land and the sea. And in no way does a leaf fall down, except that He knows it, and not a grain in the darkness (es) of the earth, not a thing wet or dry, except that it is in an evident Book.*
> – Quran 6:59

Comparatively, as minuscule as the coronavirus is to the human body, human beings are even more minuscule, when analysed from a cosmological perspective. Mankind can collectively be appreciated as a summation of insignificance evidenced by the earth's situation in the universe.

This inconsequentiality is further underpinned when the cosmos is explored via seven dimensional levels:

(1) Earth (2) Solar System (3) Milky Way Galaxy (4) Local Group (5) Virgo Supercluster (6) Observable Universe (7) Unobservable Universe.

(1) Earth is about 510 million square kilometres with roughly 7.8 billion human beings on earth.

(2) The Solar System is about 36 billion times larger than Earth and comprises the Sun and 8 planets: Mercury, Venus, Earth, Mars, Jupiter, Saturn, Uranus, and Neptune. Earth can fit into the sun1.3 million times.

(3) The Milky Way Galaxy has at least 200 billion stars and its habitable zones can accommodate at least 40 billion Earth-sized planets.

(4) The Local Group comprises the Milky Way Galaxy, which is part of at least 54 types of the galaxies.

(5) The Virgo Supercluster is a mass concentration of galaxies containing at least 100 galaxy groups and clusters, and possibly 2,000 member galaxies.

(6) The Observable Universe contains about 10 million superclusters, including the Virgo Supercluster. There could be a conglomerate of at least 2 trillion galaxies within the Observable Universe.

(7) The Unobservable Universe is anything beyond the Observable Universe.

Evidently, planet earth, with its millions of species and over 7.8 billion human population contained within its earthly space, is just a tiny spec in the universal scheme of affairs.

> *It is He Who hath created for you all things that are on earth; Moreover His design comprehended the heavens, for He gave order and perfection to the seven firmaments; and of all things He hath perfect knowledge.*– Quran 2:29

CHAPTER 7

RATIOCINATIVE ALLEGORIES

The following allegories are derived from legends and human reasoning, which logically elucidate the concept of God as The Creator, and further buttresses human limitations.

THE WOMB

The intricacies involved in pregnancy and childbirth are intellectually provocative. Imagine a baby in its mother's womb. All the baby knows is its mother's womb – its entire existence is based on the curvatures of its mother's stomach. In this idyllic state, the baby eats when it wants and sleeps when it wants. The baby is in its own paradise literally because the parameters of womb are all it knows! Assuming someone manages to communicate with the baby and informs the baby, this current residential abode (mother's womb) is nothing compared to the world the baby is going to be born into following childbirth. Apart from the mystery of childbirth, the world being described would be unfathomable to such a baby. As far as the baby is concerned, nowhere compares to the seemingly utopian surroundings of the womb. Unfortunately, it would be impossible for the baby to leave its mother's womb to experience the world being described and return. The baby would have to wait till it is born to experience the world it cannot yet fathom or comprehend. This is the similitude of man living on earth. Life on earth is ephemeral and is a transition to the afterlife, where the soul dominates. The incomprehensibility of an afterlife is similar to those who say that life ends here on earth, and believing, once you die – that is it! Man living on earth is like the baby stuck in its mother's womb – the afterlife is simply incomprehensible.

However, in both scenarios, the baby and man have been informed, and in both instances, it is impossible to return.

Imagine the absurdity of a human being born into the world, but still trying to feed through the umbilical cord of its mother's womb. Trying to feed as it did, during the womb period, would not only be ridiculous, but an extremely deleterious misadventure. The rules of eating in the world are very much different from the confines of a womb. The womb analogy further highlights the irony of creation, and the contumacy of man is brought to fore. Man, as a fragile and helpless embryo in the womb, develops and acquires little knowledge about the world, and then based on life's mesmerising effects, denies the existence of The Creator.

THE DESERT BEDOUIN

As an allegorical example, I will cite an excerpt from "The Breath of Perfumes" by the famous scholar and historian Ahmad ibn Muhammad al-Maqqari (1577-1632), about a brief encounter with a Bedouin in the deserts of Arabia. A sceptic quizzed the Bedouin about his conviction in the existence of God, considering he had never seen God, and the Bedouin replied:

> *Camel dung indicates camels, donkey dung indicates donkeys and footprints indicate travel. So the sky, with its constellations and the seas with its waves, do not these indicate the All-Knowing, the All-Powerful?*

The succinct response from the Bedouin underpins the advantages of ratiocinating. As simplistic as the Bedouin's response may seem, it is rooted in wisdom. Through intriguing responses, the Bedouin demonstrated the causation and effectuation governing creation. Fundamentally, a variable must have caused another variable to exist. Based on existential realities, the

Bedouin's thought processes extrapolated thus; if camels did not exist, there will be no camel dung. If donkeys do not exist, there will be no donkey dung. Furthermore, the existence of footprints signifies the reality of their ownership and evidence peregrination. Most importantly, the existence of the sky with its constellations and the sea with its waves indicate precision and intelligent design, and thoroughly establishes the existence of a Creator.

Essentially, the Bedouin established himself as a thinker and chose to appreciate the existence of God through the visibility of creation in his milieu. This position affirms that you do not have to see God to appreciate the existence of God. God The Creator can be appreciated through His creation. The Bedouin's certitude affirms that manifestations of wisdom will naturally elude those who abandon or underutilise their god-gifted reasoning faculties.

ABU HANIFA AND THE ATHEIST

History is rife with many great thinkers, especially in the Islamic tradition. Abu Hanifa is an example of a wise man who engaged his intellectual adversaries logically. This is a rendition of Abu Hanifa's classic encounter with an atheist. In the era when the ancient city of Baghdad was a citadel of knowledge and scientific advancement, was a story about an atheist and Abu Hanifa. On one side of River Tigris were royal palaces and on the other side was the city. One fateful day an atheist approached the Muslims gathered at the royal palace and said to them, "I don't believe in God, there cannot be a God, because you cannot see or hear Him; you are all wasting your time! Bring me your best debater and I will debate the issue with him."

After the atheist literally threw down the gauntlet, the decision was made to contact the best debater at the time, which happened to be Imam Abu Hanifa.

A messenger from amongst the Muslims was sent over the River Tigris to the city where Abu Hanifa resided, to inform him about the challenge from the atheist. After crossing the River Tigris, the messenger conveyed the atheist's challenge to Abu Hanifa, and he confirmed his intention to attend the debate. The messenger returned, travelling over the River Tigris once again to the Royal Palaces, where everyone, including the atheist, awaited the arrival of Abu Hanifa. It was sunset at the time and one hour had passed, but Abu Hanifa still had not arrived. Another hour had passed, and there was still no sign of Abu Hanifa. The Muslims started becoming tense and worried about Abu Hanifa's absence and lateness. The Muslims were confronted with a dilemma, they did not want the atheist to think that Muslims were too scared to debate him, yet they did not want to take up the challenge themselves, because Abu Hanifa was the best of debaters from amongst the Muslims. Again, another hour passed, and suddenly the atheist started laughing and remarked, "Your best debater is too scared! He knows he is wrong; he is too frightened to come and debate with me. I guarantee he will not turn up today!" After many hours of waiting, the Muslims increased in apprehension, and the atheist had a haughty smile on his face. The clock ticked on and on, until Abu Hanifa finally arrived. The Muslims inquired about his lateness and remarked, "O Abu Hanifa, a messenger sent for you hours ago, and you arrive now, do explain your tardiness to us." Abu Hanifa apologises for his lateness and begins to explain, as the atheist listens to his story. Abu Hanifa stated: "Once the messenger delivered the message to me, I began to make my way to the River Tigris, and on reaching the riverbank, I realised there was no boat available for me to cross the river. As it was getting dark, I looked around, and there was no boat anywhere nor was there a navigator or a sailor in sight, for me to cross the river to the Royal Palaces. I continued to look around for a boat, as I did not want the atheist to think I was running away from debating him. As I was contemplating my next move, I stood by the riverbank looking for a navigator or a boat, when something strange caught my attention in the middle of the river. I looked forward, and to my surprise I saw planks of wood rising to the surface from the riverbed. I was shocked and confounded, and I could not believe what I was seeing. Readymade planks of the same width and length were rising to the surface and adjoining seamlessly. I was truly astounded by what was happening and wondered if my eyes were deceiving me. I continued to look at the middle of the river, and then I saw nails emanating from the river. The nails were properly positioned by the planks, and without anything effort or tools, the nails held all the planks together firmly. I stood in amazement and thought to myself, 'O Allah, how can all this be happening; planks of wood rising to the surface by itself, and then nails affixing without any hammering' I could not understand what was happening before my eyes."

Meanwhile, the atheist was listening to Abu Hanifa's story with a wry smile on his face. Abu Hanifa continued, "I was still standing by the riverbank watching these planks of wood join with nails when I noticed water seeping through the gaps in the wood. Suddenly, I saw a sealant appear from the river and it began sealing all the gaps by itself. Again, I thought, 'Ya Allah how is this possible, how can a sealant appear and seal the gaps without any visible effort, and nails appear without anyone hammering them?' Then, I looked closer, and I could see a boat forming before my very eyes! As I stood in astonishment, a sail suddenly appeared, and I pondered, 'How is this happening, a self-created boat has appeared before my eyes, and now a sail?' So, I thought 'how can I use this boat to cross the river to the Royal Palaces?' I stood staring in wonderment when the boat suddenly began to move. The boat came towards me, by sailing against the current, and parked floating beside me at the riverbank. I felt as if the boat was informing me to embark onto it. So, I boarded the boat, and yet again, it began to move. There was no navigator or sailor on the boat, but it was able to sail towards the direction of the royal palaces, without any instruction as to my intended destination.

I really could not comprehend what was happening! This boat had formed and was taking me to my destination. The boat eventually reached the other side of the River Tigris and I disembarked. As I turned around, the boat had vanished, and that is why I arrived late."

At that moment, the atheist bursts out laughing hysterically and remarked, "O Abu Hanifa, I heard you were the best debater from amongst the Muslims, I heard that you were the wisest, the most knowledgeable from amongst your people." The atheist continued, "From seeing you today, I can confirm that you possess none of those qualities. You speak of planks appearing from nowhere, nails positioning without being hammered, self-applying sealant, and the boat sailing to your destination without a navigator, and it was against the tide! You are talking gibberish! Your story is ridiculous, I am having none of it and I do not believe a word of it!" Abu Hanifa turned to the atheist and replied, "You do not believe a word of it? You do not believe that planks and nails can appear from nowhere and self-affix? You do not believe sealants can be self-applying? You do not believe a boat can move without a navigator; hence, you do not believe that a boat can appear from nowhere without a boat maker?" The atheist remarked defiantly, and reiterated, "Yes, I do not believe a word of it!" Abu Hanifa calmly replied, "If you cannot believe that a boat came into being without a boat maker, how can you believe that the whole world, the universe, the stars, the oceans, the planets and everything that exists came into being without a creator?" Utterly befuddled by Abu Hanifa's sapient response, the atheist fled the debate venue.

The encounter between the atheist and Abu Hanifa is very intriguing and filled with much wisdom. Contemporarily, there are many people in the category of the atheist, with their major problem being inherent hubristic tendencies obstructing their imaginative pathways, which manifests as a limitation to their ratiocinative capabilities.

How can you, as a creation, acknowledge the intelligent design of yourself and environment, which is also a creation, then deny the existence of an Intelligent Designer – The Creator? The denial of this reality is self-defeatist and is tantamount to denying your very own existence!

CHAPTER 8

REALISM, ABSTRACTS, AND SIMULATIONS

REALITY

For many centuries, philosophers and scientists have been preoccupied with issues concerning reality and consciousness, including various epistemological propositions such as materialism, idealism and ascertaining realism – the intricacies of reality, and understanding what is real and what is unreal. Between reality, abstracts, and simulations are many variations that transcend the ontological to the epistemological. For instance, The Computer Maker Analogy, as postulated, highlights mankind's vulnerabilities and incapacities. When such an analogy is juxtaposed with life in general, certain scenarios can be appreciated from a causation premise, such that, the plug can be pulled on the computer, as the plug can literally be pulled on life!

THE ABSTRACTIVE

In dealing with the abstractive, the consideration of various abstracts such as pride, joy, courage, trust, anger, hate and love must be taken into cognizance. These aforementioned abstracts fall under the category of emotions. Taking an emotion like love, as a simplistic similitude, a lot can be extrapolated. Whilst such emotions cannot be physically seen, the manifestations of such emotions exist. In view of this, it would be ridiculous to say, I want to see love or have a discussion with love or that is love crossing the road over there. So, the inability to see love as a physical entity does not prove its nonexistence.

This position further establishes why theories that primarily focus on tangible or observable evidence – seeing is believing – often have limitations, because not everything is physically observable. The emergence of quantum physics, and related interdisciplinary advancements, actually proves physical imperceptibility. Delving deeper into the abstractive realm, there are the complexities of incorporeality, and abstracts such as the mind, consciousness, dreams and the soul.

Matters of The Soul

The soul and its composition are one of the many unknowns that confound science. Mankind has long pondered on matters of the soul. For instance, Aristotle described the soul from the "actuality" premise and stated, "The soul, then, must be substance as the form of a natural body that is potentially alive."[7] From that point onwards, there have been various propositions.

As scientists continue to grapple with the matter, there are scientific studies that tend to confine the soul to neuroscience and psychological concepts. For example, the quantum theory of consciousness concentrates on understanding the nature of the soul. Such enduring scientific paradigms are being expounded by theories such as Biocentrism. Robert Lanza posited the possibility of life after death and discusses the existence of the soul.[8]

Also, two renowned quantum scientists, Dr. Stuart Hameroff and Sir Roger Penrose posited, through a quantum theory of consciousness process called Orchestrated Objective Reduction (Orch-OR), that souls are contained inside "microtubules", which reside in brain cells. [9]

According to Hameroff, if "the heart stops beating, the blood stops flowing, the microtubules lose their quantum state, but the quantum information, which is in the microtubules isn't destroyed, it can't be destroyed – it just distributes and dissipates to the universe at large". Hameroff further stated that in the event of death, the "quantum information can exist outside the body, perhaps indefinitely, as a soul." [10]

As intriguing as the foregoing postulations may seem, an explication of the Islamic viewpoint is necessary to fully grasp the concept of the soul. One of the words used to refer to the soul in the Quran is *Nafs*, including its linguistic derivatives. The Quran states:

> *Every soul must taste of death, then to Us you shall be brought back.*
> —Quran29:57

In another section, the Quran states:

> *Allah takes the souls at the time of their death, and those that do not die [He takes] during their sleep. Then He keeps those for which He has decreed death and releases the others for a specified term. Indeed, in that are signs for a people who give thought.* — Quran 39:42

Interestingly, both verses mention death. The first verse explicitly states that everyone with a soul must die and return to The Creator. However, the second cited verse further explains the dynamics of the soul during sleep. Basically, when humans sleep, they somehow die. So, the process of sleeping can be understood as a form of death, or near-death experience, because the soul is taken away, and only returned for those who are destined to be awakened. Below is a Hadith that mentions the near-death experience point:

> *Narrated by Abu Qatadah: When the people slept till so late that they did not offer the (morning) prayer, the Prophet ﷺ said, "Allah captured your souls (made you sleep) when He willed, and returned them (to your bodies) when He willed." So the people got up and went to answer the call of nature, performed ablution, till the sun had risen and it had become white, then the Prophet ﷺ got up and offered the prayer.*— Sahih al-Bukhari 7471

The above-mentioned near-death explanation makes logical sense, especially when the nature of dreams is taken into cognizance. Science has long been preoccupied with the dream phenomenon; Sigmund Freud and Carl Jung are a few examples of scientists who have done extensive work on the nature of dreams. In the entertainment industry, there has also been an artistic preoccupation with the dreams phenomenon. The Matrix (1999) and Inception (2010) are a couple of examples of dream-oriented movies. The Inception movie has aspects about lucid dreams – in which a dreamer is conscious of their dream. Personally, I have experienced many lucid dreams. I remember a particularly strange incident where I dozed off behind the wheel. On that day, I was driving on a motorway and suddenly nodded off, then I started to dream, and in my dream, I realised I was dreaming about driving a car on a motorway. This dream realisation led me to remembering my reality of driving a car. By the time I woke up from my momentary sleep, the car was already veering off my lane of the motorway and was about to enter the median strip. I immediately regained control of the car's steering wheel and thanked God there were no other cars within my vicinity, during the incident. In a scene from The Matrix movie, Morpheus asked Neo about ever having a dream that felt so real. In fact, every time we sleep should be a reminder for those who reflect. At times we sleep for just a few hours and dream. In the dream we live an entire life and do so many things that would normally take decades in real time. I have had dreams that were so real; I thought I existed in another realm. I dreamt I lived a detailed and fulfilled life, just as I would in the real world. But alas, it was just a dream! This sort of reality-oriented dream can be appreciated as a wondering soul – ethereal – without its body. Thus, making it clearer, that humans are spirit-like creatures trapped in a physical body. During dreams, the soul wonders off and returns during the point of awakening. The Quran explains the process thus:

And it is He who takes your souls by night and knows what you have committed by day. Then He revives you therein that a specified term may be fulfilled. Then to Him will be your return; then He will inform you about what you used to do. – Quran 6:60

In view of these points, the soul must be appreciated as what it is – a distinct creation in its own right. In explaining the phases preceding the actual creation of man, the Quran states:

When your Lord said to the angels, "Indeed, I am going to create a human being from clay. So when I have proportioned him and breathed into him of My [created] soul, then fall down to him in prostration.—Quran38:71-72

What the above-mentioned verse establishes is that, after man was created from dust in a complete and well-proportioned form, his perfected body was created a soul by The Creator. Basically, the body was created, and the soul was created, and these two creations (body and soul), are separate entities that complement each other – working in unison to fulfil optimal human functionality. Without the soul, the body of man will just be an empty shell. To further buttress the phases of man's creation, a Hadith on the creation of Adam states that he was created and was left hollow for a certain period. Following this period of hollowness, Adam was brought to life with a soul. Anas reported, the Prophet ﷺ saying:

When Allah fashioned Adam in Paradise, He left him as He liked him to leave. Then Iblis roamed round him to see what actually that was and when he found him hollow from within, he recognised that he had been created with a disposition that he would not have control over himself.
– Sahih Muslim 2611 a, Book 45, Hadith 146

The existence of the soul undoubtedly highlights the limitations of science. Advancements in science can, for example, replicate human bodies and prosthetics, but cannot bring the human body to life. The most that can be achieved by science are robotic replications of the human form, particularly via artificial intelligence. The absence of a soul during replications of creations buttresses man's inabilities, despite the oft-purported scientific advancements. Contemporarily, scientists are exploring the boundaries of artificial intelligence and attempting the programming of consciousness into computers. Mind uploading and emulation are theoretical possibilities. Despite such supposed developments, the inability of humans to create a soul still culminates in futility. The soul is an exclusive creation that can only be created by The Creator. In essence, man (science) can only copy but cannot create. The act of creation is solely exclusive to The Creator. The soul is the software that powers the hardware (body). Just like computer hardware, without the appropriate software, the computer is functionless.

and when the souls ⸢and their bodies⸣ are paired ⸢once more⸣, – Quran 81:7

SIMULATIONS

Vital lessons can be learnt from contemporary technological developments and emerging digital trends. We live in a world of advanced technologies that include artificial intelligence, cybernetics, computer simulations, and the possibilities of quantum computing and simulation.

Artificial intelligence or machine intelligence revolves around utilizing algorithms and data that mimic human intelligence. Cybernetics involves systems study and adaption, through feedback, of environments for functional improvement. Computer simulations involve mathematical modelling and are attained by running computer programs. There has been a rapid evolvement of quantum information sciences, and an expansion of frontiers in computing and teleportation. Quantum computing involves developments in quantum mechanics and entanglement for computation, which also includes the theoretical possibilities of simulation.

Technological advancements have evolved to a phase where what humans observe to be reality, can be replicated. As a result, there are various types of computer-generated realities – augmented reality, simulated reality and virtual reality. Primarily, these pseudo realities are attempting to simulate immersion – escapism – in some sort of alternate reality. Computer simulations can be used for training in various industries to help improve human performance through perception and execution of remote tasks. Motion controllers can track motion via accelerometer sensors. Haptic, kinaesthetic or 3D touch technology can be used to control virtual objects. Holographic User Interface (HUI) is being advanced for better 3D experience.

I remember during my postgraduate studies; I travelled to Japan and visited the Panasonic Center Tokyo. As part of my excursion, I was treated to a futuristic exhibition – a spectacular edutainment session. The highlight of futuristic technologies for me was Panasonic's Life Wall. It was an interactive wall where projected images could be controlled with hand gestures and movements. Panasonic's Life Wall could simultaneously act as a TV, computer, CCTV, gadget control, gaming and study area. Principally, the objective was to depict the capabilities of the Life Wall as it executes daily tasks, and its essentiality in futuristic households.

Simulations can be used in cybernetics, robotics, training of military personnel, pilots and astronauts. Astronauts can be trained to perform replicated tasks in a simulated outer space environment. There are various movies that have utilised these technologies to project various forms of simulated or alternate reality. The 1999 movie, The Matrix, depicts humanity being trapped in a simulated reality. In the 2017 Movie, Valerian, the scene at the Big Market portrays an extra-dimensional realm, which is accessible through special virtual reality-type equipment; this enables interaction between two realms. The 2018 movie, Ready Player One typifies the manifestation of virtual reality and gaming. Gaming is a multi-billion industry that has continually pushed the boundaries of simulated reality. The world of gaming (video games, arcade games, computer games), has come a very long way from Spacewar! (1962) and Pong (1973). Nowadays, computer games are trying hard to simulate reality. The virtual world is a computer-based simulated environment that is commonplace in gaming. Also, within this virtual world, there are instances; which are a copy of game areas for a select group of players, isolated from the wider game world. So, this can be perceived as a game within game – creation within a creation. Such gaming platforms permit user-generated content (UGC) or user-created content (UCC) by users. These permitted instances can manifest in various contents like the metaverse – portmanteau of "meta" (beyond) and universe. There are virtual world platforms that simulate reality and permit user-generated content such as Second Life or the life simulation games of The Sims franchise. These games are often referred to as MMOG (Massively Multiplayer Online Game). Such platforms involve a combination of role-playing video games (RPGs) and massively multiplayer online games where a large number of players interact via a virtual world platform. Examples of some of these games include, World of Warcraft, Star Wars: The Old Republic, Realm Online, Lord of The Rings Online, Anarchy Online, Final Fantasy, and Star Trek Online. The gaming world keeps developing and the games can be deployed on smartphones. Some of these smartphones utilise GPS technology to simulate augmented reality and gives the user another experience. Games such as Ingress and Pokémon Go are part of this gaming sub-genre. There are some downsides to these sorts of games. For instance, Pokémon Go was blamed for causing "deaths", and accidents to gamers, passersby and bystanders caught in its gaming web.[11] Nevertheless, computer gaming continues to broaden its scope with the metaverse, virtual world evolution to 3D – three dimensional – spaces, shared with the internet of things. Interestingly, the gaming world has a sub-genre referred to as 'god-games'. The irony!

There are propounded theories based on the advancement of technological patterns and trajectories, developments may metamorphose to a point where simulation is indistinguishable from reality. That reality is simulation. For example, there are theorists such as the French sociologist and philosopher, Jean Baudrillard whose works included simulacra and simulation, and hyperreality, highlighted the inability to consciously distinguish between reality and the simulation of reality.[12]Also, American writer and science fiction enthusiast, Philip K. Dick, had his own theories about simulation; at the 1977 METZ Sci-Fi Conference in France, he informed his audience that "we are living in a computer-programmed reality".[13]More recently, I came across discussions about the possibility of mankind living in a computer simulation. Elon Musk and Neil deGrasse Tyson are examples of those who have respectively discussed the topic via different platforms.[14] The computer simulation theory is not new. In 2003, Nick Bostrom published "Are You Living in a Computer Simulation?" in Philosophy Quarterly.[15] Bostrom's probabilistic analysis propounds the possibility of mankind living in a computer simulation. However, I am of the opinion that as intellectual beings, we must not stop at the hypothetical phase – the ultimate quest is to identify the initiator of the 'computer simulation'. The self-inflicted, and often hubristic, epistemological boundaries must be shattered to include the possibility of a supreme being – a creator. The objective is not just to identify our existence in a supposed computer simulation, nor is it the futile preoccupation of breaking out of a presumed encapsulated system. Rather, the objective is to appreciate the computer simulation as a logical similitude to understanding our existence – as creations created within a created system by The Creator. Notably, the computer simulation position aligns with The Computer Maker Analogy, as posited, with divinity being the distinctive factor. There are simulation theories attempting to expound the potential of civilizations becoming advanced enough to escape the simulation in which they live. Those in this category theorize possibilities of escaping from a virtual prison and consequently experiencing a supposed real world. In reality, though this may seem merely theoretical, and the breaking out of a simulation an impossibility, the theory can actually be expounded from the Islamic position. The simple explanation is that mankind evolves from Earth to the afterlife. From an Islamic viewpoint, there are various examples of citations in an afterlife. The post-human phase of the simulation theory can be appreciated by exploring human transfiguration. Essentially, mankind goes through a phase of their souls being trapped in the human form, until it is released to manifest to its fullest potential. One example where the Quran explains transfiguration in the afterlife states:

> *In that We will change your likeness and produce you in that [form] which you do not know* – Quran 56:61

A loosely translated saying attributed to Ali ibn Abi Talib – a cousin of Prophet Muhammad ﷺ – explains mankind's transcendence thus:

> *People are asleep, when they die they wake up* – Ali ibn Abi Talib

CHAPTER 9

PURPOSE OF LIFE

What is the meaning of life? What is life's purpose? These are recurring questions that have preoccupied humankind from inception. To understand the purpose of life, an elucidation of the initial creation is vital. From an Islamic position, absolutely nothing existed before creation was created by The Creator – Allah. The Quran emphasizes that the world was not created without purpose and the primary purpose of life is to worship Allah.

> *Those who remember Allah (always, and in prayers) standing, sitting, and lying down on their sides, and think deeply about the creation of the heavens and the earth, (saying): "Our Lord! You have not created (all) this without purpose, glory to You! (Exalted be You above all that they associate with You as partners). Give us salvation from the torment of the Fire.* – Quran 3:191

Based on Islamic exegesis, mankind is not the first creation. Also worthy of note is that the Quran does not specify a timeline about the era Adam existed, unlike some other religious scriptures. Moreover, the environment Adam was created into already existed. The Quran mentions the story of Adam's creation and the conversation with the angels.

> *⸢Remember⸣ when your Lord said to the angels, "I am going to place a successive ⸢human⸣ authority on earth." They asked ⸢Allah⸣, "Will You place in it someone who will spread corruption there and shed blood while we glorify Your praises and proclaim Your holiness?" Allah responded, "I know what you do not know."*

He taught Adam the names of all things, then He presented them to the angels
and said, "Tell Me the names of these, if what you say is true?"
They replied, "Glory be to You! We have no knowledge except what You have
taught us. You are truly the All-Knowing, All-Wise."
Allah said, "O Adam! Inform them of their names." Then when Adam did,
Allah said, "Did I not tell you that I know the secrets of the heavens and the
earth, and I know what you reveal and what you conceal?"
– Quran 2:30-33

The clarity the angels sought was based on apprehensions of something
ruinous that may have occurred with a previous creation or creations. Also, the
angels stated their knowledge is based on what Allah has taught them.
However, Adam appeared to have been a special creation, presumably with a
unique form of intellect. When the angels could not fulfil the naming task,
Allah told Adam to inform the Angels of all the things created. Another way
of explicating the scenario is that Adam was created after other creations – a
prior environment filled with other creations. In this regard, the Islamic
viewpoint is in tandem with the scientific position that some organisms have
existed for millions of years, just as the universe has existed for billions of
years. The reality is that humankind came much later than its habitual
environment and no detailed information is revealed about the timeframe
between the respective creations.

THE STRUGGLE

Following the episode of the naming contest – an advanced form of
taxonomy, and Adam had identified the creations, Allah told all the angels
present to prostrate to Adam out of reverence (not worship). All those present
prostrated as instructed, except Iblis.

Notably, Iblis was a jinn, whose refusal to prostate to Adam, transformed him to the accursed aka Satan.

> *(Allah) said: "Then get thee out from here; for thou art rejected, accursed.*
> –Quran 15:34

It is important to state that Jinn are a prior creation, created from smokeless fire, before Adam. And similar to human beings, the Jinn were given free will. Angels on their part, were not created with free will, so can only obey their Creator. This position is starkly contrastive to some religious doctrines that believe Satan (Iblis) was an angel that rebelled. The default composition of angels as creatures of conformity to their Creator does not permit rebellion.

Explicating from a legal viewpoint, the taxonomical event can be perceived as a special court. When Allah instructed those present to bow to Adam, and Iblis did not comply, Allah gave Iblis the opportunity to explain himself – a defence, and questioned Iblis about his reason for not bowing to Adam as the angels did. A possible reason for this sequence is that, if Allah had immediately sanctioned Iblis, the angels may be unaware of the reason for his disobedience, or the angels wait until they are made aware afterwards by Allah. Rather, Allah allowed Iblis a self-incriminating testimony for all those present to witness and for the benefit of all future generations of creations – especially mankind and jinn. For reasons best known to Iblis, he refused to bow down to Adam, with the presumptuous notion that he was better than Adam.

Following his transgression, the preposterous justification Iblis gave for his transgression was that Allah created him from fire, whilst Allah created Adam from clay. The Quran captures the interrogation and response of Iblis:

Allah asked, "What prevented you from prostrating when I commanded you?"
He replied, "I am better than he is: You created me from fire and him from
clay." – Quran 7:12

Contextually, another interpretation of Allah informing the angels about His awareness of what the angels were unaware of is that Allah was fully aware of the pride and imperious tendencies within Iblis and the angels were not. The pride of Iblis became manifest after the creation of Adam, and for this reason Iblis was banished.

> *[Iblis (Satan)] said: "See? This one whom You have honoured above me, if*
> *You give me respite (keep me alive) to the Day of Resurrection, I will surely*
> *seize and mislead his offspring (by sending them astray) all but a few!"*
> – Quran 17:62

Still prideful, Iblis maintained he was better than Adam, and pleaded for respite for his disobedience, only so he can mislead mankind. Iblis managed to expedite the eviction of Adam and Eve from their initial paradisiacal abode, by causing them to disobey Allah. Unlike Iblis, Adam immediately admitted his guilt, sought repentance and hoped in the Mercy of Allah. Adam was forgiven, and he and his progeny are allowed to dwell on earth for a period and given the opportunity to decide their eternal abode in the hereafter, based on individual actions. Eventually, Iblis will exculpate himself from those he misleads, and the Quran mentions the future encounter:

> *And Satan will say ⸢to his followers⸣ after the judgment has been passed,*
> *"Indeed, Allah has made you a true promise. I too made you a promise, but I*
> *failed you. I did not have any authority over you. I only called you, and you*
> *responded to me. So do not blame me; blame yourselves. I cannot save you, nor*

can you save me. Indeed, I denounce your previous association of me with
Allah ⌐in loyalty⌐. Surely the wrongdoers will suffer a painful punishment."
– Quran 14:22

Nevertheless, mankind must be fully cognizant that the mission of Iblis is still in motion, and he is still dedicated to using the period of respite granted him to mislead the progeny of Adam. Mankind's protracted struggle against evil has existed ever since. To be successful in the struggle, mankind must fulfil their purpose of existence. The struggle involves sacrificing certain desires to earn the right of entry into paradise. The greater Jihad (struggle) is the internal struggle – against oneself. Internal struggles include hate, jealousy, envy, pride, arrogance, lust, greed, selfishness and other self-detrimental emotions manifesting as evil.

> *The one striving in jihad in the way of Allah is the one who*
> *wages jihad against himself in obedience to Allah.*
> – Musnad Aḥmad 23438

Purification of the Soul

Self-purification is vital to living a successful life and integral to being victorious in the hereafter. The Quran mentions self-purification in various verses, and some examples include:

> *The Day when neither wealth nor children will be of any benefit.*
> *Only those who come before Allah with a pure heart ⌐will be saved⌐*
> – Quran 26:88-89

> *Successful indeed are those who purify themselves,* – Quran 87:14

Successful indeed is the one who purifies their soul,
and doomed is the one who corrupts it! – Quran 91:9-10

More importantly, Allah knows what is in the hearts of all His creation. For instance, the hate, envy, jealousy, discrimination, pride and arrogance Iblis harboured internally, manifested after Adam's creation and reverence.

[Iblis (Satan)] said: "I am not the one to prostrate myself to a human being,
whom You created from sounding clay of altered black smooth mud."
– Quran15:33

It is instructive to note that in the aforementioned verse, Iblis specifically mentions the black colour of the muddy substance which Adam was created with. Also, from a linguistic perspective, Adam means black. This is a crucial lesson for mankind, particularly those who exhibit racism and other forms of discrimination. Iblis was basically the first racist and can be described as the progenitor of all racists. Because what the human heart possesses tends to manifest, it is rather better to think good thoughts, exude positivity and be hopeful in the Mercy of Allah. In a Hadith Qudsi (special narrations from Prophet Muhammad ﷺ attributed to Allah); "Allah the Almighty said: I am as My servant thinks I am". In this regard, human beings must be careful about their innermost thoughts, because it is from such thoughts that actions manifest. Human beings tend to divagate with tangential thoughts that are largely counterintuitive and negate the primary purpose of existence.

DIVINE MERCY AND LOVE

Allah is more merciful to his servants than a mother is to her child
– Prophet Muhammad ﷺ

The Mercy of Allah is boundless, even though some human beings tend to misconstrue what that mercy actually entails. There are people who believe they are the only ones entitled to God's mercy, though that is not the actual case. Some people are comfortable condemning others, usually without introspection. I refer to such people as the self-appointed 'bouncers' of paradise. However, it is the mercy of The Creator that will ultimately decide everyone's fate. In a Hadith, Allah states that His mercy outweighs His wrath:

> *Narrated Abu Huraira: The Messenger of Allah, peace and blessings be upon him, said, "When Allah completed the creation, He wrote in His book with Him upon the Throne: Verily, My mercy prevails over My wrath."*
> – Sahih al-Buhkari 3194

There is a misconception about divine mercy because what is often referred to as God's love is actually God's mercy. Primarily, it is because of the mercy of God that everything exists. Naturally, people will want to be loved by God; however, a self-declaration of God's love would be rather presumptuous. Such a bold declaration remains an assumption because it is not verifiable. Whatever factors that can be used as evidence, or any parameters that can be used to assess God's love, are not exclusive. For example, if someone associates wealth with God's love; that is not factual, because there are those who do not believe in God that are also wealthy. Anyone can be wealthy. The possession of wealth does not necessarily mean God loves the wealthy. Material possessions are never ideal determinants of God's love.

There is a common misconception about God's love, particularly from other religious theological positions. Hence, the concept of an "All-loving" God could be problematic. In practical terms, such a misunderstood concept tends to confuse and is often abused. For instance, people cannot reconcile the existence of an "All-loving" God and the evil that exists in the world. Rather, God is All-Merciful because mercy encompasses everything. It is out of God's mercy that human beings were created and given the opportunity to attain paradise. However, not everyone takes that opportunity. For instance, if for some reason, certain human beings decide not to have a relationship with God and conclude there is no hereafter and paradise was invented by men, then, they have excluded themselves from that divine love, but not from the mercy of God. The implication of God's mercy is that God is the Sustainer of His entire creation including those that believe and those that disbelieve. In other words, everyone is entitled to God's mercy, but specific actions determine the entitlement to God's love. The Quran associates love with abiding by religious dictates and righteousness.

> *O you who have believed, whoever of you should revert from his religion - Allah will bring forth [in place of them] a people He will love and who will love Him [who are] humble toward the believers, strong against the disbelievers; they strive in the cause of Allah and do not fear the blame of a critic. That is the favor of Allah; He bestows it upon whom He wills. And Allah is all-Encompassing and Knowing.* – Quran 5:54

Everything mankind is bestowed falls under the mercy of God. Mercy encompasses everything, but the love of God is exclusive. God is the most Merciful because His mercy is required in everything. Meaning, His doors of mercy are open to all. For example, any evil-liver or sinner can repent and attain His mercy at any time. After that, possibly the love of God can be worked towards and attained. Also, a person cannot claim God's love whilst killing innocent people, including women and children. A person cannot claim God's love whilst having whimsical sexual intercourse with anything; including, both sexes of adults and children (paedophilia), and even animals (bestiality). Such atrocious actions are obviously flagrant abuses of human privileges and an abuse of the concept of God's love. God's love is a driving force of positivity – to promote peaceful human coexistence.

Generally, mankind needs the mercy of God for its existence and sustenance. Mankind's very existence on earth is a testament to God's mercy. God's mercy accommodates everything from good to evil and all that is in between. Nonetheless, God's love cannot be categorically claimed on earth, because such a position cannot be substantiated. Hypothetically, those that make it to paradise can incontrovertibly claim God's love, because their claim is evidenced by their being in paradise. However, whilst still dwelling on earth, God's love is an exclusive category that has to be earned.

To further buttress the difference between God's love and God's mercy, I will cite a desperate scenario as an example. Assuming someone is in a fix or a difficult problem and needs urgent divine help. When such a person prays for divine intervention, the prayer would most likely be for God to have mercy – 'God have mercy upon me'. In such a desperate scenario, it would be rather odd for the person in need of divine intervention to pray for God's love – such as a drowning man saying, 'God love me'. So, in that scenario, the mercy is more useful than love. Personally, I have never come across such a prayer for God's love, especially in desperate circumstances, but I have come across numerous prayers for God's mercy. I will cite a couple of examples from the Quran, about how desperate scenarios make human beings remember their Lord and are naturally inclined to call out to Him in times of need.

Say, ˹O Prophet,˺ "Who rescues you from the darkest times on land and at sea? He ˹alone˺ you call upon with humility, openly and secretly: "If You rescue us from this, we will be ever grateful."
– Quran 6:63

He is the One Who enables you to travel through land and sea. And it so happens that you are on ships, sailing with a favourable wind, to the passengers' delight. Suddenly, the ships are overcome by a gale wind and those on board are overwhelmed by waves from every side, and they assume they are doomed. They cry out to Allah ˹alone˺ in sincere devotion, "If You save us from this, we will certainly be grateful." – Quran 10:22

Furthermore, there are common conflations of God's love and God's mercy, which can lead to confusion, and in some cases, ingratitude. Analysing mercy from a perspective of ingratitude reveals that, though the Mercy of Allah is extraordinary, human beings tend to be unappreciative. This underappreciation is based on a lack of understanding about the concept of God. At the core of all this is arrogance – the absence of humility. Some people spend their entire life complaining about their lives and some complain about world problems. For example, some people will present arguments along the lines of, 'if God loves us or if there is a God, then why are there world problems?' The fact of the matter is that people cannot claim the nonexistence of God and in the same breath blame that nonexistent God for world problems. Blaming God for man-made problems is typical of people with such mindsets. However, it is crucial for human beings to understand the problems of the world are a primary consequence of man's excessiveness and not God's incapacity. Rather than bother about world problems and using that as an excuse to deny God's existence, mankind must come to terms with its seeming insignificance – man is but a creation among other creations, existing within other creations. It is out of the special Mercy of Allah a creation like mankind was created, and by default, was given the opportunity to strive for a paradisiacal eternal life.

> *O mankind, worship your Lord, who created you and those before you, that you may become righteous* – Quran 2:21

Evidently, every creation will be given the opportunity to earn paradise. And the Quran mentions that there is no gain or benefit for Allah in the punishment of His creation.

> *What would Allah do with [i.e., gain from] your punishment if you are grateful and believe? And ever is Allah Appreciative and Knowing.*
> – Quran 4:147

In summary, the purpose of mankind can be appreciated as a process of initial confusion that ought to culminate in reconciliation – an epiphanic journey of enlightenment. A part of humankind's quest is to discover their purpose on earth. Whilst on this path of discovery, the usual questions arise – Who am I? What am I doing here? From an Islamic perspective, the Quran categorically states that man's primary purpose is to worship The Creator.

> *I created the jinn and humankind only that they might worship Me*
> – Quran 51:56

Based on this premise of being created primarily to worship God, all other objectives are secondary. Other secondary objectives involve, among other things, worldly pursuits with the cognizance of ultimate accountability, forming a harmonious relationship with other co-creations and taking care of the environment – which is also a creation. However, the act of worship should not be seen as just a divine injunction, but a natural process of identifying the magnificence of The Creator.

Following the process of self-awareness and the identification of The Creator, the inclination to glorify and worship such an All-Powerful being should only come naturally. In other words, the prerequisite to worshipping God is actually identifying The Creator. In this regard, identifying the correct God becomes vital and the next crucial phase would be the establishment of the proper means of communication, i.e., religion.

PART TWO

RELIGION

CHAPTER 10

DECONSTRUCTING RELIGION

Religion! The oft-discussed issue with a unique pervading tendency: an inescapable topic with the potential to manifest one way or another. The irony of our dynamic world is that the irreligious cannot escape the religious and vice versa. Be it the atheist, agnostic or nullifidian, the matter of religion is inescapable. Society is structured in such a way that you are either dealing with matters of religion or the manifestations of religion. Karl Marx described religion as "das Opium des Volkes"– the opium of the people, but even those who claim to be irreligious are about as concerned, if not more concerned, about religion as the religious folk: it is an unavoidable phenomenon – one of life's many mysterious necessities.

Alas, not all those who are religiously oriented are delusional or out of touch with reality. Some of those concerned about religion, have in certain instances, attained the peak of their respective sciences, and came to the realisation that religion and science go hand in hand. The scientific approach to religion can be appreciated as an advocacy of a tradition where religion and science are complementary. After all, Albert Einstein stated: "Science without religion is lame, religion without science is blind". Also, Carl Sagan stated: "Science is not only compatible with spirituality; it is a profound source of spirituality… The notion that science and spirituality are somehow mutually exclusive does a disservice to both."

Ideally, religion should be the guiding light of science. History confirms that the unfortunate mishandling of state and religious matters, elicited public distrust and suspicion. Those saddled with the responsibility of managing religious affairs for the populace, particularly in the West, abused institutional privileges, which resulted in a dichotomy.

The manifestation of the dichotomy between religion and science is inextricably linked to the rise of ideologies such atheism, agnosticism and other related isms. Ironically, those claiming atheism and similar ideological positions have a somewhat convoluted understanding of the views of some scientists they revere and sometimes quote out of context, to propagandize their agenda. For instance, Charles Darwin never unequivocally claimed to be a God-denying atheist.[16] Analysing the matter from a creationist perspective, the evolution of societies sometimes gives a faux sense of delusional hubris, which manifests in an antirealism cocoon. The manifestation of societal evolution is underpinned by the realism of man's existentiality, but the quandary of not fully comprehending the primary purpose of existence has been an ongoing challenge for mankind. The world has gone through many phases, and at various point in history, religion has played indelible roles in different societies. Citing the Western world as a contemporary example, societal evolution had reached a point whereby there seems to be a general aversion to the 'G' word and its deliberate evisceration from public discourse. This wilful disinclination is intricately connected to reservations about the 'R' word. In this particular context, the 'G' denotes God and 'R' represent religion. It is noteworthy to emphasize that an aversion to God or religion is not exactly a science; rather, it is just an opinion – personal or collective.

Societies have evolved to a point where the tendency to question the need for religion is prevalent and such ideologies validate the necessity of this discourse. What exactly is religion? What is the history of religion? What was the first religion? Why are there so many religions? Why do we even need religion? So many questions!

NULLIFYING THE NULLIFIDIAN

The nullifidian in this context can be appreciated as a catch-all term or symbolic representative of all those with an aversion to religion, and to some degree, God. This grouping includes atheists, agnostics, freethinkers and other forms, combinations and manifestations of supposed irreligiosity. These peculiar groupings have manifested as a religion in their own right. For example, those who say they do not believe in religion, belong to the religion of those who claim not to believe in religion. Also, those who say they do not believe in God, belong to the religion of those who claim not to believe in God. This extrapolative definition is applicable to any group of people, wherever they may exist. From the perspective of the nullifidian, the 'religious' dilemma, becomes even more problematic, particularly because of the laxity or lack of articulated set of rules. In my explication of matters concerning religion, it must be emphatically stated that everyone is entitled to their belief and non-belief. My *ad rem* research is primarily an intellectual discourse exploring religion from a universal perspective.

There are many human beings existing across the globe who can carry on their daily activities without the seeming need for religion. If there seems to be no apparent need for religion, typically, people can wake up in the morning, brush their teeth, have a bath, eat breakfast, wear their clothes and go to work – for those working, or go to school – for those studying, or lazing around – for nothing-doers generally. In such quotidian scenarios, however monotonous, everyone, in whatever category they may belong, returns home to sleep and do it all over again the next day. These are just some examples of daily activities, to highlight why some people question the need for religion in their lives.

The questioning of religion is often intertwined with the questioning of God, though these views are sometimes distinct. Some people may decide to reject religion and God, whilst some people may choose to reject religion, but do not necessarily reject God.

Some dictionary definitions of religion state thus: the American Heritage dictionary of the English language describes religion as, "Belief in and reverence for a supernatural power or powers regarded as creator and governor of the universe"[17]. Merriam Webster defines religion as "a personal set or institutionalized system of religious attitudes, beliefs, and practices", "scrupulous conformity: conscientiousness", "a cause, principle, or system of beliefs held to with ardour and faith".[18]The Cambridge dictionary describes religion as, "the belief in and worship of a god or gods, or any such system of belief and worship", "an activity that someone is extremely enthusiastic about and does regularly: Football is a religion for these people."[19]

In view of these explanations, some of the foregoing definitions can be applied to other non-conventional groups of people, or what would not typically be classified as the conventional meaning of religion. Also, it can be argued that through certain activities, some human beings instinctively fulfil their human religious requirement. This religious requirement is fulfilled by filling the associative spiritual void with an alternative, even if done subconsciously. Anything that is valued, or any set of values that are sacred to an individual, has essentially fulfilled the role of 'god' to that individual. Those values could be science, tradition or ancestry or anything at all. And when there is an assemblage of such people, they are effectively a religion. There are certain scenarios where the vacuum of spirituality–cum–religion, in its traditional sense, gets fulfilled. Based on its definition, religion could be any cause or principle dedicated with ardour. So, atheism, for example, can be considered a religion. As a similitude, there are atheists who believe in scientism and are proponents of Darwin's theory of evolution.

Based on this premise, an atheist has faith in the works of scientists who developed and propagate evolution and would also profess it accordingly.

As there is one atheist, there are also groupings of atheists who share such beliefs among themselves and with others. In this regard, those in this category are part of a belief system. Technically, atheists in this category accept this belief as fact, despite inherent infallibilities in the theory. The impediments faced in proving its veracity, affirm its theoretical nature, and one can choose to believe or reject the postulations of that belief system. This similitude is applicable to any religion, because one can choose to accept or reject any belief system. For instance, theists are sometimes challenged to prove the existence of God. In some situations, some of those who choose to believe in God might not actually be able to prove such an existence. In some other instances, theists might want to prove the existence of God to an atheist, through the utilization of the creations of God – the works of the forerunners of that belief system. Similarly, when atheists are confronted with the same challenge, they too cannot prove evolution; because neither did any of those who propounded and developed the theory of evolution actually witnessed evolution. For example, nobody witnessed man supposedly evolving from apes! Despite not witnessing the evolution of apes, those who believe in this theory present books about related studies. So, scientists, atheists, agnostics and other forms of ideologies belonging to a similar spectrum of belief, can present evolution and other theories as evidence for their belief. This is the same manner theists present their arguments from their religious viewpoint.

In particular, Muslims can present the Quran as evidence for their conviction in that belief system. Importantly, it must be emphasized, that there is diversity within any belief system, and those with a general aversion to God or religion or both, fall within the same category. Furthermore, all those who belong to the same category usually congregate based on shared beliefs. For instance, there are atheists' conferences and conventions, including humanities congregations. However, this does not mean all those within this belief system will attend such gatherings. This situation is applicable to other belief systems;

for instance, not all those who claim to be Muslims attend Islamic conventions or gatherings. In this regard, atheists are at times passionately committed to their cause of atheism, even if some atheists deny it, their actions speak otherwise. For a certainty, some atheists – especially militant atheists, are devoted to their atheism cause and fervently attack theism at every given opportunity. This position can be appreciated as the same dedication or ardency, by which certain religious folk are committed to their religious causes. Also, within any religious grouping, there are those not as committed, even though they share the same beliefs.

Theory of Natural Inclusion: I posit the Theory of Natural Inclusion as a pragmatic explication of the inclusivity process. Based on the inclusivity premise, various sets of people with shared ideologies or beliefs can be collectively grouped and identified. Furthermore, those within the same category do not necessarily have to formally identify, acknowledge or admit being part that belief system, because their thought-processes and faith in whatever they claim to believe and profess, has naturally included them within the associative belief system.

Ironically, in the field on evolution, a prominent evolutionary biologist and proponent of the Endosymbiotic theory, Lynn Margulis, in describing Neo-Darwinism, stated that history will ultimately judge the theory "a minor twentieth century religious sect within the sprawling religious persuasion of Anglo-Saxon Biology".[20]

In the world of entertainment, music has a huge followership and somewhat fulfils a 'religious' requirement for certain groups of people. At times, fans of music artists follow their favourite musicians around the globe, and some music festivals can be likened to a religious pilgrimage.

The energetic atmosphere at some music concerts is similar to a revered religious figure preaching from the pulpit to ardent followers. Also, calmer atmospheres with operatic and soulful music exist, with their respective fervid devotees. Interestingly, in an archived interview of American artist, Kanye West, he stated: "Hip-hop is a religion to a certain extent, and the rappers are the preachers, the music is the scriptures, you know. It's just like church, because you go to a concert, you raise your hands in the air, you get dressed up, you sing songs, and you definitely pay some money. It's just like church".

In the sports world, football is considered a religion in some parts of the globe. For instance, the Brazilian football legend, Pelé stated: "Football is like a religion to me. I worship the ball, and I treat it like a god". Also, Argentinean football legend, Diego Maradona stated "football isn't a game, nor a sport; it's a religion".[21] Sports fans follow their teams across the world, and sporting events like the football world cup, are effectively a religious pilgrimage. The fanatical followership prevalent in football is not exclusive and is applicable to other sports. The word 'fan' is etymologically linked to fanatic and denotes 'insane' or 'enthusiasm' – extremism.[22]

Potential Extremism: Any cause dedicated to with avidity has the potentiality of extremism. The fervency and followership of football can be equated to religious fanaticism. In the United Kingdom for example, the notoriety of football fanaticism, particularly hooliganism is established. Football clubs have had historical hooligan firms and rival fans have clashed for decades. During the 2018 Russia World Cup, over 1200 football hooligans were banned from attending by the Home Office.[23] To some football followers, football is basically their religion, and the actions of the hooligans amongst them should not define the entire sport.

In South America, football fanaticism is rife. Some years ago, there was a news story about a gruesome incident in Brazil. During a football match, the officiating referee was decapitated – beheaded![24] In any extreme situation, sports or football should not be put on trial, rather, the culprits who commit heinous crimes should. The purpose of highlighting the preceding extreme position is for juxtaposition. Those with an axe to grind with religion, or what would be considered conventional religion, usually do not consider the reality of extremism in every sphere of life. Religion is the convenient scapegoat for those with an obsessive fixation on the religion, primarily because of their unresolved issues with religion.

At this juncture, it is pertinent to note that in spite of the aforementioned points, a crucial factor to be acknowledged is that there are categories of people who would never accept facts, even when confronted with the most elucidative of presentations. A classic example are people who claimed the earth was flat centuries ago, but when it was later proved that the earth was spherical, there are people who still refused, and insisted on the debunked theories. They are effectively saying, despite all enumerated evidence, they would not change their minds, and would refuse to accept these new facts, because their mind is made up.

Ultimately, religion is a choice, if or whenever anyone is interested in matters of religion, it is only logical to undertake the adequate research required. There are so many religions in the world, including those that are considered religions and those that religion is ascribed unto, and those that deny being religions. Whether organized or disorganized, conventional or neo-religious, once a group of people share certain interests, then such an assemblage can be considered a religion, in the descriptive sense. In practical terms, religion can be defined as a pursuit or interest followed with great devotion. This can be applied to any pursuit or interest followed with great devotion.

Evidently, man's gregarious inclination and the need for affiliation and affirmation is second nature. The default human tendency to seek association, particularly with the like-minded, can also lead to the congeniality of the faithless. In summary, a nullifidian – including those with similar ideologies – can claim faithlessness or irreligiosity in the conventional sense, nonetheless, a similar type of devotion, as exerted by those who are faithful or religious, is comparably expended on nullifidianism.

CHAPTER 11

DISSECTING WORLD RELIGIONS

Contextually, world religions encompass all the religions across the world. Anyone can have, or claim to have, a relationship with God, just as anyone can claim to have religion, or even formulate their own religion – cult – movement. To some segments of society, religion is not necessary, and a life with rules makes religion unattractive to others. A common question I hear is – why are there so many religions?

The question about the existence of many world religions is quite valid, however, based on experience, some, if not most, of those who ask about the enormity of world religions, are not necessarily interested in the answer. The question often stems from the criticism of religion generally. For those with an aversion to religion, it is not uncommon to lump all religions together, for the convenience of excoriation. Also, it would be cumbersome and a bit tiring for critics of religion to go through the arduous process of analysing world religions to determine authenticity. This is where the work of specialists in world religions is useful. There are currently thousands of religions in the world, and possibly a new religion is being founded as I write these words. In order not to dissipate intellectual energies on every religion that exists in the world, religions will be adequately analysed for fair geographical coverage. Notable world religions include Bahá'í, Buddhism, Confucianism, Hinduism, Jainism, Shintoism, Sikhism, Taoism, Zoroastrianism and of course the Abrahamic religions – Judaism, Christianity and Islam. Based on previously elucidated definitions of religion, atheism and other related ideologies are classified as a religion in their own right. Some religions are autochthonous or ethnic-oriented whilst some religions have a universal outlook – without any ethnic, national or racial boundaries.

Autochthonous religions can be analysed via continental and geographical categorizations, including Eastern, Western, and African classifications. Africa, America, Asia, Australia, and Europe are the generally accepted continents, and a presumed continent like Antarctica would not be analysed, because it is largely uninhabited.

Religion on the Australian continent cannot be analysed without the Indigenous Australians. The indigenous people are the inhabitants of Australian mainland, and some Islands include Fraser Island, Galiwinku Island, Groote Eylandt, Hinchinbrook Island, Tasmania, Tiwi Islands, and Torres Strait Islands. Notably, the Torres Strait Islanders are usually not associated with the Western-oriented exonym – Aboriginal Australians. The Dreaming is a widespread cultural religious belief involving the reverence of ancestral figures. It is believed these ancestral figures have supernatural capabilities and performed heroic feats. The term is also referred to as Dreamtime or in some local dialects as Alchera, Alcheringa, Mura-Mura, and Tjukurpa. Dreaming tracks or Songlines in the form of traditional art, dance and stories, are connective paths used to traverse the routes established by ancestral figures to create sacred sites. Also, totemism plays an integral role in linking people with their ancestors in the spiritual realm. Totems could exist in various forms. For instance, the Arrernte people of Australia utilise the Tjurunga for sacred ceremonies, passage rites and religious purposes. For identification purposes, the Tjurunga often has an associative group totem that could be in the form of a stone or wooden object. In some circumstances, the Tjurunga a person is paired with during initiation will accompany the corpse of that person to the grave after death. Generally, Australian indigenous religion can be appreciated as ancestral worship.

On the Asian continent, there are some relatively known religions such as Buddhism, Confucianism, Hinduism, Shintoism, Sikhism, Taoism, and Zoroastrianism. Also, there are other religions that include Bahá'í, Caodaism, and Jainism. Religions of Asian origin are sometimes classified with different demographic terminologies, which include Eastern religions, East Asian religions, South Asian religions, and Middle Eastern religions. Historically, the term Inner Asia has been used interchangeably with Central Asia. Tengrism or Tengri Religion was practiced in parts of Central Asia, such as Kazakhstan, Kyrgyzstan, Mongolia and parts of Siberia. Sometimes, classifications include more geographical specificity, such as the Indic or Dharmic religions, Chinese religions and Japanese religions. For example, Hinduism, Jainism, Buddhism, and Sikhism are classified Indic or Dharmic religions, primarily because they originated from the Indian subcontinent. Similarly, Confucianism and Taoism are of Chinese origin, just as Shinto and Tenrikyo originate from Japan, and Jeungsanism is of Korean origin. Also, animism is still practiced in some parts of Southeast Asia, such as the Orang Asli of Malaysia and their indigenous religion. Religious syncretism, ancestral worship totemism and shamanism are rife on the Asian continent.

Religion in Europe has gone through various transitions and external influences in history. Western religions are really syncretized manifestations of Christianity; Catholicism, Puritanism, Protestantism, and Evangelicalism. However, from an historical viewpoint, Europe had a diverse tradition of autochthonous religious beliefs.

For instance, the Hellenic religion that was practiced among the Greeks, involved the veneration of Greek gods and the Twelve Olympians.

The Romans on their part, strived to attain *pax deorum* – peace of the gods – in their society. Similar indigenous religious practices existed among other Western cultural groups such as the Slavic, Celtic, Germanic, and Norse, etc. Generally, European religion had as part of their tradition, the adulation of ancestral and mythological figures.

Religions in Africa involve various aspects of syncretism, animism, fetishism, tutelary deities, spirits, nature and ancestral worship. Traditional African religions include Akan, Bantu, Dinka, Dogon, Kemetism, Maasai, Vodun, Waaqeffanna, Yoruba, and Zulu. Furthermore, African religions are not only limited to the African continent, due to the emergence of religious practices amongst the African Diaspora in places such as the Caribbean, Latin America and United States. Some African Diaspora religions include the Afro-Brazilian Candomblé, Quimbanda and Umbanda, Afro-Guyanese Comfa, Afro-Jamaican Kumina and Rastafari, Afro-Saint Lucian Kélé, Afro-Cuban Arará and Santería, Cuban Vodú, Dominican Vudú, Haitian Vodou, Louisiana Voodoo, Surinamese Winti, and the Yoruba religion.

Religion in the Americas can be categorized based on past and present-day demographics. These classifications include North America, South America, Caribbean and Mesoamerica. Historically, there were the pre-Columbian civilizations, which had their respective religious traditions. For example, the Inuit Religion consisted of animism, shamanism and reincarnation, and was practiced among Arctic peoples indigenous to Alaska and Canada. The indigenous Americans of North America had various cultural religious beliefs, which include the Crow religion, Ghost Dance and Midewiwin.

In the South America region, there were various cultures, like the Inca. The Inca had their indigenous religion, which included human sacrifice. In the Caribbean, the Arawak and Taino people worshipped spirits called Zemi. Mesoamerica had various cultural and religious traditions such as the Aztec, Huastec Olmec, Maya, Mixtec, Toltec, and Zapotec. For instance, the Aztec religion, like other Mesoamerican religions, is ethnocentric in nature and involves elements of human sacrifice. This element of human sacrifice is not exclusive and is fundamental to various autochthonous religions globally.

In view of this contextual reality, imagine a modern-day scenario where an adherent is informed that their first son has been chosen by the high chief priest to be sacrificed to the gods – well, your guess is as good as mine: *Hasta la vista* to you and your human-oblation religion! Evidently, no right-thinking human being would willingly want a human being killed as offering, especially theirs or any other person's child, as human sacrifice for purported deities. These supposed deities are integral to autochthonous religions and are labelled in various forms, including ancestors and forefathers, and are supposed to act as intermediaries to a spirit world. Based on research into autochthonous religious beliefs, or what is considered traditional religion and spirituality in certain respects, the séance, or any form of spirit communication or divination, and spiritism, is effectively Jinn-oriented or direct Jinn worship. Basically, those who claim to be indigenous religion practitioners are giving the Jinn the opportunity to prove that mankind is unworthy of the exalted position given to them by God. This has been the paramount goal of the Jinn; to establish they are better than mankind. So, when men abase themselves in the name of cultural or indigenous religious practices, they are scoring a point for the Jinn against themselves. As the adage goes: the greatest trick of the devil is convincing the world of his nonexistence!

On the surface, indigenous religions may seem attractive, but delving deeper reveals something much darker and the rudiments are the same as the dark arts or black magic. A scrutiny of indigenous religions, religious practices and spirituality, exposes such quiddities.

As a precursory caveat, I often emphasize, religion is not actually a compulsion for anyone. However, if anyone does decide to choose a religion, it is best to seek out the religion that literally ticks all the right boxes. Surely, there are benefits that could be derived from any religion, and people are entitled to choose whatever path suits their spiritual needs. Nonetheless, it is crucial to appreciate that not all religions were divinely ordained.

I am of the opinion that the issue of religion requires serious scrutiny, for those interested in the subject. All world religions should be treated as a subject matter, and thoroughly scrutinized via universally applicable methods, based on certain criteria. In this regard, the research of world religions becomes imperative for those interested in the authentication of religion from a pro-humanity viewpoint, and particularly from the universal perspective. For authentication objectives, a process of elimination, via certain criteria, can be employed to ascertain which religion is universally acceptable – historically and contemporarily, even if, for theoretical or academic purposes.

The postulated authentication criteria can be applied by any dedicated and research-oriented individual or group, regardless of individual religious affiliations or inclinations.

HOLISTIC ANALYSIS

The holistic analytical approach is primarily about dissecting world religions through historical, scriptural, comparative and contemporary perspectives. As world religions could be examined via various viewpoints, it becomes necessary to analyse religions from a foundational angle. More importantly, the primary concentration should never be about the behavioural attributes of the so-called adherents of a particular faith, but the actual framework of the faith itself. The reason for this approach is because adherents are not usually the ideal representatives of their professed religion, and in many cases, they are not the epitome of what the religion actually stipulates. The primary purpose of this analytical approach is not necessarily aimed at comparing or contrasting adherents of any faith. Rather, the principal focus is on the historicity of foundations, scriptural evidence and contemporary manifestations.

In essence, the concern is not to highlight individual differences between adherents of various religions; for example, Muslims are bad, and Christians are good, or Buddhists are barbaric, and Jews are angelic. Based on personal experiences, I have seen good agnostics, atheists and secularists that are better behaved than so-called Muslims.

As an analogy, if I am training to be a doctor in medical college, an unhygienic doctor or a doctor who murders patients routinely would not deter me from studying medicine; neither should such an unethical doctor affect the noble profession of medicine. Primarily, religion should be analysed via its tenets and not adherents. The science of religion is a discipline in its own right, and it has its dedicated learning students.

The science of dissecting world religions should consider criteria such as origins, institutionalization, inclusivity, universality, scriptural evidence, concept of God and a combination of related factors. For this specific purpose, I posit five criteria termed CORSU: Creator, Origin, Reverence, Scripture, and Universality. See Appendix 1 for a sample of the CORSU form. The five criteria will be discussed individually; CORSU: (1) Creator (2) Origin (3) Reverence (4) Scripture (5) Universality.

CORSU CRITERIA

1. Creator

The Creator criterion entails the concept of God from a creationist viewpoint. The specificity of the criterion is deliberate. The oft-discoursed concept of God could have been the primary selected criterion, but that particular selection would not fulfil specific requirements. God may mean different things to different people and some world religions have plenty gods. Whilst acknowledging the existence of many gods in our dynamic world, there is only one Creator. The Creator did not self-create and cannot be a creation. If it were possible for a creator to be created, there would have been many creators.

The Creator is a unique entity and not part of a pantheon or a co-equal in existence, and possesses the sole responsibility of creating creation, without the reliance on creation or the process of creation.

Based on this unique creator criterion, any god that is a manifestation of creation cannot be equated to The Creator. For instance, Taoism and Jainism are religions that do not exclusively believe in a Creator. In fact, Jainism refutes the idea of a supreme divine creator, owner or preserver of the universe exists. Fundamentally, if any supposed, acclaimed or proclaimed god does not possess creation capabilities, then such a god is not a worthy contender.

2. Origin

The origin criterion primarily concentrates on the history of the religion. The historicity of the religion is analysed based on available facts, covering how long the religion has existed and its manifestation in our contemporary world. Another important factor to be taken into consideration, are the historical processes involved in the institutionalization of the religion.

3. Reverence

The reverence criterion specifically deals with the most revered figure of the religion. The revered figure could sometimes be the founder, protagonist or the most notable person associated with the religion.

4. Scripture

The scripture criterion involves the scriptural analysis of any sacred text associated with the religion. The genesis of the scripture is analysed for authenticity and originality. Furthermore, the evolution, modifications and manifestations of the texts sacred to the religion, will be scrutinized, particularly from a contemporary perspective.

5. Universality

The universality criterion deals with the exclusivity or inclusivity of a religion from its universal applicability – global application of faith. In this regard, any world religion can be analysed from the universality perspective, particularly via its exclusivity or inclusivity.

Theory of Natural Exclusion: I posit the theory of natural exclusion; which involves any religion that excludes potential adherents based on intrinsic preconditions. A religion that is exclusively autochthonous, ethnic or racial, excludes groups that do not fall within the stipulated criteria of that particular religion. Also, religious exclusion could be natural – based on intrinsic characteristics and does not require any stipulation to qualify adherents.

For instance, a person of African descent is naturally excluded from Hinduism, because the primary criterion for Hinduism is to be from the Indian subcontinent. Whilst those of Indian origin may decide to be Hindu, those who are not ethnically Indian do not have that special privilege. In this regard, Hinduism is primarily exclusive and cannot fulfil the universality criterion. All world religions that are autochthon- oriented are inclined to natural exclusion. A critical analysis of all world religions reveals a common pattern; majority of world religions are intrinsically ethnocentric and tend to exclude. I daresay, almost all world religions have autochthonous origins or have manifested into something parochial: either limited in scope or culminated in the deification of central human figure(s).

Notably, when world religions are analysed historically, an argument that cannot be discounted is the possibility that certain central figures across some global religions, including those euhemerized by some cultures, may actually have been people who at some point in history, propagated pure monotheistic messages of worshipping a sole and All-Powerful Creator.

However, over a period, the message of monotheism somehow became adulterated. The eventuality of such adulterated messages, manifested in the transformation of human beings into deities to be worshipped in place of, or along with, God The Creator.

In the case of Islam, Muhammad ﷺ never claimed divinity; he acknowledged his humanness and stated he was a messenger and prophet, like those that came before him – the only exception was his being the seal (last) of the prophets. Prophet Muhammad ﷺ was emphatic about not being deified or worshipped. Islam stipulates that Muslims worship Allah and not Muhammad. Principally, this position underscores why the promoters – especially Orientalists – of the 'Mohammedan' terminology can be accused of mislabelling, and in some extreme cases, failed in their attempt to taint Islam via such spurious portrayals. The followers of Islam are not referred to as Mohammedans but Muslims. Also, the word 'Muslim' is not a linguistic derivative of Muhammad. The terminology 'Muslim' is not primarily based on Muhammad. The Quran confirms that the terminology was used to refer to those who existed before Muhammad, right to the very first human being – Adam. The term Muslim is universally constant and has been utilized from inception. The word 'Muslim' translates as 'Submitter' and submission to God The Creator did not start with Prophet Muhammad – it only culminated during his era, when it was formally designated as Islam: The Submission. Analysing from a universalism perspective, both Christianity and Islam have a seemingly universal outlook; however, Islam is unique because of its timeless transcendence. In comparison to other religions, Islam is distinctive because other religions are mainly based around a figure and involves the worship of that figure: nobody worships Muhammad ﷺ – definitely not Muslims. The fundamental reason underpinning the 'Mohammedan' attribution to Muslims was because Islam was perceived through the prism of Christianity.

CHAPTER 12

THE CHRISTIANITY PARADIGM

Christianity is unique, and in some respects, it fulfils the CORSU (Creator, Origin, Reverence, Scripture, Universality) criteria. For instance, the universal aspect is fulfilled, as there are no obstacles for anyone to claim association with Christianity, contemporarily. Also, the concept of Christianity and salvation is not applicable to those who existed before the advent of Jesus. Nonetheless, there are other issues relating to the origin, reverence and scripture that require further analysis. Superficially, the Creator criterion is fulfilled. However, a critical analysis reveals more complexities. Historically, Christendom and those who claim to associate with Jesus, accept there is an omnipotent God. As time evolved, there have been variations to the understanding, and appreciation of the conceptualization of the All-Powerful God. A recurring issue often encountered is the perception of God, primarily from a Christian theological premise. This approach in and of itself is problematic, because of its inherently flawed concept of God. For instance, to some Christians, Jesus is God, and to others, Jesus is the son of God, whilst others believe Jesus is part of a trinity that includes God. It must be categorically stated that all these supposed permutations of God are predominantly based on conjectural premises and imprecise parameters. Once God is fully-appreciated as The Creator, then understanding what God is comes naturally. The Creator cannot be reduced to the level of the creation, similarly, the creation of The Creator should not be adored or venerated to the level of elevating the creation to the status of The Creator.

Unfortunately, Christianity – when analysed as a religion or way of life – is not unsusceptible to the deification issue and is a classic example of the adverse manifestations of hagiographical excesses and human veneration.

Also, it must be taken into cognizance that Jesus never explicitly requested that he or his mother should be worshipped, during his initial mission on earth. Sadly, what ensued afterwards was the manifestation of their respective deification, especially Jesus. Biblical evidence affirms Jesus primarily enjoined the worship of God:

> *Jesus answered, "It is written: 'Worship the Lord your God and serve him only.'"*
> – Luke 4:8

Interestingly, in certain quarters of Christendom, Mary, the holy and exceptional mother of Jesus is literally being worshipped. Though this excessive veneration is not a general practice by all Christians, some Christian sects continue with these practices, particularly Catholics.

From the Islamic perspective, but for the explicit emphasis of not turning human beings into deities, Islam would have ended up with a major deification issue. Sahih al-Buhkari 3261 states:

> *Do not exaggerate my praises as the Christians have done with the son of Mary. Verily, I am only a servant, so refer to me as the servant of Allah and his messenger.* – Prophet Muhammad ﷺ

Islam honours Mary exceptionally, but does not elevate her to the level of deification. In fact, Chapter 19 in the Quran is named after Mary. Islam acknowledges Mary's righteous ancestry and lineage, her interaction with Angel Jibreel (Gabriel), the miraculous conception and birth, and the instruction to point to baby Jesus when she returns to town with a newborn.

At this juncture, it is important to note that speaking as a baby, in defence of his righteous mother –Mary, and stating his God-sent mission, was actually the first miracle of Jesus, as documented in the Quran.

The Quranic verse about Jesus and his mother Mary, states:

> *[And mention] when the angels said, "O Mary, indeed Allah gives you good tidings of a word from Him, whose name will be the Messiah, Jesus, the son of Mary - distinguished in this world and the Hereafter and among those brought near [to Allah].*
> *He will speak to the people in the cradle and in maturity and will be of the righteous." –* Quran 3:45-46

The miraculous birth of Jesus and subsequent miracles are testament to the greatness of God, and a trial for mankind, particularly those who claim to follow Jesus. Also, the miraculous birth of Jesus is a test to appreciate the manifestation of the power of God, with primary concentration on The Creator and not the creation. Apart from speaking as a baby, other miracles of Jesus documented in the Quran include: a table laden with food from heaven (Quran 5:112-114); a designed clay bird brought to life; healing the blind and leper; raising the dead; awareness of people's consumed edibles and stored provisions (Quran 3:49). Importantly, it must be emphasized that those who claim to be Jesus' followers but reject this first miracle of Jesus (speaking as a baby), because the miracle is not documented in the current form of the Bible, must expressly be reminded that, the Bible also states that not all the miracles of Jesus are documented in the Bible:

> *Jesus worked many other miracles for his disciples, and not all of them are written in this book.–* John 20:30

> *Jesus did many other things. If they were all written in books, I don't suppose there would be room enough in the whole world for all the books.*
> – John 21:25

The Bible also affirms that miracles are done by the permission of God:

> *Men of Israel, listen to these words: Jesus the Nazarene, a man attested to you by God with miracles and wonders and signs which God performed through Him in your midst, just as you yourselves know*—Acts 2:22

Emphasizing the permission of God to perform miracles is crucial, so people do not miss the import of the divine message – miraculous signs. Also, as written in the Bible, Jesus affirms that he can by himself do nothing:

> *I can do nothing on my own. I judge as God tells me. Therefore, my judgment is just, because I carry out the will of the one who sent me, not my own will.* –John 5:30

The specificity of the Quran regarding miracles is clear, especially as it concerns Jesus. For instance, the phrase *Bi'ithnillah*– "by permission of Allah" accompanies the miracles of Jesus:

> *... Indeed I have come to you with a sign from your Lord in that I design for you from clay [that which is] like the form of a bird, then I breathe into it and it becomes a bird by permission of Allah . And I cure the blind and the leper, and I give life to the dead - by permission of Allah...*– Quran 3:49

Furthermore, the Quran is specific about Allah –The Creator, having the exclusive power to grant resurrection – raising the dead:

> *And that it is He (Allah) Who causes death and gives life;* – Quran 53:44

Following the revelation about Jesus' miraculous birth, the Quran also gives details of the conversation Jesus – as a baby, had with the people that gathered to interrogate his mother. During the conversation, Jesus, not only defended the honour of his mother, but mentions some aspects of his earthly assignment.

> *Then she brought him to her people, carrying him. They said, "O Mary, you have certainly done a thing unprecedented.*
> *O sister [i.e., descendant] of Aaron, your father was not a man of evil, nor was your mother unchaste."*
> *So she pointed to him. They said, "How can we speak to one who is in the cradle a child?"*
> *[Jesus] said, "Indeed, I am the servant of Allah. He has given me the Scripture and made me a prophet.*
> *And He has made me blessed wherever I am and has enjoined upon me prayer and Zakah as long as I remain alive*
> *And [made me] dutiful to my mother, and He has not made me a wretched tyrant.*
> *And peace is on me the day I was born and the day I will die and the day I am raised alive."*
> *That is Jesus, the son of Mary – the word of truth about which they are in dispute.*
> *It is not [befitting] for Allah to take a son; exalted is He! When He decrees an affair, He only says to it, "Be," and it is.* – Quran 19: 27-35

Notably, whilst the first miracle of Jesus was speaking to mankind as a baby, his last miracle was effectively evading his scheduled crucifixion, as plotted by the Roman authorities – Tiberius Caesar Augustus as Emperor and Marcus

Pontius Pilatus as Governor of Judaea. The Quran details the ultimate miracle of Jesus that has mystified mankind ever since:

> *And because of their saying (in boast), "We killed Messiah 'Iesa (Jesus), son of Maryam (Mary), the Messenger of Allah," - but they killed him not, nor crucified him, but the resemblance of 'Iesa (Jesus) was put over another man (and they killed that man), and those who differ therein are full of doubts. They have no (certain) knowledge, they follow nothing but conjecture. For surely; they killed him not [i.e. 'Iesa (Jesus), son of Maryam (Mary)]: But Allah raised him ['Iesa (Jesus)] up (with his body and soul) unto Himself (and he is in the heavens). And Allah is Ever All-Powerful, All-Wise.*
> — Quran 4:157-158

The special prayer of Jesus is captured in the Bible:

> *"My soul is overwhelmed with sorrow to the point of death," he said to them. "Stay here and keep watch."*
> *Going a little farther, he fell to the ground and prayed that if possible the hour might pass from him.*
> *"Abba, Father," he said, "everything is possible for you. Take this cup from me. Yet not what I will, but what you will."* — Mark 14:34-36

In a related point about the crucifixion, contrary to the belief that Jesus was sacrificed – crucified – at the cross, the Bible states that no man can redeem another:

> *No man can redeem the life of another, nor can he give to God a sufficient payment for him* – Psalms 49:7

As the crucifixion plans were being enacted, the prayer of Jesus was indeed answered, and in spectacular manner, Jesus was rescued. Also, based on biblical evidence, Jesus being rescued is a manifestation of Psalms 91:10-15, particularly Psalms 91:14-15:

> *"Because he loves me," says the LORD, "I will rescue him; I will protect him, for he acknowledges my name.*
> *When he calls to me, I will answer him; I will be with him in trouble; I will rescue him and honor him.*
> – Psalms 91:14-15

The Bible affirms that Jesus prayed to God – in Aramaic: Elahi. The following are some Biblical examples of Jesus praying to God:

> *During the days of Jesus' life on earth, he offered up prayers and petitions with fervent cries and tears to the one who could save him from death, and he was heard because of his reverent submission*
> – Hebrew 5:7

> *And about the ninth hour Jesus cried out with a loud voice, saying, "Eli, Eli, lema sabachthani?" that is, "My God, my God, why have you forsaken me?"*–
> Matthew 27:46

> *One of those days Jesus went out to a mountainside to pray, and spent the night praying to God.*
> – Luke 6:12

According to the Bible, Jesus was a servant of God:

The God of Abraham, the God of Isaac, and the God of Jacob, the God of our fathers, glorified his servant Jesus, whom you delivered over and denied in the presence of Pilate, when he had decided to release him. – Acts 3:13

The Bible affirms that God is not human, and that Jesus is a man not God:

God is not human, that he should lie, not a human being, that he should change his mind. Does he speak and then not act? Does he promise and not fulfill?– Numbers 23:19

As it is, you are looking for a way to kill me, a man who has told you the truth that I heard from God. Abraham did not do such things. – John 8:40

Christianity is generally associated with the life and teachings of Jesus – The Christ. However, Jesus never formally institutionalized a religion called Christianity, nor is the religion explicitly mentioned anywhere in the Bible. Apart from the issue of institutionalization, considering there are Christians who do not actually consider Christianity a religion, the terminology 'Christian' has its limitations from an historical perspective. Christian is derived from Christ. Christ is derived from the Greek word *Khristos*, meaning "the anointed", and translated from the Hebrew term *Mashiah* (Messiah in English).A person, who adheres to Christianity, is considered a Christian. Christian is a derivative of Jesus' title – Christ (Messiah).Elucidating on that point, can the term 'Christian' be applied to people who existed before the emergence of Jesus? Basically, is the term 'Christian' applicable to all those who preceded Jesus, up till the first acknowledged human: Adam? – The answer is No! Ironically, from an historical viewpoint, and chiefly based on biblical evidence, the origin of the term 'Christian' can be traced to the story of Barnabas and Paul at Antioch, in the Acts of the Apostles 11:26.

and when he found him, he brought him to Antioch. So for a whole year
Barnabas and Saul met with the church and taught great numbers of people.
The disciples were called Christians first at Antioch. —Acts 11:26

In essence, according to the Bible, the term 'Christian' manifested many decades after Jesus walked the earth. It was from the word Christian that Christianity was coined. So, Jesus never heard of the term 'Christian', nor did he ever endorse or establish a religion called Christianity. It can be deduced that Paul founded 'Christianity'. Paul was a Hellenistic-Jew, who had his own geopolitical agenda; but he needed the actual teachings of Jesus for acceptance and veracity. For instance, Paul preached to Gentiles and took decisions on circumcision and the Sabbath.

According to all documented evidence and accounts, including the Bible, Jesus never heard of the term 'Christian' during his gospel on earth. Furthermore, this reality establishes Jesus knew nothing of Christianity, because the word 'Christianity' is a derivative of Christian. More importantly, Jesus spoke Aramaic and was only aware of the Aramaic – Semitic word *Meshiha* (*Mashiah* in Hebrew), meaning he could not have sanctioned words of Greek origin to be the foundations of any religion – especially one that he knew nothing about, but is often associated with. Based on historical evidence, Jesus is actually '*Meshiha*' –which is the word Jesus, and his contemporaries would have been more accustomed. The Greek translations and consequent definitions came much later, with integral contributions from "Saint Paul" (Saul). In reality, Paul is responsible for the establishment of the religion called Christianity. Ideally, those who adhere to Paul's teachings should be referred to as Paulinites and their religion labelled Paulinity, and not Christians and Christianity. The influence of Paul can be appreciated as Paulism, or a manifestation of the Hellenization of Christianity.[25]

Paul hijacked Christ; Paul tactically used the holy name of Jesus to authenticate his preaching and mission of spreading his gospel – one which, nonetheless, had Greco-Roman socio-religious and geopolitical underpinnings.

Paul had an enormous impact on the Bible, as it is currently constituted. The authorship of 13 books in the New Testament is usually ascribed to Paul. Interestingly, Paul claimed he met Jesus spiritually, though his epiphanic claim is contradicted by biblical evidence. Paul's supposed 'conversion' is made spurious by two Biblical verses – Acts 9:7and Acts 22:9.

Acts of the Apostles 9:7:

> *The men who were traveling with him stood speechless because they heard the voice but saw no one.* – Acts 9:7

Acts of the Apostles 22:9:

> *Now those who were with me saw the light but did not hear the voice of the one who was speaking to me.* – Acts 22:9

The two aforementioned Biblical verses in Acts of the Apostles depict an apparent contradiction. It is rather intriguing that such revelations emanate from someone responsible for writing most of the books contained in the New Testament; which is more than anyone has written in the entire Bible. More worrisome is the historical fact that Paul used to be known a Saul of Tarsus – a notorious bounty hunter who specialized in hunting Christians. The fact of the matter is, when a supposed conversion appears paradoxical, it is only wise that anything associated with a Hellenistic-Jew like Paul, is thoroughly scrutinized for authenticity.

Based on his past endeavours and possible exposure to the corridors of power, Paul was learned and had a lot of influence on the establishment of what we call Christianity today, including the later infusion of Greek philosophical concepts to form the new religion (Christianity). Furthermore, to acknowledge the immense influence Paul has had on Christianity, the religion is sometimes referred to as Pauline Christianity. This is a sharp distinction from the authentic message of Jesus Christ, the Messiah and son of Mary.

CHAPTER 13

TRINITY ON TRIAL

The trinity has been a contentious issue within Christendom for centuries and is as confusing as it is complicated, even for some Christians. Generally, the Trinitarians are in support of the trinity and Nontrinitarians are against the trinity. The Trinitarians believe the trinity involves God (father), Jesus (son) and the Holy Spirit coexisting, coequal and coeternal. There are other dimensions to Nontrinitarianism, which includes concepts such as the Unitarians and Arians. Unitarians believe that Jesus is not a deity nor God incarnate, but just a saviour. The Arians believe Jesus is a son but not coeternal – a subordinationist position. Despite all the tripersonal variations and theological divergence within Christendom, it is crucial to identify the origin of the trinity concept. Historically, the concept of the trinity, triad or triune, has been integral to many cultural traditions and religions. The worship of three deities has existed since the Babylonian era and predates the advent of Christianity. For example, the Sumerian traditions of Mesopotamia included a triad of deities named Anu, Enlil and Ea. Egyptian traditions had triads of deities as part of their pantheon, and some of them included Amun, Mut, and Khonsu. Another triadic set were Amun, Re and Ptah. Also, the triune of Osiris, Isis, and Horus were a set of trinities. Khnum, Satis and Anukis, including Ptah, Sekhmet and Nefertum, were some of the trinity sets that existed in ancient Egypt. Ancient Arabs traditions had their triad of deities such as Al-lat, Manat and Al-Uzza. The Phoenicians had the triune deities called Ulomus, Ulosuros and Eliun. The Hinduism trinity of deities are named Brahma, Vishnu, and Shiva. The Persian triad included Ahura Mazda, Anahita and Mithra. The triune of Irish Paganism consists of Criosan, Biosena and Seeva. The Norse mythology trinity includes Thor, Wodan and Fricco.

In Greek mythology, the triad included the triple goddess Hecate, and another triune of Zeus, Poseidon and Hades. Roman mythology had a triad of deities which included Diana aka Diana triformis – triple goddess and is part of the triad of Egeria and Virbius. There is another trinity that includes Jupiter, Neptune and Pluto. The aforementioned trinity examples existed centuries before the advent Christianity.

The emergence of Jesus was perceived as a usurpation of constituted authority. The Romans literally worshiped their supreme rulers, who were considered god and saviour of mankind; for example Julius Caesar and Emperor Augustus. A protracted strife led to concessions within Christendom, and the trinity concept was infused into the teachings of Jesus, centuries after his departure. For instance, St. Justin Martyr, an early Christian Apologist and philosopher from around the 2nd century, wrote in Chapter XXI of The First Apology to the Roman Emperor Antoninus Pius:

> *And when we say also that the Word, who is the first-birth of God, was produced without sexual union, and that He, Jesus Christ, our Teacher, was crucified and died, and rose again, and ascended into heaven, we propound nothing different from what you believe regarding those whom you esteem sons of Jupiter.*

Unfortunately, Christianity accepted the syncretization of certain customs that were not initially part of Christian doctrine, and the trinity is just one example. The first usage of the term 'trinity' was in Latin – *trinitas*, and has been traced to the 2nd century, theologian, Quintus Septimius Florens Tertullianus, also known as Tertullian. Following centuries of polemics, debates and controversies, by the 4th century, ecumenical councils were convened to address issues and hopefully attain a consensus with the Clergy in attendance. The first ecumenical council was convened by the Roman Emperor,

Constantine, in the city of Nicaea (modern-day Iznik, Turkey). The First Council of Nicaea was in 325 and it effectively established, through the Nicene Creed, the full divinity of Jesus as son of God. About 56 years later, in 381, there was the second ecumenical council convened in Constantinople (modern-day Istanbul, Turkey) – the First Council of Constantinople. During this convention, the matter of the Holy Spirit's divinity was declared, through the Nicene-Constantinopolitan Creed. In 431, a third ecumenical council was convened in Ephesus (modern-day Selçuk, Turkey) – the First Council of Ephesus. The main objective was to deal with the conflict created by the teachings of Nestorius, who was the Patriarch of Constantinople from 428 to 431 and Cyril, the Patriarch of Alexandria from 412 to 444.

The convention affirmed the position of the two previous ecumenical councils (Nicaea and Constantinople), and addressed the position of the Nestorian doctrine; which emphasised the distinctive composition of Jesus – human and divine nature. Another contention was the title of Mary as the *Theotokos* (God-Bearer) and not *Christotokos* (Christ-Bearer). The fourth ecumenical council, which was the First Council of Chalcedon in 451, also dealt with the repudiation of Nestorianism and the extremist contrarian position on consubstantiality and Monophysitism by Eutyches – presbyter and archimandrite at Constantinople. Notably, the canons and declarations from the First Council of Ephesus in 431, led to a schism between different Christian denominations, which has lasted centuries. A prominent split within Christendom that cannot be ignored was between the Roman Catholic Church of the West and the Eastern Orthodox Church of the East – Great Schism.

Within Christendom were enduring issues that fuelled the dichotomy, such as the Filioque controversy, Papal supremacy, mutual excommunications, and the necessitation of the Athanasian Creed.

Essentially, historicity establishes that polytheism, the worship of numerous gods, specifically three Gods and the concept of the trinity, had aforetime existed as part of numerous traditions; right from mythology in Mesopotamia to Greco-Roman mythology, and other religious beliefs.

The following excerpts are from various sources, which underline the history of the trinity and its eventual manifestation within Christendom.

The Larousse Encyclopedia of Mythology highlights that the trinity was part of ancient Sumerian mythology:[26]

> *The universe was divided into three regions each of which became the domain of a god. Anu's share was the sky. The earth was given to Enlil. Ea became the ruler of the waters. Together they constituted the triad of the Great Gods*

Babylonian mythology trinity is described in the 1867 published Dionysius book, titled "The Mystical Woman and the Cities of the Nations: Or, Papal Rome and Her Secular Satellites": [27]

> *The ancient Babylonians recognised the doctrine of a trinity, or three persons in one god—as appears from a composite god with three heads forming part of their mythology, and the use of the equilateral triangle, also, as an emblem of such trinity in unity*

Regarding the trinity, Volume 2 of the Nouveau Dictionnaire Universel (New Universal Dictionary) by Maurice La Châtre, published in 1870, states: [28]

> *The Platonic trinity, itself merely a rearrangement of older trinities dating back to earlier peoples, appears to be the rational philosophic trinity of*

attributes that gave birth to the three hypostases or divine persons taught by the
Christian churches. This Greek philosopher's (Plato, 4th century BC)
conception of the divine trinity . . . can be found in all ancient (pagan) religions

The British aristocrat and Countess of Caithness, Marie Sinclair, in her 1876 book titled "Old Truths in a New Light", stated the trinity existed before the advent of Christianity:[29]

> *It is generally, although erroneously, supposed that the doctrine of the Trinity is*
> *of Christian origin. Nearly every nation of antiquity possessed a similar*
> *doctrine. [The early Catholic theologian] St. Jerome testifies unequivocally, 'All*
> *the ancient nations believed in the Trinity'.*

English Historian and Archivist, James Bonwick, in his 1878 book titled, "Egyptian Belief and Modern Thought" mentioned the prevalence of trinity (triads) across the world:[30]

> *It is an undoubted fact that more or less all over the world the deities are in*
> *triads. This rule applies to eastern and western hemispheres, to north and*
> *south. Further, it is observed that, in some mystical way, the triad of three*
> *persons is one. The first is as the second or third, the second as first or third, the*
> *third as first or second; in fact, they are each other, one and the same individual*
> *being. The definition of Athanasius, who lived in Egypt, applies to the trinities*
> *of all heathen religions.*

English Egyptologist, Arthur Weigall, in his 1928 book titled "Paganism in Our Christianity", described the trinity in ancient Greece, with an excerpted quote from Aristotle:[31]

> *In the Fourth Century BC Aristotle wrote: 'All things are three, and thrice is all: and let us use this number in the worship of the gods; for, as the Pythagoreans say, everything and all things are bounded by threes, for the end, the middle and the beginning have this number in everything, and these compose the number of the Trinity'*

The Swiss psychiatrist, Carl Jung, wrote "Psychology and Religion" initially published circa 1938. In an essay titled "A Psychological Approach to the Dogma of the Trinity", Carl Jung stated:[32]

> *Triads of gods appear very early, at the primitive level. The archaic triads in the religions of antiquity and of the East are too numerous to be mentioned here. Arrangement in triads is an archetype in the history of religion, which in all probability formed the basis of the Christian Trinity.*

Furthermore, there are various Christian scholars critical of the trinity, and clearly associate it with paganism or heathenism. Some theologians are vehemently against Trinitarianism and espouse that the trinity is a manifestation of forgery. For example, Victor Paul Wierwille released a publication in 1978 titled, "Forgers of The Word", in which he stated:

> *The truth of Jesus Christ the son of God was deliberately forged into the doctrine of God the Son. Seeds of Jesus Christ as God the Son were planted and sprouted during the life-time of Paul, continued growing during Timothy's life-time and flourished shortly thereafter, reaching full bloom for all future creeds by 325 A.D.*
>
> *The doctrine that Jesus Christ the son of God was God the Son was decreed by worldly and ecclesiastical powers. Men were forced to accept it at the point of the sword or else. Thus, the error of the trinity was propounded to the end that*

ultimately people believed it to be the truth. Thus, Christianity became in essence like Babylonian heathenism, with only a thin layer of Christian names. Throughout the centuries following 325 A.D., unknowledgeable believers, because of previous teaching and believing, deliberately forged scriptures in support of the doctrine of God the Son by purposely tampering with manuscripts and by false translations.

The trinitarians demanded the insertion of I John 5:7, 8 because it speaks about "these three are one," and then they could speak of three persons in one.

In the 1998 book titled "The Doctrine of the Trinity: Christianity's Self-Inflicted Wound", written by Sir Anthony F. Buzzard and Charles F. Hunting, the authors argued against the Trinity. In the book, the authors stress that God is one and is the same God of Moses, Isaiah, Jesus and the apostles.

That "in spite of prodigious mental gymnastics" by Trinitarians, whatever has been fractionalized into parts cannot remain one. Sir Anthony F. Buzzard and Charles F. Hunting consider it a great historic marvel that Christians were convinced of the trinity: [33]

> *One of the great marvels of Christian history has been the ability of theologians to convince Christian people that three persons are really one God.*

Interestingly, the third president of the United States, Thomas Jefferson, considered trinity an "unintelligible proposition of platonic mysticisms that three are one and one is three".[34]

Also, a scriptural explication of the Bible reveals that 'trinity' as a term or doctrine is not explicitly mentioned or taught anywhere in the Old and New Testament. The concept of the trinity is at variance with some aspects of the Bible. For instance, the trinity clearly contradicts core aspect of The Shema: "Hear, O Israel: The Lord our God is one Lord" (Deuteronomy 6:4).

Other Bible verses that do not conform to the trinity doctrine include:

That they may know that You, whose name alone is the LORD, Are the Most High over all the earth. –Psalm 83:18

There is only one God, and he makes people right with himself only by faith, whether they are Jews or Gentiles. – Roman 3:30

A mediator, however, implies more than one party; but God is one.
– Galatians 3:20

You heard me say, 'I am going away and I am coming back to you.' If you loved me, you would be glad that I am going to the Father, for the Father is greater than I.–John 14:28

The aforementioned points asseverate the trinity was integral to many ancient civilizations that predated Christianity, and establishes the trinity was not part of early Christianity doctrine.

DISSECTING THE TRINITY INTEGRANTS

Father

It is vital to establish that the usage of 'Father' in the Bible, particularly by Jesus, is not biological, but contextual. The usage represents a fatherly attribute that can easily be appreciated as a generic term applicable to all humans.

For example, within the Jewish traditions, the usage of 'Father' as God is metaphorical in Aramaic and Hebrew –*Abba*.

Another good example is among the Yoruba speaking people of modern-day Nigeria; 'Father' means '*Baba*', but also denotes God based on linguistic preferences.

Furthermore, a thorough analysis of the Bible reveals there are biblical evidence that attest to the 'Father' contextuality.

> *"Do not cling to Me," Jesus said, "for I have not yet ascended to the Father. But go and tell My brothers, 'I am ascending to My Father and your Father, to My God and your God.'*–John 20:17

The Bible profiles Jesus' genealogy, and below are a couple of examples:

> *The book of the genealogy of Jesus Christ, the son of David, the son of Abraham.* – Matthew 1:1

> *Jesus was about thirty years old when he began his public ministry. Jesus was known as the son of Joseph. Joseph was the son of Heli.* – Luke 3:23

Son

Sons of 'God': The Son of God is a title accorded different biblical figures. The Bible contains many occurrences of the usage of 'son', and it also uses 'sons' (*Bene Elohim*). Also, in some versions of the Bible, 'Children' is used interchangeably. Below are some examples:

> *Then say to Pharaoh, 'This is what the LORD says: Israel is my firstborn son* – Exodus 4:22

> *...for I am a father to Israel, and Ephraim is my firstborn*– Jeremiah 31:9

> *When Israel was a child, then I loved him, and called my son out of Egypt.* –Hosea 11:1

Kenan was the son of Enosh. Enosh was the son of Seth. Seth was the son of Adam. Adam was the son of God. –Luke3:38

Again there was a day when the sons of God came to present themselves before the LORD... – Job 2:1

For as many as are led by the Spirit of God, they are the sons of God – Romans 8:14

That ye may be blameless and harmless, the sons of God, without rebuke, in the midst of a crooked and perverse nation, among whom ye shine as lights in the world;– Philippians 2:15

But as many as received him, to them gave he power to become the sons of God, even to them that believe on his name– John 1:12

Behold what manner of love the Father hath bestowed upon us, that we should be called the sons of God: therefore the world knoweth us not, because it knew him not. – 1 John 3:1

Beloved, now are we the sons of God, and it doth not yet appear what we shall be: but we know that, when he shall appear, we shall be like him; for we shall see him as he is.– 1 John 3:2

Now there was a day when the sons of God came to present themselves before the LORD,– Job 1:6

When the morning stars sang together, and all the sons of God shouted for joy? –Job 38:7

That the sons of God saw the daughters of men that they were fair
– Genesis 6:2

...when the sons of God came in unto the daughters of men,– Genesis 6:4

I will be his father, and he shall be my son. If he commit iniquity, I will chasten him with the rod of men, and with the stripes of the children of men
– 2 Samuel 7:14

You are the children of the LORD your God; you shall not cut yourselves nor shave the front of your head for the dead. – Deuteronomy 14:1

(King David) I will declare the decree: the LORD hath said unto me, Thou art my Son; this day have I begotten thee– Psalms 2:7

Blessed are the peacemakers: for they shall be called the children of God.
– Matthew 5:9

Neither can they die any more: for they are equal unto the angels; and are the children of God, being the children of the resurrection.– Luke 20:36

Son of Man: The term 'Son of man' occurs 81 times in the Bible – 30 times in Matthew, 14 times in Mark, 25 times in Luke and 12 times in John. The 'son of man' reference in the Bible emphasizes the human nature of Jesus. According to the Academic American Encyclopedia:[35]

During his earthly life Jesus was addressed as rabbi and was regarded as a prophet. Some of his words, too, place him in the category of sage. A title of respect for a rabbi would be "my Lord." Already before Easter his followers, impressed by his authority, would mean something more than usual when they addressed him as "my Lord."…. it is unlikely that the title "Son of David" was ascribed to him or accepted by him during his earthly ministry. "Son of God," in former times a title of the Hebrew kings (Psalms 2:7), was first adopted in the post-Easter church as an equivalent of Messiah and had no metaphysical connotations (Romans 1:4). Jesus was conscious of a unique filial relationship with God, but it is uncertain whether the Father/Son language (Mark 18:32; Matt. 11:25-27 par.; John passim) goes back to Jesus himself.

The Spirit

The Spirit is acknowledged as the Holy Spirit. There are various Biblical verses that confirm the Spirit as a separate entity, and generally supportive of Jesus. Below are a couple of examples about the Holy Spirit in the Bible:

How God anointed Jesus of Nazareth with the Holy Spirit and with power. He went about doing good and healing all who were oppressed by the devil, for God was with him. – Acts 10:38

Likewise the Spirit helps us in our weakness. For we do not know what to pray for as we ought, but the Spirit himself intercedes for us with groanings too deep for words. – Romans 8:26

Based on Islamic exegeses, Angel Jibreel (Archangel Gabriel) is actually the Holy Spirit – in Arabic transliteration: *Ruh Al-Qudus.* The following Quranic verses mention the Holy Spirit:

And We did certainly give Moses the Scripture [i.e., the Torah] and followed up after him with messengers. And We gave Jesus, the son of Mary, clear proofs and supported him with the Pure Spirit [i.e., the angel Gabriel]. But is it [not] that every time a messenger came to you, [O Children of Israel], with what your souls did not desire, you were arrogant? And a party [of messengers] you denied and another party you killed.

– Quran 2:87

Of those messengers, some of whom We have caused to excel others, and of whom there are some unto whom Allah spake, while some of them He exalted (above others) in degree; and We gave Jesus, son of Mary, clear proofs (of Allah's Sovereignty) and We supported him with the holy Spirit. And if Allah had so willed it, those who followed after them would not have fought one with another after the clear proofs had come unto them. But they differed, some of them believing and some disbelieving. And if Allah had so willed it, they would not have fought one with another; but Allah doeth what He will.

– Quran 2:253

And ˹on Judgment Day˺ Allah will say, "O Jesus, son of Mary! Remember My favour upon you and your mother: how I supported you with the holy spirit so you spoke to people in ˹your˺ infancy and adulthood. How I taught you writing, wisdom, the Torah, and the Gospel. How you moulded a bird from clay—by My Will—and breathed into it and it became a ˹real˺ bird— by My Will. How you healed the blind and the lepers—by My Will. How you brought the dead to life—by My Will. How I prevented the Children of Israel from harming you when you came to them with clear proofs and the disbelievers among them said, "This is nothing but pure magic."

– Quran 5:110

In view of the above enumerated evidence, Jesus is primarily human, and the trinity is inherently problematic. So, whatever explanation or rationalization that is applied to the matter, or whatever gimmickry that is spun around it, the trinity remains three, and can never be equal to one. In actuality, the trinity completely nullifies the exceptionality of The Creator; because if all the integrants of the triune were equal, then who exactly is The Creator. There can only be one Creator. Evidently, The Creator cannot be created because He exists outside the realms of all His creation. The Quran emphatically warns about the venerative excesses of those professing the trinity doctrine:

> O People of the Scripture, do not commit excess in your religion or say about Allah except the truth. The Messiah, Jesus the son of Mary, was but a messenger of Allah and His word which He directed to Mary and a soul [created at a command] from Him. So believe in Allah and His messengers. And do not say, "Three"; desist – it is better for you. Indeed, Allah is but one God. Exalted is He above having a son. To Him belongs whatever is in the heavens and whatever is on the earth. And sufficient is Allah as Disposer of affairs. – Quran 4:171

The Quran explicitly discounts the trinity and affirms the oneness of God:

> They have certainly disbelieved who say, "Allah is the third of three. "And there is no god except one God. And if they do not desist from what they are saying, there will surely afflict the disbelievers among them a painful punishment.– Quran 5:73

> Say: He is Allah, the One and Only;
> Allah, the Eternal, Absolute;
> He begetteth not, nor is He begotten;
> And there is none comparable unto Him.– Quran 112:1-4

CHAPTER 14

SCHISMATIC DIMENSIONS

THE BIBLE AND "GRAVE DEFECTS"

There have been debates about the authorship and authenticity of the Bible, based on some identified issues. It may come as a surprise to some people that the Bible contains 'grave defects'. The preface section of the Revised Standard Version of the Bible categorically states:

> *The King James Version has grave defects and that these defects are so many and so serious as to call for revision.*

Also, the Bible highlights some of the historical fabrications that have occurred within Christendom through the scheming of scribes:

> *'How can you say, 'We are wise, and the law of the LORD is with us'? But behold, the lying pen of the scribes has made it into a lie.–* Jeremiah 8:8

For many centuries, there have been long-lasting issues around the authenticity of the Bible, from an originality standpoint; translations (Hebrew to Greek, Latin, etc.), Vulgate, Apocrypha, Canonicity, Deuterocanonical and Protocanonical Books, and the enduring matter of the addition of the end of Mark (Mark 16:9-20). The Reformations and the rise of Protestantism, following Martin Luther's 95 Theses of 1517 and the Edict of Worms decree by Emperor Charles V of 1521, had a lasting effect on Christendom. Then in 1534, the Anglican (Church of England) emerged based on a contention between Pope Clement VII and King Henry VIII's marital entanglements.

In 1545, the Council of Trent commenced, at the instance of Pope Paul III, and was concluded in 1563. The gathering was the 19th ecumenical council and is also referred to as the Counter-Reformation. Amongst other Reformation issues addressed, were the matters of seven sacraments, indulgences, Protestant Communion and transubstantiation, salvation and faith, and scripture and authority. Consequent schismatic manifestations resulted in deeper chasms; further church divisions and denominations, and various versions of the Bible. There is literally a Bible to fit every denomination's requirement.

The Bible is essentially a bibliography – a collection of manuscripts. Each version of the Bible comprises aspects – particularly the New Testament's gospels and letters – that any of the sanctioning authorities believe is worthy of inclusion. The authorship of the Bible is loosely based on non-primary accounts and themed according to some sources that never coexisted with Jesus. The narrator is essential to identifying any narration in the Bible that is why some aspects are presented as the 'Gospel according to'. For example, in the Bible you will find the Gospel according to – Matthew, Mark, Luke, John. However, there is nowhere in the Bible about the Gospel according to Jesus, or better yet, the actual Gospel of Jesus.

The disparity between the Synoptic Gospels and the Gospel of John is just one example of existent incongruities. Though the purpose of this discourse is not to dwell on the historical inaccuracies and contradictions within the Bible, it is important to highlight these disparities, and the critical views that arise about its authenticity, especially from the divinity perspective.

Evidently, the Bible, as it is currently constituted, has lost its authenticity. Based on deliberate distortions and interpolations that lasted over a protracted period, combined with numerous ideological aberrations, Christians, sadly, came to believe concocted falsities as truth.

Unfortunately, not too many Christians are ready to research these findings, and those that become aware, may decide to conceal the truth or dismiss for spiritual comfort, believe their faith in Jesus is enough, become irreligious or change their faith completely – may be become Muslims. From an Islamic perspective, the altering of scriptures is detailed in the Quran:

> *So woe to those who write the "scripture" with their own hands, then say, "This is from Allah," in order to exchange it for a small price. Woe to them for what their hands have written and woe to them for what they earn.* – Quran 2:79

> *And indeed, there is among them a party who alter the Scripture with their tongues so you may think it is from the Scripture, but it is not from the Scripture. And they say, "This is from Allah," but it is not from Allah. And they speak untruth about Allah while they know.* – Quran 3:78

> *The similitude of those who were charged with the (obligations of the) Mosaic Law, but who subsequently failed in those (obligations), is that of a donkey which carries huge tomes (but understands them not). Evil is the similitude of people who falsify the Signs of Allah: and Allah guides not people who do wrong.* – Quran 62:5

JESUS AND HIS MISSION

> *He ['Iesa (Jesus)] was not more than a slave. We granted Our Favour to him, and We made him an example to the Children of Israel (i.e. his creation without a father).* – Quran 43:59

Based on Islamic exegesis, the likeness of Jesus' miraculous birth is juxtaposed with Adam. Whilst Jesus had no biological father, Adam had neither a father nor mother. The similitude of Adam and Jesus is mentioned in the Quran:

> *The similitude of Jesus before Allah is as that of Adam; He created him from dust, then said to him: "Be". And he was.* – Quran 3:59

Jesus' miraculous birth was one of the many divine signs from God. Also, Jesus was sent with a scripture named the *Injeel* – The Gospel.

However, the Injeel no longer exists in its original form, and as a result, a lot of distortions and conjecture have ensued about Jesus. The reality is that Jesus never claimed to be God. Sadly, some Christians still believe Jesus is God and totally misconstrued the actual purpose of his mission on earth, thereby missing the import of the wisdom behind his God-gifted powers. Jesus, like all his divinely inspired predecessors, was a prophet sent by God, and this is affirmed in the Bible:

> *And they took offense at him. But Jesus said to them, "A prophet is not without honor except in his own town and in his own home."*
> –Matthew 13:57

> *And the crowds said, "This is the prophet Jesus, from Nazareth of Galilee."*
> –Matthew 21:11

> *Although they wanted to arrest him, they were afraid of the crowds, who considered Jesus to be a prophet.* –Matthew 21:46

> *And Jesus said to them, "A prophet is not without honor, except in his hometown and among his relatives and in his own household."* – Mark 6:4

Fear gripped everyone, and they began to praise God. "A great prophet has appeared among us," they said, and "God has helped his people." – Luke 7:16

Nevertheless I must journey today, tomorrow, and the day following; for it cannot be that a prophet should perish outside of Jerusalem. – Luke 13:33

"What things?" he asked. "About Jesus of Nazareth," they replied. "He was a prophet, powerful in word and deed before God and all the people. – Luke 24:19

The woman told him, "Sir, I see that you are a prophet! –John 4:19

Then those men, when they had seen the miracle that Jesus did, said, This is of a truth that prophet that should come into the world. –John 6:14

So they asked the formerly blind man again, "What do you say about him, since it was your eyes he healed?" He said, "He is a prophet. –John 9:17

Also, in a previously quoted verse, the Quran affirms Jesus as a prophet:

[Jesus] said, "Indeed, I am the servant of Allah. He has given me the Scripture and made me a prophet. – Quran 19:30

An especially important discourse is the actual mission of Jesus, whilst on earth. According to the Bible, Jesus was actually sent to the "lost sheep" of the house of Israel and claims of him being sent to the world were added to the doctrine much later.

The historic schisms were chiefly motivated by geopolitics enshrouded in ethnicism. The actual mission of Jesus is mentioned in the Bible:

Do not think that I have come to abolish the law or the prophets; I have come not to abolish but to fulfill.—Matthew 5:17

Just then a Canaanite woman from that region came out and started shouting, "Have mercy on me, Lord, Son of David; my daughter is tormented by a demon."
But he did not answer her at all. And his disciples came and urged him, saying, "Send her away, for she keeps shouting after us.
He answered, "I was sent only to the lost sheep of the house of Israel."
—Matthew 15:22-24

The above verses indicate that Jesus is affirming the Law of Moses that preceded his Gospel and confirming the uniformity of the mission of the prophets that antedated his own mission.

And I have come confirming that which was before me of the Taurat (Torah), and to make lawful to you part of what was forbidden to you, and I have come to you with a proof from your Lord. So fear Allah and obey me.
—Quran 3:50

At this juncture, it would be useful to highlight that the Judaic view of Jesus is highly critical, especially when juxtaposed with the Islamic view and the honour accorded to Jesus. The Jews categorically reject Jesus as Messiah and believe the expected Messiah is yet to come and fulfil that messianic role. For instance, the prominent Jewish philosopher and Torah scholar named Maimonides aka Rambam, who authored the 13 Principles of Faith, considers Jesus the most influential, but a false messiah, nonetheless. From an Islamic viewpoint, the Quran highlights the dispute between Jews and Christians:

The Jews said that the Christians follow nothing (i.e. are not on the right religion); and the Christians said that the Jews follow nothing (i.e. are not on the right religion); though they both recite the Scripture. Like unto their word, said (the pagans) who know not. Allah will judge between them on the Day of Resurrection about that wherein they have been differing. –Quran 2:113

In this regard, Islam can be appreciated as the arbiter that resolves the age-long dispute between Judaism (Jews) and Christianity (Christians). Islam is the middle path between two extremes regarding Jesus – Christianity elevating Jesus to the level of God, including the son of God claim, and Judaism labelling Jesus a false messiah and magician. Islam acknowledges Jesus as a prophet who performed miracles by the permission of Allah. Islam honours Jesus as the actual Messiah with a divine mission. Jesus is the only figure referred to as Messiah in the entire Quran and the return of Jesus is one of the signs of the last days – before the Day of Judgement. It is instructive to note that Prophet Muhammad ﷺ is the last prophet and messenger and when Jesus returns, he is coming as a Messiah to fulfil the messianic mission. Jesus is not bringing a new message or scripture and will abide by the last Holy Scripture from God – The Quran. Also, Jesus will expose and annihilate a false messiah – anti-Christ – *Dajjal*. The mission of Jesus – first and second coming – is detailed in numerous Islamic exegeses.

And [make him] a messenger to the Children of Israel, [who will say], 'Indeed I have come to you with a sign from your Lord in that I design for you from clay [that which is] like the form of a bird, then I breathe into it and it becomes a bird by permission of Allah . And I cure the blind and the leper, and I give life to the dead - by permission of Allah. And I inform you of what you eat and what you store in your houses. Indeed in that is a sign for you, if you are believers.

And [I have come] confirming what was before me of the Torah and to make lawful for you some of what was forbidden to you. And I have come to you with a sign from your Lord, so fear Allah and obey me.

Indeed, Allah is my Lord and your Lord, so worship Him. That is the straight path'"

But when Jesus felt [persistence in] disbelief from them, he said, "Who are my supporters for [the cause of] Allah?" The disciples said, "We are supporters for Allah. We have believed in Allah and testify that we are Muslims [submitting to Him]. −Quran 3:49-52

Evidently, Jesus never heard of, nor sanctioned the creation of a new religion, especially the religion that was to be called Christianity. The mission of Jesus was to affirm the Law of Moses and confirm the mission of predecessor prophets (Matthew 5:17). More importantly, the Bible explicitly states that Jesus was sent to the Jews who had strayed from the straight path: the Law − Lost sheep of the house of Israel (Matthew 15:24).

The Quran mentions the straight path message Jesus delivered to the Children of Israel:

[Jesus said], "And indeed, Allah is my Lord and your Lord, so worship Him. That is a straight path."

Then the factions differed [concerning Jesus] from among them, so woe to those who disbelieved - from the scene of a tremendous Day. −Quran 19:36-37

An historical analysis of Christianity establishes the theological differences that occurred and many denominations that emerged afterwards.

The creation of a religion called Christianity occurred long after Jesus departed earth and can be traced to the aftermath of the protracted strife that existed between the Jews and Roman authorities.

Though Christianity is a religion with Middle Eastern roots, it is highly influenced by Greco-Roman history. From a socio-political prism, Christianity was literally hijacked by the West and became weaponized for parochial geopolitical and socio-political agendas globally.

THE DEIFICATION DILEMMA

Deification and concomitant manifestations are problematic. The process of deification manifests in various forms, whether anthropomorphic or anthropocentric. Deification is the apotheosis of humans – elevation to divine status. Creations are sometimes ascribed these 'godly' characteristics, even if honorific, the veneration is sometimes taken to extremes.

From an Islamic perspective, Allah has many known and unknown attributes; which are sometimes referred to as His glorious names. There are certain attributes that human beings have been exposed to such as *Ar-Rahman* (The Beneficent) and *Ar-Rahim* (The Most Merciful). Also, there are attributes that are unknown and those that will manifest; such as *Al-Hakam* (The Judge) or *Al-Malik* (The Master) of the day of judgement. Even the term 'God' can be perceived as an attribute that represents a powerful being. The term 'Creator' can be seen as an attribute that represents inimitable creative capabilities.

There are many other attributes that deal specifically with the matters affecting His creation. However, some religious and cultural traditions deified the attributes and manifestations of attributes of God and made them gods in their own right. Historically, deification has been part of every cultural tradition and sometimes manifests radically, with interminable societal challenges. The world is currently dealing with deification manifestations.

The deification issue would have taken a solid foothold in Islam and manifested into an established deviance if the Prophet had not specifically cautioned against such excessive practices. This specific admonition is documented in a Hadith – Sahih al-Bukhari 3445, Book 60, Hadith 115:

> *Do not exaggerate my praises as the Christians have done with the son of Mary. Verily, I am only a servant, so refer to me as the servant of Allah and his messenger.* – Prophet Muhammad ﷺ

In fact, Prophet Muhammad ﷺ defended Jesus when the polytheist of Arabia debated with him about the status of Jesus. The polytheists compared Jesus with their idols and insinuated that Jesus too was a worshipped idol, like the idols they worshipped. However, the Prophet clarified that Jesus did not instruct anyone to worship him during his lifetime and that his deification occurred after he departed the world. Despite such admonitions, certain people still indulge in the excesses of deifying fellow creations – human beings. The citation of Christian excesses as an example is important because deification has been an ongoing issue within Christendom for centuries. Christological, exegetical, and historiographical narratives confirm the various manifestations of the deification issue. The Bible warned against making idols and graven images in some verses – Exodus 20:23, Deuteronomy 4:16-18 and Leviticus 26:1.

On the day of reckoning, when Prophets are gathered to be questioned about their missionary affairs whilst on earth, the questioning of Jesus is primarily about the deification of himself and his mother, by others. However, Jesus will exculpate himself of such insubordination and will categorically state: "I was a witness over them as long as I was among them; but when You took me up, You were the Observer over them, and You are, over all things, Witness."

And [beware the Day] when Allah will say, "O Jesus, Son of Mary, did you say to the people, 'Take me and my mother as deities besides Allah?'" He will say, "Exalted are You! It was not for me to say that to which I have no right. If I had said it, You would have known it. You know what is within myself, and I do not know what is within Yourself. Indeed, it is You who is Knower of the unseen.

I said not to them except what You commanded me - to worship Allah, my Lord and your Lord. And I was a witness over them as long as I was among them; but when You took me up, You were the Observer over them, and You are, over all things, Witness. – Quran 5:116 -117

The above statement is evidence that whilst Jesus was carrying out his mission, he never claimed to be a deity, and the deification of his character, which occurred afterwards, is not his responsibility. The exculpation of Jesus applies to Mary as well and is a symbolic precept for all those practicing apotheosis – the deification of mortals. The importance of this specificity stems from the manifestational reality of Jesus being the only prophet that was exceptionally apotheosised after his departure. Analysing the deification issue from a global perspective, the confusion that would emanate from having multiple autochthonous deities from various geographical regions, cannot be overstated. In addendum, graven images, idols or man-made gods can offer no help or assistance to themselves, and definitely not to others.

If there were, in the heavens and the earth, other gods besides Allah, there would have been confusion in both! but glory to Allah, the Lord of the Throne: (High is He) above what they attribute to Him! –Quran 21:22

CHAPTER 15

THE ABRAHAM POSER

Abraham was a righteous man from Mesopotamia (modern-day Iraq) who is revered and synonymous with the so-called Abrahamic religions – Judaism, Christianity and Islam. And herein lays the critical aspect about Abrahamic religions, which is sometimes not given proper consideration, especially by those who claim Abraham as a patriarch or have a religious affiliation with Abraham. The crux of the issue with the claimants of Abraham, particularly among the "Abrahamic Religions", stems from the fact that Abraham only had one religion during his lifetime. Although all the Abrahamic Religions that lay claim to Abraham may have rights to such entitlements, only one of those religions must be the authentic religion of Abraham. For authentication purposes, the Abrahamic assessment will be adopted. The primary purpose of the exercise is to determine the actual religion of Abraham.

What exactly was the religion of Abraham?

Before elucidating on the religion of Abraham, some scriptural evidence on why Abraham is revered by the Abrahamic religions will be highlighted. From the Judeo-Christian position, Abraham is mentioned in some parts of the Torah (Pentateuch) and the Bible (Old Testament and New Testament). The following Bible verses are a few examples:

> *Neither shall thy name any more be called Abram, but thy name shall be Abraham; for a father of many nations have I made thee.* – Genesis 17:5

> *And God said unto Abraham, Thou shalt keep my covenant therefore, thou, and thy seed after thee in their generations.* – Genesis 17:9

But thou, Israel, art my servant, Jacob whom I have chosen, the seed of Abraham my friend.
– Isaiah 41:8

Even as Abraham believed God, and it was accounted to him for righteousness.
– Romans 3:6

Analysing from an Islamic viewpoint, Ibrahim (Abraham) is highly regarded and considered a friend of God. Abraham was gifted with divinely inspired wisdom – a unique form of esotericism. His curiosity about existential realities and the purpose of life made Abraham constantly ratiocinate about his milieu and spurred his observation of celestial phenomena.

We also showed Abraham the wonders of the heavens and the earth, so he would be sure in faith.
When the night grew dark upon him, he saw a star and said, "This is my Lord!" But when it set, he said, "I do not love things that set."
Then when he saw the moon rising, he said, "This one is my Lord!" But when it disappeared, he said, "If my Lord does not guide me, I will certainly be one of the misguided people."
Then when he saw the sun shining, he said, "This must be my Lord—it is the greatest!" But again when it set, he declared, "O my people! I totally reject whatever you associate ˹with Allah in worship˺.
I have turned my face towards the One Who has originated the heavens and the earth—being upright—and I am not one of the polytheists."
– Quran 6:75-79

The above verses affirm the celestial bodies – sun, moon and stars – are part of creations that serve specific purposes and are not to be worshipped.

It is Allah Who created the heavens and the earth and sends down rain from the sky, causing fruits to grow as a provision for you. He has subjected the ships for your service, sailing through the sea by His command, and has subjected the rivers for you.

He has ˹also˺ subjected for you the sun and the moon, both constantly orbiting, and has subjected the day and night for you.

— Quran 14:32-33

And of His signs are the night and day and the sun and moon. Do not prostrate to the sun or to the moon, but prostrate to Allah, who created them, if it should be Him that you worship.

–Quran 41:37

At various stages of his life, Abraham faced and overcame many trials. For instance, as a youth, Abraham confronted his father – an established idol sculptor – about idol worship. Also, Abraham publicly confronted his idol-worshipping townsmen and the King – acknowledged by some historians to be Nimrod.

And recite to them the story of Ibrahim (Abraham).
When he said to his father and his people, "What do you worship?"
They said: "We worship idols, and to them we are ever devoted."
He said: "Do they hear you, when you call (on them)?
"Or do they benefit you or do they harm (you)?"
They said: "Nay, but we found our fathers doing so."
— Quran 26:69-74

Following the public confrontation with the idolaters, the king ordered that Abraham should be catapulted into a specially prepared blazing fire. Based on the exegetical narrative of events that preceded the planned public immolation, Angel Jibreel appeared to Abraham as he was being bound to be flung into the inferno. Then Angel Jibreel asked Abraham if he needed assistance, and he responded that he required assistance, though not from Angel Jibreel exclusively, but from his Creator – Allah, especially. Abraham then recites the prayer: "Sufficient for us is Allah, and [He is] the best Disposer of affairs."–*HasbunAllahu wa ni'mal Wakeel* (Quran 3:173).

The special and timely prayer of Abraham was indeed answered, and the extraordinary miracle is documented in the Quran:

> *We [i.e., Allah] said, "O fire, be coolness and safety upon Abraham."*
> – Quran 21:69

Miraculously, and to the surprise of those present, Abraham emerged from the blazing fire unscathed and his reputation amongst the people grew. The king was threatened by Abraham's growing reputation, so challenged him to a debate. Abraham was gifted with wisdom, and he often debated people with success, and on this occasion, he debated with a king.

> *Have you not considered the one who argued with Abraham about his Lord [merely] because Allah had given him kingship? When Abraham said, "My Lord is the one who gives life and causes death," he said, "I give life and cause death." Abraham said, "Indeed, Allah brings up the sun from the east, so bring it up from the west." So the disbeliever was overwhelmed [by astonishment], and Allah does not guide the wrongdoing people.*
> – Quran 2:258

The life of Abraham was truly unique and epitomizes what it means to have unshakeable faith in God. Abraham followed divine instruction without doubt and his life highlights the benefits of not questioning certain things that happen in our lives, even though certain occurrences may not make sense at that point in time, particularly from a human reasoning point of view.

Abraham was confronted with another trial: this time he was commanded to leave his family (Hajar and Ishmael) at an uncultivable valley. The valley region has been identified as modern-day Makkah (Mecca), and the entire area used to be arid. Makkah is blessed today because of the prayer of Abraham. Also, the travails Hajar endured whilst searching for water to care for Ishmael led to the legacy of Zamzam, Ka'bah, and Hajj (pilgrimage).

> *O our Lord! I have made some of my offspring to dwell in an uncultivable valley by Your Sacred House (the Ka'bah at Makkah); in order, O our Lord, that they may perform As-Salat (Iqamat-as-Salat), so fill some hearts among men with love towards them, and (O Allah) provide them with fruits so that they may give thanks.* – Quran 14:37

Notably, whilst Abraham's first wife, Sarah was childless, his second wife, Hajar, had a son Ismail (Ishmael), though Sarah later had Ishaq (Isaac).

> *My Lord, grant me [a child] from among the righteous."*
> *So We gave him good tidings of a forbearing boy.*
> *And when he reached with him [the age of] exertion, he said, "O my son, indeed I have seen in a dream that I [must] sacrifice you, so see what you think." He said, "O my father, do as you are commanded. You will find me, if Allah wills, of the steadfast."*
> *And when they had both submitted and he put him down upon his forehead,*

We called to him, "O Abraham,

You have fulfilled the vision." Indeed, We thus reward the doers of good.

Indeed, this was the clear trial.

And We ransomed him with a great sacrifice,

And We left for him [favorable mention] among later generations:

"Peace upon Abraham."

Indeed, We thus reward the doers of good.

Indeed, he was of Our believing servants.

And We gave him good tidings of Isaac, a prophet from among the righteous.

– Quran 37:100-112

Evidently, Abraham passed his test and did not have to sacrifice his son because an animal – probably ram, appeared as a replacement. A noteworthy point is that there has been an ongoing debate for centuries, especially among Christians and Muslims, about which of Abraham's sons was put up for sacrifice: whether it was Ishmael or Isaac?

Logically, Isaac could not have been the child involved in the test of sacrifice, because Ishmael was the first-born and Isaac was the second-born, and Abraham would have had two children at the time. Hypothetically, it would be a less excruciating experience to sacrifice one of two sons, than to sacrifice an only son. Based on this logic, it is safe to deduce that the sacrifice trial occurred when Abraham had just one son – Ishmael. Furthermore, due to the sequence of events from the previously highlighted verses, Abraham was given glad tidings of another son (Isaac), after he passed the test of sacrificing his son (Ishmael). And Quran 37:112 specifically mentions Isaac as the son to come after the trial episode. Indeed, Abraham was grateful for the favour bestowed upon him, and the Quran confirms this:

Praise to Allah, who has granted to me in old age Ishmael and Isaac. Indeed, my Lord is the Hearer of supplication. –Quran 14:39

Abraham's life contains many lessons, and a classic example of obeying divine injunction was when Abraham was instructed to sacrifice his child as a test of obeisance. What makes Abraham's story more intriguing is because he had longed and prayed for offspring. The aforementioned points were necessary, because the elucidation on some aspects of Abraham's life, gives credence to why he is exceptionally revered by the so-called Abrahamic religions.

At this juncture, the crux of this section and the initial poser must be addressed: to determine the religion of Abraham. To ascertain the religion of Abraham, a comparative analysis of the contending religions (Abrahamic) is a necessity. Though there are some other religious groups that are sometimes associated with Abraham, the primary focus will be on the major contenders: Judaism, Christianity and Islam.

A comparative analysis will explore linguistic and descriptive paradigms, via historical and contemporary perspectives. The objective is to determine whether Abraham practiced Judaism as a Jew, Christianity as a Christian or Islam as a Muslim, and the historical and contemporary applicability of those identities. Furthermore, the resulting paradigm from the comparative analysis will be historically applicable; ideally starting from the first human creation, down to our contemporary times, and the future.

ABRAHAM AND JUDAISM

Was Abraham a Jew and his religion Judaism?

To address these questions, an explicative of the words 'Jew' and 'Judaism' becomes necessary. Historically, the sons of Jacob were initially divided into twelve tribes, and following the death of Solomon, were further divided into ten tribes and two tribes. The divisions were recognised as two kingdoms – northern Kingdom of Israel and southern Kingdom of Judah. The Jews are meant to be the descendents of Judah – the fourth son of Jacob and his wife Leah. From an etymological perspective, Jew was derived from Anglo-French *Iew* or *Iuw*. The elision of the letter 'd' occurred during the Greek (*Ioudaios*) and Latin (*Iudaeus*) translations from the original Semitic languages – Hebrew *Y'hudi* and Aramaic *Y'hudah* (Judah) – which means "celebrated" or "praised". Notably, Hebrew alphabets do not include the equivalent of the letter 'J'. From around the 16th century, the letter 'J' became predominantly used as a Latinized replacement, and by extension in the English language, for some words with Aramaic and Hebrew roots. [36]

In view of this historical perspective, what is Judaism and who is a Jew? Jews (*Y'hudim*) are an ethnoreligious group that trace their ancestry to the Kingdom of Judah. Jews are the descendants of Judah – the person and Kingdom (region), and ethnocentrism was the primary basis for the formation of the religion – Judaism (*Yahadut*). In essence, if you cannot trace your ancestry to the Kingdom of Judah, you cannot be a Jew.

As Judaism is an ethnic religion, you cannot be Jewish if your ancestry is Malay for example, because being Jewish has its roots in Judean ethnos. From a Biblical perspective, Abraham was from the Ur of the Chaldees or Chaldeans (Ur Kasdim), which was in Babylonia – Mesopotamia (modern-day Baghdad, Iraq), and he was referred to as 'the Hebrew':

> *You are the LORD God, who chose Abram and brought him out of Ur of the Chaldeans and named him Abraham.* – Nehemiah 9:7

> *Then one who had escaped came and told Abram the Hebrew*
> –Genesis 14:13

In view of the aforementioned points, Abraham could not have been a Jew, nor could his religion be Judaism, because the terminology and practice of the ethnoreligious group and faith, originated centuries after Abraham, which emanated from Judah.

ABRAHAM AND CHRISTIANITY

Was Abraham a Christian and his religion Christianity?

To address these questions, an explicative of the words 'Christian' and 'Christianity' becomes imperative. From an etymological perspective, Christian is a derivative of Christ. The word 'Christ' is derived from the Greek word *Khristos – Christus* in Latin – meaning "the anointed"; which is a translation of the Hebrew term *Mashiah* (Messiah in English). A Christian is considered to be any person who adheres to Christianity. Based on historical evidence, the first usage of the term 'Christian' was in the Bible. The term 'Christian' was used pejoratively during the story of Barnabas and Paul at Antioch, in Acts of the Apostles in the Bible:

> *and when he found him, he brought him to Antioch. So for a whole year Barnabas and Saul met with the church and taught great numbers of people. The disciples were called Christians first at Antioch.* –Acts 11:26

It is important to emphasize that Paul, who was a bounty hunter named Saul of Tarsus, was a Hellenistic-Jew who emerged many decades after the primary mission of Jesus on earth, and literally claimed to have 'seen the light', even though, his supposed epiphany – based on Biblical evidence – are contradictory. Acts 9:7 (The men who were traveling with him stood speechless because they heard the voice but saw no one) versus Acts 22:9 (Now those who were with me saw the light but did not hear the voice of the one who was speaking to me.)

Essentially, according to all documented historical evidences and accounts, especially the Bible, Jesus never heard of the phrase 'Christian' or its derivative; which is where the name for the religion 'Christianity' is derived. More importantly, Jesus spoke Aramaic and was only aware of the Aramaic word *Mashiach* – *Mashiah*, which is *Meshiha* in Hebrew and Messiah in English. *Mashiach* is probably the word Jesus, and his contemporaries would have been more conversant with; the Septuagint renditions, Greek translations, and consequent definitions emerged much later. In view of this, Jesus could never have sanctioned words of Greek origin (*Khristos*) to be the foundations of any religion (Christianity). According to the Bible, Jesus was never referred to as a Christian, nor did he ever sanction the establishment of a religion named Christianity. Christianity is actually attributed to the works of Paul – hence the religion is sometimes referred to as Pauline Christianity. Basically, the term 'Christian' cannot be applied to people who existed before the emergence of Jesus, and even to Jesus. If Jesus, who emerged many centuries after Abraham cannot be referred to as a Christian, then, it is impossible for Abraham to be referred to as a Christian, neither can his religion be Christianity.

In the light of these revelations, it has been established that Abraham was neither Jew nor Christian, nor did he practice Judaism or Christianity. So, the poser remains – what was the religion of Abraham? From an Islamic position, the Quran categorically states that Abraham was neither Jew nor Christian. Furthermore, it establishes Abraham was given a scripture and emphatically associates Abraham with the religion of monotheism – *"Hanifan Musliman"* (true Muslim), and he is especially honoured as the "friend" of Allah.

> *Ibrahim (Abraham) was neither a Jew nor a Christian, but he was a true*
> *Muslim Hanifa (Islamic Monotheism - to worship none but Allah Alone) and*
> *he was not of Al-Mushrikun* – Quran 3:167

And who is better in religion than one who submits himself to Allah while being a doer of good and follows the religion of Abraham, inclining toward truth? And Allah took Abraham as an intimate friend.– Quran 4:125

Say, "Indeed, my Lord has guided me to a straight path - a correct religion - the way of Abraham, inclining toward truth. And he was not among those who associated others with Allah."–Quran 6:161

Then We revealed to you, [O Muhammad], to follow the religion of Abraham, inclining toward truth; and he was not of those who associate with Allah.– Quran 16:123

He has ordained for you of religion what He enjoined upon Noah and that which We have revealed to you, [O Muhammad], and what We enjoined upon Abraham and Moses and Jesus — to establish the religion and not be divided therein. Difficult for those who associate others with Allah is that to which you invite them. Allah chooses for Himself whom He wills and guides to Himself whoever turns back [to Him]. –Quran 42:13

And this is in the Books of the earliest (Revelation), -
The Books of Abraham and Moses – Quran 87:18-19

These foregoing Quran verses reveal Abraham had a religion and was bestowed with his divinely inspired book (revelation). The religion of Abraham is the same religion as all other prophets and messengers that traversed the earth at various points in history.

In the Quran, God The Creator – Allah, posed this burden of proof to mankind, especially to the Jews and Christians:

And they say, "Be Jews or Christians [so] you will be guided." Say, "Rather, [we follow] the religion of Abraham, inclining toward truth, and he was not of the polytheists."

Say, [O believers], "We have believed in Allah and what has been revealed to us and what has been revealed to Abraham and Ishmael and Isaac and Jacob and the Descendants [al-Asbāt]and what was given to Moses and Jesus and what was given to the prophets from their Lord. We make no distinction between any of them, and we are Muslims [in submission] to Him."

So if they believe in the same as you believe in, then they have been [rightly] guided; but if they turn away, they are only in dissension, and Allah will be sufficient for you against them. And He is the Hearing, the Knowing.

[And say, "Ours is] the religion of Allah. And who is better than Allah in [ordaining] religion? And we are worshippers of Him."

Say, [O Muhammad], "Do you argue with us about Allah while He is our Lord and your Lord? For us are our deeds, and for you are your deeds. And we are sincere [in deed and intention] to Him."

Or do you say that Abraham and Ishmael and Isaac and Jacob and the Descendants were Jews or Christians? Say, "Are you more knowing or is Allah?"And who is more unjust than one who conceals a testimony he has from Allah? And Allah is not unaware of what you do.

−Quran 2:135-140

These set of verses highlight the sayings of Jews and Christians regarding guidance and salvation, via their religion solely, without taking into cognizance the actual religion of the common patriarch they both share in Abraham. The Quran invites the People of the Book (Jews and Christians) to dialogue and discuss these issues with incontrovertible facts and hard evidence; and come to "common terms" with Islam and Muslims.

Say: "O People of the Book! come to common terms as between us and you: That we worship none but Allah; that we associate no partners with him; that we erect not, from among ourselves, Lords and patrons other than Allah." If then they turn back, say ye: "Bear witness that we (at least) are Muslims (bowing to Allah's Will).

Ye People of the Book! Why dispute ye about Abraham, when the Law and the Gospel Were not revealed Till after him? Have ye no understanding? Ah! Ye are those who fell to disputing (Even) in matters of which ye had some knowledge! but why dispute ye in matters of which ye have no knowledge? It is Allah Who knows, and ye who know not!

Abraham was not a Jew nor yet a Christian; but he was true in Faith, and bowed his will to Allah's (Which is Islam), and he joined not Gods with Allah (not of the polytheists).

Without doubt, among men, the nearest of kin to Abraham, are those who follow him, as are also this Prophet and those who believe: And Allah is the Protector of those who have faith.

It is the wish of a section of the People of the Book to lead you astray. But they shall lead astray (Not you), but themselves, and they do not perceive!

Ye People of the Book! Why reject ye the Signs of Allah, of which ye are (Yourselves) witnesses?

Ye People of the Book! Why do ye clothe Truth with falsehood, and conceal the Truth, while ye have knowledge?" –Quran 3: 64-71

Based on the above verses, Abraham could not have been a Jew, nor did he practice Judaism, neither could he have been a Christian nor did he practice Christianity, because the Law of Moses and Gospel of Jesus were revealed much after the era Abraham sojourned on earth.

In conclusion, Abraham was neither Jew nor Christian, but followed the monotheistic religion of all previous prophets – Islam: The Submission.

When his Lord said to him, "Submit," he said, "I have submitted [in Islam] to the Lord of the worlds."

And Abraham instructed his sons [to do the same] and [so did] Jacob, [saying], "O my sons, indeed Allah has chosen for you this religion, so do not die except while you are Muslims."

Or were you witnesses when death approached Jacob, when he said to his sons, "What will you worship after me?" They said, "We will worship your God and the God of your fathers, Abraham and Ishmael and Isaac - one God. And we are Muslims [in submission] to Him." – Quran 2:131-133

CHAPTER 16

THE SUBMISSION: ISLAM

Islam essentially means The Submission to The Creator. Specifically, Islam is stating that Allah is the sole incomparable Supreme Being and Creator and is the only one worthy of praise and worship. From a linguistic perspective, Islam is a verbal noun and a derivative of the triconsonantal root S-L-M (Salam), and its meaning is associated with peace, safety, security, submission, surrender. Hence, the reason Islam is often translated as peace. Peace can be defined as tranquillity and serenity. Peace can also be divided into personal peace and societal peace. Personal peace relates to the individualistic, whilst societal peace, or in some regards, communal peace, relates to the collective. Islam is a systemic panacea to issues that affect individuals and society. Also, Islam is a system that deals with people's daily tasks and struggles, and proffers solutions for socio-economic and socio-political matters. Principally, Islam is being at peace with your Creator and with co-creations – essentially all living and non-living things, and the environment in which all created things and their creative manifestations exist. In order to attain peace, one must humbly submit to The Creator. Basically, once a creation goes through the process of submission, peace is attained. However, the only way anyone can submit is through humility: by accepting you are a mere creation, incapable of creating life and created by the only one capable of creation, who was not created: The Creator. The basics of Islam are straightforward and devoid of complexities. The fundamentals of Islam involve the articles of faith, which is belief in God, Angels, Revelations, Prophets, Resurrection and Predestination, and the Five Pillars: *Shahadah* (Testimony), *Salat* (Prayer), *Sawm* (Fasting), *Zakat* (Charity) and *Hajj* (Pilgrimage). There are some Hadith that highlight Islam's simplicity and moderation.

Narrated Abu Abdullah Jabir bin Abdullah al-Ansaree: A man questioned the Messenger of Allah ﷺ *and said, "Do you think that if I perform the obligatory prayers, fast in Ramadan, treat as lawful that which is halal, and treat as forbidden that which is haram, and do not increase upon that [in voluntary good deeds], then I shall enter Paradise?" He* ﷺ *replied, "Yes."*
– 40 Hadith Nawawi 22

Narrated Aisha: The Prophet ﷺ *used to say, Observe moderation (in doing deeds), and if you fail to observe it perfectly, try to do as much as you can do (to live up to this ideal of moderation) and be happy for none would be able to get into Paradise because of his deeds alone. They (the Companions of the Holy Prophet) said: Allah's Messenger, not even you? Thereupon he said: Not even I, but that Allah wraps me in His Mercy, and bear this in mind that the deed loved most by Allah is one which is done constantly even though it is small.*
– Sahih Muslim 2818 a, Book 52, Hadith 75

Narrated Abu Huraira: The Prophet ﷺ *said, "Religion is very easy and whoever overburdens himself in his religion will not be able to continue in that way. So you should not be extremists, but try to be near to perfection and receive the good tidings that you will be rewarded; and gain strength by worshipping in the mornings, the afternoons, and during the last hours of the nights."*– Sahih al-Bukhari 39, Book 2, Hadith 32

It is germane to point out that intentions play a vital part in actions and the consequential determination of reward or recompense. There is a well-known Hadith about intentions:

Narrated 'Umar bin Al-Khattab: I heard Allah's Messenger ﷺ *saying, "The reward of deeds depends upon the intentions and every person will get the reward according to what he has intended. So whoever emigrated for worldly benefits or for a woman to marry, his emigration was for what he emigrated for."*
– Sahih al-Bukhari 1, Book 1, Hadith 1

Ultimately, it is the Mercy of Allah that will determine salvation. The Mercy of Allah is vast, and any sin will be generally forgiven, except dying in the state of *Shirk* – the association of partners with Allah. Nonetheless, though Allah is the most merciful, He is also The Just. Allah being The Just means He is the ultimate giver of justice and everyone will get justice.

Indeed, Allah does not do injustice to mankind in anything, but mankind do injustice to themselves.– Quran 10:44

(Remember) the Day when every person will come up pleading for himself, and every one will be paid in full for what he did (good or evil, belief or disbelief in the life of this world) and they will not be dealt with unjustly. – Quran 16:111

On the day of reckoning everyone will be given the opportunity to plead their case and all indisputable evidence of their actions on earth will be presented. In a situation where a sin is committed, Allah can forgive that sin because He is The Merciful – the most merciful; however, if the sin involves wrongdoing against another being or creation, then the wronged party will deservedly get justice from Allah. As Allah is the Creator, He is aware that His creation will definitely sin. Hence, what Islam recommends is constantly seeking forgiveness from Allah for committed sins. In a related Hadith, mankind is expected to sin and seek forgiveness:

Narrated Abu Huraira: Allah's Messenger 🕋 *said: By Him in Whose Hand is my life, if you were not to commit sin, Allah would sweep you out of existence and He would replace (you by) those people who would commit sin and seek forgiveness from Allah, and He would have pardoned them.*
– Sahih Muslim 2749, Book 50, Hadith 13

Islam has a wide spectrum of sins from major to minor. Though there is long list of sins, some of the identified major sins include, associating others with Allah (Shirk), disobeying one's parents, killing a soul (murder), speaking falsely (bearing false witness), devouring the orphan's wealth, usury, gambling, magic, adultery (fornication), intoxicants (alcohol), etc.

The Quran mentions the path to salvation is the avoidance of the major sins, though ultimately, it is the forgiveness of Allah that supersedes everything.

If you avoid the major sins which you are forbidden, We will remove from you your lesser sins and admit you to a noble entrance [into Paradise].
– Quran 4:31

And to Allah belongs whatever is in the heavens and whatever is in the earth - that He may recompense those who do evil with [the penalty of] what they have done and recompense those who do good with the best [reward]
Those who avoid the major sins and immoralities, only [committing] slight ones. Indeed, your Lord is vast in forgiveness. He was most knowing of you when He produced you from the earth and when you were fetuses in the wombs of your mothers. So do not claim yourselves to be pure; He is most knowing of who fears Him. – Quran 53:31-32

PRIMAL RELIGION

Essentially, the lack of religious uniformity manifests as religious confusion. I posit that God The Creator is not a God that would establish confusion; rather, it is the creation (mankind), that is responsible for religious multiplicity, its unpredictable consequences and emanating imbroglios that have long plagued mankind. I reckon that if a religion is not universal and all-accommodating, then it cannot be from God. No religion should exclude or be exclusive. From an historical viewpoint, there must have been one primary accepted religion which God The Creator ordained for His creation, while the other religions were man-made for selfish and parochial objectives.

Islam is not necessarily a new religion. Preceding paths of righteousness had been revealed in parts at various points in history, and its complete embodiment manifested in its current form, as the perfected religion of Islam. For instance, previous generations were instructed to observe some rites that are practiced by contemporary Muslims, and there were those who abided and those who abandoned their duties. The Quran mentions such instances:

> *And We made them leaders, guiding (mankind) by Our Command, and We inspired in them the doing of good deeds, performing Salat (Iqamat-as-Salat), and the giving of Zakat and of Us (Alone) they were worshippers.* – Quran 21:73

> *Then, there has succeeded them a posterity who have given up As-Salat (the prayers) [i.e. made their Salat (prayers) to be lost, either by not offering them or by not offering them perfectly or by not offering them in their proper fixed times, etc.] and have followed lusts. So they will be thrown in Hell.* – Quran 19:59

The ability of Islam to transition through time cannot be replicated by any other religion. Islam is a systemic culmination of belief, whereby the oneness of God is manifested in the perfection of religion – The Submission.

Islam came in phases and is the culmination of a religious continuum that has existed to challenge all forms of idolatry or ungodly religious activities over time. Possibly, if monotheism happens to be part of the teachings by any revered figure, or religion, including autochthonous beliefs, then it may possibly be an adulterated or corrupted version of the original monotheistic message. Comparatively, a cardinal difference between Islam and Christianity is the belief in the revered figure as a deity, or part of a triplicate deity or deities. Also, the Christianity position raises questions about the fate of those who existed before the advent of Jesus. The seeming lack of consecution is an approach that problematizes religion, particularly from a historical viewpoint. Hypothetically, all monotheistic beliefs should lead to the one and only God The Creator. Islam is as old as time, and the meaning has never changed, particularly from a practical implementation of submission position. There is no ambiguity of definition or clarity required for the meaning of submission. Islam has always been and would always be Islam.

> *Mankind were but one community (i.e. on one religion - Islamic Monotheism), then they differed (later), and had not it been for a Word that went forth before from your Lord, it would have been settled between them regarding what they differed.*– Quran 10:19

Unequivocal Declaration

A distinctive and rather intriguing aspect about Islam is that it is the only religion in the world that makes an unequivocal statement about the divinity of religion. There is no other religion in the world that can make such an audacious claim of divinity, and back it up scripturally – explicit documentation in scripture. Citing Christianity as a comparative example, there is no unanimity within Christendom about the Bible being the word of God.

The Bible is based on divergent assumptions about the Gospel of Jesus, but certainly not the actual Gospel. Historic disparities and disaccords on the Gospel led to series of synods and councils. For example, the name 'Jesus' is not contained in the original 1611 King James Version.

Furthermore, another crucial point that cannot be overemphasized is that the word 'Christianity' is not mentioned anywhere in any version of Bible. Based on this premise, if the word 'Christianity' is not contained in the Bible – Christianity's Holy Scripture – then the actual concern should be investigating, on whose authority the religion of Christianity was officially institutionalized.

> *And they worship besides Allah that for which He has not sent down authority and that of which they have no knowledge. And there will not be for the wrongdoers any helper.*– Quran 22:71

Islam is not affected by the authorization and institutionalization incongruity. The Quran contains verses attesting to the approval of a religion named Islam:

> *There is no compulsion in religion. Verily, the Right Path has become distinct from the wrong path. Whoever disbelieves in Taghut and believes in Allah, then he has grasped the most trustworthy handhold that will never break. And Allah is All-Hearer, All-Knower.* – Quran 2:256

> *Truly, the religion with Allah is Islam. Those who were given the Scripture (Jews and Christians) did not differ except, out of mutual jealousy, after knowledge had come to them. And whoever disbelieves in the Ayat (proofs, evidences, verses, signs, revelations, etc.) of Allah, then surely, Allah is Swift in calling to account.* – Quran 3:19

Do they seek other than the religion of Allah (the true Islamic Monotheism worshipping none but Allah Alone), while to Him submitted all creatures in the heavens and the earth, willingly or unwillingly. And to Him shall they all be returned. – Quran 3:83

So whoever Allah wants to guide - He expands his breast to [contain] Islām; and whoever He wants to send astray - He makes his breast tight and constricted as though he were climbing into the sky. Thus does Allah place defilement upon those who do not believe. – Quran 6:125

He it is Who has sent His Messenger (Muhammad SAW) with guidance and the religion of truth (Islam), that He may make it (Islam) superior over all religions. And All-Sufficient is Allah as a Witness. – Quran 48:28

In summary, there are various world religions and The Creator sent reminders through messengers at various points in history, about the authentic religion. It is noteworthy to highlight the general assumption by non-Muslims and some 'Muslims', that Islam (The Submission) is a brand-new religion founded by Prophet Muhammad ﷺ; which is a common misconception. Islam – The Submission to The Creator of all creation – did not start with Prophet Muhammad ﷺ. Essentially, the message of submission is not limited to Arabs or the region that came to be known as the 'Middle East' – post Western colonial incursion. Prophet Muhammad ﷺ only came to complete the mission – as the pinnacle – of an established religious system that was initiated by his predecessors: Proclamation of The oneness of God.

Historically, there was never a prophet or messenger sent by God that did not proclaim "One God": Deuteronomy 6:4 and Mark 12:29 are just a couple of Biblical examples.

Islamic exegesis explicates that Submission to The Creator is mankind's default setting – the immanent proclivity. The natural inclination of humankind is called the *Fitrah*, and it remains that way until it is corrupted by various external influences, that may end up having temporary or permanent effects on any individual. The Quran explains religion and Fitrah.

> *So direct your face [i.e., self] toward the religion, inclining to truth. [Adhere to] the fiṭrah of Allah upon which He has created [all] people. No change should there be in the creation of Allah. That is the correct religion, but most of the people do not know.* – Quran 30:30

Such expositions establish that all religions were man-made and only one in particular can be classified as God-made. The Quran is explicit about Islam being the only divinely accepted religion.

> *And whoever desires other than Islam as religion – never will it be accepted from him, and he, in the Hereafter, will be among the losers.* –Quran 3:85

The word used for religion in the foregoing verse is *Deen*. The meaning of Deen includes religion but is actually meant to be the complete guide to life. Islam can be appreciated as the Primal Deen – the primal mode of instructions that has been communicated between Creator and creation from inception. In other words, Islam is the Primal Religion – Islam in its pristine form, not the Arabized, Asianized, Africanized, Americanized, Europeanized, or any other form, but just Islam: The Submission. Islam can be traced to the earliest periods of mankind's existence. Right from the point Adam existed – his initial blissful life, after being created, to the point that he transgressed and was sent to earth. The primal religious instruction was for Adam and Eve to avoid eating from a certain tree in The Garden.

This incident is mentioned in Quran 7:20-23. After their transgression, they repented. Effectively, Islam was initiated from the period of Adam and Eve's repentance onwards and was succeeded by instructions which manifested in various forms, for different eras, and ultimately culminated in the revelation of the Quran. Furthermore, apart from Islam being repeatedly mentioned throughout the Quran, a categorical statement is made regarding the divine approval of Islam as a religion. Islam has been perfected through a divine process and represents a completed favour from The Creator.

> *This day, I have perfected your religion for you, completed My Favour upon you, and have chosen for you Islam as your religion.*– Quran 5:3

According to a Hadith, a Jew remarked about its significance and what it would mean to them, had they been the recipients of such a momentous declaration.

> *Narrated Umar bin Al-Khattab: Once a Jew said to me, "O the chief of believers! There is a verse in your Holy Book Which is read by all of you (Muslims), and had it been revealed to us, we would have taken that day (on which it was revealed as a day of celebration." 'Umar bin Al-Khattab asked, "Which is that verse?" The Jew replied, "This day I have perfected your religion For you, completed My favor upon you, And have chosen for you Islam as your religion."(5:3) 'Umar replied, "No doubt, we know when and where this verse was revealed to the Prophet. It was Friday and the Prophet ﷺ was standing at 'Arafat (i.e. the Day of Hajj)"*
> – Sahih al-Bukhari 45, Book 2, Hadith 38

Islam can be appreciated as a favour bestowed upon mankind – especially those who have chosen the path of submission unto their Creator.

The same favour was bestowed on the contemporary Submitters (Muslims). A critical analysis of the definition reveals the universality of the submission concept. Islam simply means "The Submission" and those who 'submit' to God The Creator or the 'Submitters' are Muslims.

THE SUBMISSION PROCESS: ACCEPTANCE OF ISLAM

There are various reasons people submit to The Creator – accept Islam, and the reasons may be exceptional to every individual. However, a fundamental aspect that is vital to accepting Islam is through the mercy of The Creator. I am of the humble opinion, that there must have been an initial level of sincere soul-searching and dedicated guidance-seeking, to eventually attain a unique level of identifying The Creator, and wanting to be at peace with Him and His creation, through submission. Those that eventually decide to submit can be referred to as submitters, i.e., Muslims, meaning they have decided to follow the age-long practice of The Submission. The acceptance of Islam can be broken into three stages, though the act of faith is instant, and the levels of spirituality can be in phases, acceptance has some prerequisites. Though it is possible, a person cannot just declare one day, "I am a Muslim". Ideally, if there are any knowledgeable Muslims around, they should quiz such a person about why and how such a decision was attained, and not just say: '*Allah-u-Akbar*' or '*Alhamdulillah*' – praise the lord. The reason for questioning is to determine if the mental faculties of the declarer are intact and to assess their understanding of the implications of the declaration.

The acceptance of Islam can be categorised into three stages:

(1) The Conviction (2) Formal Declaration (3) Practical Implementation

People often misunderstand or misconstrue the most important aspect of the acceptance of Islam (becoming a Muslim) - The Conviction.

Conviction of the heart is the first stage and most important prerequisite. Every other aspect follows this vital stage – which can be termed 'The Foundation'. Predictably, a house built on a shaky or questionable foundation will either crash or disintegrate gradually. As is often the case in some scenarios, it is quite possible to carry on with the other stages of acceptance of Islam: i.e., stage (2) Formal Declaration – with the mouth, and stage (3) Practical Implementation – with the body, without stage (1) The Conviction - of the heart. In the physical sense, such a person will be perceived as a Muslim, but in the spiritual sense, the heart would contain a vacuum because of the absence of the vital stage, the foundation: stage (1) The Conviction. In such a situation, a spiritual chasm exists in the hearts of those who bypass the conviction of the heart. In most cases, such people cannot last as *'Muslims'*, because such internal doubts are unsustainable – one can only pretend and live in such a dilemma for so long. This serves as evidence that there is no leeway for fence-sitting in Islam; it is either you believe, or you do not, it is either you are convinced, or you are not. Basically, there are no half measures. So, the issue of doubt must have been dealt with from inception i.e., Stage (1) The Conviction. The easiest aspect the 'evil whisperer' can capitalize on is doubt, which is related to stage (1) The Conviction –the foundation. Conviction is crucial because it eliminates doubt. There is a no room for doubt after conviction. The process of doubt ought to culminate in conviction. A state of perpetual doubt is self-detrimental. Once the seed of doubt is sown and the matter is not addressed, the manifestation in disbelief is guaranteed.

As I often quip, is it possible to 'un-convince' oneself? Therefore, I am certain those who claim to be 'ex-Muslim', were not convinced initially; as they did not fulfil the most important perquisite stage (1) – The Conviction of the heart – hence, the basis of their dilemma. So, it is not uncommon for those who affiliate with the 'ex-Muslim' insignia to take extreme positions.

In some cases, the actions of those in the 'ex-Muslim' category appear to be underpinned by melancholia bordering on psychosis. The decision to be 'ex-Muslim' is one thing, and another thing entirely to attack those who decide to be Muslim. It is simply a form of extremism to force a personal position on others. I will explicate this point with an analogy of a university dropout.

The Dropout Analogy

Imagine a set of students enrol at a university to study medicine, and a male student decides to drop out of university; because he is not convinced about medicine and cannot visualize himself as a medical practitioner. Based on this scenario, the dropout is free to study anything else or nothing at all. But rather than live with the consequences of his unilateral decision, the dropout takes it upon himself to attack medicine and discourage and deride those who decide to be medical students and practitioners. That is the similitude of those who cannot live peacefully with their decision of abandoning Islam but have taken it as their sole mission in life to attack Islam, Muslims and in some cases, religion and God – as if such extreme positions would make any difference.

Following the dropout analogy, certain realities must be taken into cognizance. For instance, being born into a Muslim family or exposure to a purportedly Islamic-oriented culture is not enough to be a Muslim – conviction is fundamental. There are numerous examples of people who claimed religiosity but abandoned their religiosity or faith when they migrated from less developed environments to more advanced societies. The reason for this desertion is because their religiosity was based on certain societal constraints or prevailing socioeconomic factors. There are many instances of familial or cultural-oriented exposures to Islam that have been counterproductive.

In some families and societies, those who claim to be adherents of Islam actually know absolutely nothing about Islam. They just follow ritualistic instructions because of their parents, or because that is the prevailing norm or what their society demands. In sooth, no genuine effort is made to understand Islam or why they are practising Islam. In certain instances, such people tend to take Islam for granted, unlike those who struggled to seek out the truth before accepting Islam. In practical terms, anyone claiming to be Muslim must have total conviction from the bottom of the heart – the soul! Hence, I am of the opinion, the 'ex-Muslim' designate is a misnomer. Thus, the reason I often refer to people who claim to be 'ex-Muslim' as former affiliates of Islam or 'ex-affiliates' as they were never actual submitters – Muslims. A deeper analysis of the situation and introspection will reveal those who make such specious claims of being 'ex-Muslim' were never really Muslim, but people whose hypocrisy or disbelief became manifest. Certainly, people can only pretend for so long – as the truth will always prevail.

In the discourse of The Submission (Islam) and the process of submitting, a fundamental caveat must be emphasized – conviction. In a real-life scenario, if someone informs me of their intention to become Muslim, my first question is "are you sure?", and then I will follow up with "are you certain?" or "are you convinced?" Following the initial line of questioning, I must explain to such a person that Islam invites you to a journey – it is a means to an end and not an end in itself. And being a Muslim does not in any way translate to instant prosperity, neither does it guarantee material success in this world. Also, becoming Muslim does not hinder or deter your individual aspirations in this world. However, human beings must take cognizance of the ultimate accountability of all actions to The Creator, whilst pursuing worldly affairs. What Islam assures is eternal success in the hereafter because we are really spiritual beings trapped in human form. Specifically, what accepting Islam guarantees is acceptance to be tested by The Creator.

Do people think that they will be left alone because they say: "We believe," and will not be tested.— Quran 29:2

Fundamentally, it is not enough to say, 'I believe', then expect not to be tested – life is a big test. If you claim to believe whilst everything is rosy and things are going your way, will you still believe when you are broke and hungry? Will you still believe when you lose your loved ones? Will you still believe when you suffer a major mishap? That is the condition for those who chose to be believers – submitters to The Submission.

Conviction is the compelling reason why Muslims will stay in Islam no matter the condition. Also, conviction – the absence thereof – is the reason why some people would leave Islam. Those who abandon Islam do not really see the point of such beliefs, especially if adhering to the belief does not guarantee prosperity and success here and now. However, what such people seem to forget or are oblivious of is that life is transient – just a transition to the next phase. More importantly, whatever is done whilst on earth has a corresponding effect on the next phase – the afterlife. Also, the absolute conviction in Islam, no matter the situation, is not necessarily the case with other faiths, particularly those that preach immediate prosperity.

In this regard, there are those whose faith is dependent on good times – the fair-weather followers. When things are merry, they claim to believe, but when they are confronted with any trial, they abscond from the supposed belief. It is a common trait for such people to lament that, they prayed five times a day, fasted Ramadan and did this or did that, but their prayers were not answered, and because of that they left Islam. In many instances, people who lose faith – which they never really had – declare war upon religion and in extreme cases, challenge the existence of God. However, because God did not answer a prayer does not prove God's non-existence. God does not need anyone or anything. Anyone who submits does so for their own benefit.

The self-entitlement mentality leads to spiritual inimicality. The ideal position of any suppliant ought to be a humble anticipation to determine whether the supplication and other individual aspirations or plans, align with the master plan of God. Technically, God The Creator does not owe His creation anything other than sustenance and guidance. There is a universal order – a divine system, and out of God's wisdom, He grants what He wills to whom He wills, when He wills. Nobody can alter that divine system except the creator of the system. In view of this reality, when people abandon Islam for some flimsy reason – like a prayer not being answered – no matter how desperate or needy, they do a disservice to themselves and are at a greater loss. Apart from mortgaging their hereafter, their action does not guarantee they will achieve whatever they seek in this world. Evidently, one thing their abscondment from Islam establishes is that their supposed belief was conditional and not genuine.

> *And there are some who worship Allah on the verge ʿof faithʾ: if they are blessed with something good, they are content with it; but if they are afflicted with a trial, they relapse ʿinto disbeliefʾ, losing this world and the Hereafter. That is ʿtrulyʾ the clearest loss.* – Quran 22:11

There is no conditionality attached to submission; it is either conviction or non-conviction. Analysing from a linguistic perspective, there is no such thing as "un-conviction", particularly after a process of conviction. Using the English language as an example, there are two contrastive positions on conviction – being convinced or remaining unconvinced. The only instance where conviction has an opposing position is in the legal context – in matters of jurisprudence, i.e., conviction and acquittal. Accordingly, the process of conviction can be appreciated as a one-way progression – you are either convinced or not convinced. This explication is crucial in understanding the process of conviction. Genuine Muslims are meant to submit with conviction unconditionally, whether rich or poor, happy or sad, healthy or sick – the worship of The Creator is paramount. Ultimately, only God The Creator knows those who genuinely submit to Him. Importantly, a submitter is not necessarily obliged to reveal their submission to anyone, because in certain situations, some matters are strictly between the creation and The Creator.

Verily Allah knows (all) the hidden things of the heavens and the earth: verily He has full knowledge of all that is in (men's) hearts. – Quran 35:38

CHAPTER 17

THE SUBMITTERS: MUSLIMS

Muslim is a general term for those who identify with Islam. There are other terms for Muslims who have developed spiritually and are striving toward *Ihsan* – pursuit of excellence. Some other identifiers include *Muhsin – Al-Muhsineen* (the good-doers), *Muttaqi – Al-Muttaqeen* (the God-conscious), *Muqarrab – Al-Muqarrabeen* (those to be nearest [to Allah], *Mutawakkil – Al-Mutawakkileen* (the God-trusting), *Muqsit – Al-Muqsiteen* (acting equitably), *Mutatahir – Al-Mutatahireen* (the self-purifying) and the *Mumin – Al-Muminun* (the believers). Based on these classifications, there are people who may tick all the boxes, tick some of the boxes or tick one of the boxes. For instance, the Quran makes a distinction between the Muslim and Mumin, when discussing the commitment of Desert Arabs (Bedouins) to Islam.

> *The bedouins say: "We believe." Say: "You believe not but you only say, 'We have surrendered (in Islam),' for Faith has not yet entered your hearts. But if you obey Allah and His Messenger (SAW), He will not decrease anything in reward for your deeds. Verily, Allah is Oft-Forgiving, Most Merciful."* – Quran 49:14

These categorizations are necessary because there are those who profess to be Muslim but are far from righteousness. Such people could be outwardly identified as Muslim but are *Munafiq – Al-Munafiqun* (the hypocrites). Clearly, these categorizations help in understanding Allah and His relationship with His creation. Furthermore, the aforementioned categories (Muhsin, Muttaqi, etc.), include those Allah loves. In fact, the Quran states that following the Prophet Muhammad ﷺ is a guaranteed way of attaining the love of Allah:

Say (O Muhammad SAW to mankind): "If you (really) love Allah then follow me (i.e. accept Islamic Monotheism, follow the Quran and the Sunnah), Allah will love you and forgive you of your sins. And Allah is Oft-Forgiving, Most Merciful."– Quran 3:31

In contrast, there are those Allah does not love as well, which are based on the positions and actions taken by those in these categories. A few examples of those Allah does not love mentioned in the Quran include *Al-Mufsideen* (the corrupters), *Al-Murtadeen* (the transgressors), *Al-Zalimeen* (the wrong-doers) and the *Al-Mustaqbireen* (the arrogant).

A general lack of understanding of these categorizations and levels of piety sometimes confuses people, especially those who are critical of Islam and Muslims. I often argue that because someone claims to be a Muslim or associates with Islam does not mean such a person immediately become the epitome of righteousness. Islam affirms some Muslims are hell-bound. Basically, a person identifying as a Muslim is simply not enough for salvation. As a similitude, if someone is admitted into university and does not strive academically, such a person will fail resoundingly. A student matriculating does not automatically mean graduating, because matriculation and graduation are separate endeavours. University admission is not the same as university graduation – between the two ceremonies is a process that requires effort. Based on this premise, if someone becomes a Muslim, it does not mean they immediately become angelic. The real work starts after the decision of commitment to Islam, and such people must strive for the rest of their lives to attain a higher spiritual level worthy of admittance in the fold of the righteous. Islam invites you to a journey – it is a means to an end and not an end in itself. Islam is a spiritual process and not a destination.

The 'Muslim' label is primarily for identification purposes. For instance, a person can be a Muslim but not a Muhsin – doer of good. Those who claim to be Muslims, do so for various reasons. Some may have associated with Islam for individual or societal reasons. For some people it may be because of love and for others it may have been the lure of money. For some people, it is because of the family they have been born. There are those who claim to be Muslim because of societal influence – the society they happen to be residing, may be utilising Islam for socio-cultural or socio-political purposes. Hence, the reason it is quite easy for some people to disassociate with Islam after their reason for associating with Islam is removed from the equation. For those who claimed to be Muslim for love, once the relationship is dead, they are gone from Islam. And those who claimed to be Muslim for material reasons, like money, once that benefit is no longer forthcoming, they abscond from Islam. As for those who claimed to be Muslim because of the family they were born into, once they gain some independence from the family or their patriarch or matriarch is deceased, their Islam is gone with the wind. As for those who claim to be Muslim because of the society they happen to reside, once they leave that society, they leave Islam completely.

In essence, there is stark difference between claiming to believe and actually believing. One can claim belief and exhibit actions contrary to belief. This situation is one of the reasons why the scrutinization of those who claim to be Muslims is sometimes necessary. In sooth, the Creator is the ultimate Judge and only He knows what is in the hearts of his entire creation.

SUBMITTERS ENSEMBLE

From an historical perspective, submitters have existed from time, right from the very first created human being (Adam). In fact, all of creation are conscious of their Creator and submit – glorify The Creator in their own way.

The Quran mentions various instances of glorification:

Whatsoever is in the heavens and whatsoever is on the earth glorifies Allah. His is the dominion, and to Him belong all the praises and thanks, and He is Able to do all things. – Quran 64:1

See you not (O Muhammad SAW) that Allah, He it is Whom glorify whosoever is in the heavens and the earth, and the birds with wings out-spread (in their flight). Of each one He (Allah) knows indeed his Salat (prayer) and his glorification, [or everyone knows his Salat (prayer) and his glorification], and Allah is All-Aware of what they do.
And to Allah belongs the sovereignty of the heavens and the earth, and to Allah is the return (of all). – Quran 24:41-42

The seven heavens and the earth and all that is therein, glorify Him and there is not a thing but glorifies His Praise. But you understand not their glorification. Truly, He is Ever Forbearing, Oft-Forgiving. – Quran 17:44

In essence, everything glorifies The Creator, even though the creation may not be able to understand the details of this unique glorification process. Also, some verses in the Quran highlight that all of creation are in submission:

Have they not considered how the shadows of everything Allah has created incline to the right and the left ˹as the sun moves˺, totally submitting to Allah in all humility?
And to Allah ˹alone˺ bows down ˹in submission˺ whatever is in the heavens and whatever is on the earth of living creatures, as do the angels—who are not too proud ˹to do so˺. – Quran 16:48-49

Do you not see that to Allah bow down ˹in submission˺ all those in the heavens and all those on the earth, as well as the sun, the moon, the stars, the mountains, the trees, and ˹all˺ living beings, as well as many humans, while many are deserving of punishment. And whoever Allah disgraces, none can honour. Surely Allah does what He wills. – Quran 22:18

In a related Hadith:

Narrated Amr ibn Abasah: The Messenger of Allah, ﷺ, *said, "The sun does not rise over any creation of Allah but that it glorifies Allah, except for devils and fools among the children of Adam."*–Musnad al-Shamiyyin 942

The irony of this phenomenon is that those who are ungrateful may actually be in submission to the Creator and be unaware. This situation can be appreciated as mankind being a creation. Every living thing was created and is confined to another creation and can only exist based on nature's laws – Creator's permissions. As a creation, all human body parts and organs were created, and probably have their own way of communicating with the Creator, or are at least, accessible to the Creator. A typical example is when doctors diagnose someone with an ailment like cancer and have determined how long the person has to live, but the patient defies medical projections and survives. Also, a person who supposedly looks healthy could just die and medical professionals may not have a logical explanation for the cause of death. There are other scenarios underpinning mankind's subjection to a much superior force. For instance, human beings cannot live forever. Also, a man cannot decide to commit suicide and plan a resurrection – it is a one-way trip.

In a similar vein, someone cannot go the top of a skyscraper to jump down, and confidently expect to fly naturally, like a bird.

Accordingly, even if the possessor of a body is not humble or sensible enough to submit, submission is occurring through some elements beyond human control and comprehension. So, whether mankind likes it or not, approves of it or not, acknowledges The Creator or not, mankind is still subjected to the pre-existing rules that govern creation and all its manifesting dynamics.

Based on these realities, submission is manifesting all around us. Even though human beings may not be able to decipher or comprehend how other creations are submitters and fulfilling their form of submission, their Creator who created all things is very much aware. Actually, as submitters, our primary concern should be fulfilling our own submission.

A further analysis of the submitter concept gives a broader understanding of the definition and its application. Since a Muslim is anyone who submits to God, the holistic definition can, for example, be extended to the revered figures associated with other monotheistic religions, especially the Abrahamic religions. As all prophets are Submitters from the same divine source, every prophet understood the continuation of their mission and the interconnectivity with other prophets. This process was meant to continue until the last prophet and the final message – which is a compendium that affirms matters of the past and explains the future. The believers of that divine message are the Submitters and are meant to emulate the prophets by continuing the spread of that message amongst the fellow-beings.

> Say, "Allah has told the truth. So follow the religion of Abraham, inclining toward truth; and he was not of the polytheists."–Quran 3:95

Evidently, all prophets and messengers of God, including Abraham, Moses and Jesus were Submitters who submitted to God The Creator.

By extension, all these previous prophets and messengers can be called Muslims by definition. From a definitional outlook, the historical followers of Islam (The Submission), i.e., Muslims (Submitters) existed during every era. So, all prophets and Messengers were submitters (Muslims), and those who submitted during their respective prophetic missions, were the submitters (Muslims) of that era. For example, those who lived during the time of Moses were the Jews (Submitters) who submitted to God via the divinely sanctioned mode of The Submission for that era. Similarly, those who lived during the time of Jesus and submitted to God via the divinely sanctioned medium – The Submission, were the Submitters of that era. Also, the Nazarenes who followed Jesus and submitted to God would have been rightly identified during Jesus' era, as the Submitters – Muslims in the contemporary parlance.

Notably, when analysed from a biblical point of view, Jesus was a submitter:

> *During the days of Jesus' life on earth, he offered up prayers and petitions with fervent cries and tears to the one who could save him from death, and he was heard because of his reverent submission* – Hebrew 5:7

Often, when people, especially Christians, hear the phrase that Jesus is Muslim; the response varies from anger, shock, bewilderment, rebuke and prayers – "get thee behind me Satan". Only the inquisitive will prod further and ask why? Why exactly is Jesus a Muslim? The answer lies in the definition of Muslim. For purposes of clarification, 'Muslim' does not mean a follower of Muhammad; rather, it means one who has submitted to Allah – The Creator of everything that exists. Also, 'Muslim' is not a derivative of Muhammad.

Generally, when you ask people for the definition of Muslim or meaning of Islam, they simply say: religion of Prophet Muhammad ﷺ and its adherents. Rather, Islam is a divinely ordained and officially institutionalized religion, and

Prophet Muhammad ﷺ is one of many previously sent prophets/messengers, who were all Submitters – Muslims.

> *Say, [O believers], "We have believed in Allah and what has been revealed to us and what has been revealed to Abraham and Ishmael and Isaac and Jacob and the Descendants [al-Asbat]and what was given to Moses and Jesus and what was given to the prophets from their Lord. We make no distinction between any of them, and we are Muslims [in submission] to Him."* –Quran 2:136

Ideally, Muslims are meant to be the epitome of righteousness for all believers that have existed prior to the coming of the final revelation: The Quran. Every generation in history that chose to be followers of Islam (The Submission) did not suddenly decide to label themselves Muslims (submitters). The Quran affirms the usage of "Muslim" is historical and has been an established identifier from previous eras and generations. The "Muslim"designation is not new and was previously used to identify believers associated with the monotheistic belief in God; those who adhered to the religion of Abraham – The Submission (Islam).

> *And strive for Allah with the striving due to Him. He has chosen you and has not placed upon you in the religion any difficulty. [It is] the religion of your father, Abraham. He [i.e., Allah] named you "Muslims" before [in former scriptures] and in this [revelation] that the Messenger may be a witness over you and you may be witnesses over the people. So establish prayer and give ẕakāh and hold fast to Allah. He is your protector; and excellent is the protector, and excellent is the helper.* – Quran 22:78

CHAPTER 18

THE MIDDLE NATION

Thus We have appointed you a middle nation, that ye may be witnesses against mankind, and that the messenger may be a witness against you. And We appointed the qiblah which ye formerly observed only that We might know him who followeth the messenger, from him who turneth on his heels. In truth it was a hard (test) save for those whom Allah guided. But it was not Allah's purpose that your faith should be in vain, for Allah is Full of Pity, Merciful toward mankind. – Quran 2:143

The Quran refers to the submitters – adherents of Islam – as the *Ummatan Wasatan,* which can mean, a middle nation, median community or justly balanced community. This means, there are not meant to be excesses in matters of religion and Islam advocates the middle path.

A juxtaposition of the concept of the middle path with other religions, particularly Abrahamic religions, Islam is actually a good median example. Some religious traditions go to the extremes of abstaining from the world and live hermitic lives, such as mendicants, or those involved in eremitism or monasticism. There are downsides to practising a lifestyle of extreme asceticism because it is often counterproductive.

A typical example is catholic monasticism. Some priests or bishops of the Catholic Church, who in their supposed religiosity go to the extremes of practising celibacy, not only deny themselves the right to legal marriage, but also deny reality, and are undermining their own human physiology. Sadly, concupiscence envelopes some of those in monkhood and they end up committing sexual pervasions like paedophilia, which has graver consequences on themselves, their victims and their families, and the wider society. The Quran mentions monasticism as an innovation that was not divinely ordained.

> *Then in the footsteps of these ⸢prophets⸣, We sent Our messengers, and ⸢after them⸣ We sent Jesus, son of Mary, and granted him the Gospel, and instilled compassion and mercy into the hearts of his followers. As for monasticism, they made it up—We never ordained it for them—only seeking to please Allah, yet they did not ⸢even⸣ observe it strictly. So We rewarded those of them who were faithful. But most of them are rebellious.* – Quran 57:27

Another extreme, are those who are primarily world-oriented and live for the here and now – those who believe, you only live once: YOLO. Those who proclaim that if it feels good go ahead and do it! Based on such depravity, if it feels good to be a paedophile, then go ahead, or if it feels good to rape, do it, or if it feels good to sleep with animals, go for it. Where exactly are the boundaries for such feelings if everyone decides to act on such whims? Also, what about the rights of the victims of such turpitude? Self-abasement through unbridled sensuality reduces humans to the level of animals. Hedonism is the primary goal and driving force for such people, even though in reality, there are limitations to overindulgence, at a certain level.

Immoderation drives those with such views, and sometimes, such ideologies hide under the cloak of religion to promote extreme wealth, and somehow associate worldly success with divine approval. These are the merchants of the prosperity gospel. Christendom has been invaded with such people and the church platform is being utilized without any compunction, as a cover for their business – pastorpreneurship.

Have you seen him who takes his own lust (vain desires) as his ilah (god), and Allah knowing (him as such), left him astray, and sealed his hearing and his heart, and put a cover on his sight. Who then will guide him after Allah? Will you not then remember?— Quran 45:23

Islam promotes a balance in worldly and heavenly pursuits. Basically, human beings must be cognizant of the hereafter, during the pursuit and acquisition of worldly possessions. There is a constant reminder that the ultimate goal is the final abode.

Our Lord! Give us in this world that which is good and in the Hereafter that which is good, and save us from the torment of the Fire!— Quran 2:201

Furthermore, whilst Islam thoroughly combines law and theology, Judaism is generally law-centric, and Christianity is more theology-oriented. Judaism primarily concentrates on law, and according to Jewish *halakha*— the collection of Jewish religious laws, there are meant to be 613 commandments or *mitzvot* (mitzvah). So, Judaism is more about fulfilling the law than theology. Contrastingly, Christianity relegates the law and promotes the theology of just believing or having blind faith, and the attaining of salvation through Jesus' atonement – dying on the cross for the sins of mankind. From a soteriological perspective, the much-touted salvation doctrine is contradictive of some aspects of the Bible – Matthew 5:17 ("Do not think that I have come to abolish the law or the prophets; I have come not to abolish but to fulfill"), and Galatians 6:5("For every man shall bear his own burden").

Also, because the founders and practitioners of Christianity claimed the law has been abrogated, and belief is centric to salvation, there are no standard rituals, particularly those to be performed daily, obligatorily.

These are specific obligatory rituals that can be traced, in practice, to the revered figure or prophet and documented in scripture. In Christianity, there is usually a prevalence of cherry-picked rituals and not the actual rituals that can be linked or associated with the acknowledged revered figure of the religion. For example, if a Christian fasts and prays, that is a common practice by all righteous figures, but it is not an obligatory daily requirement that can be associated with worshipping God. In this regard, Christianity is devoid of daily obligatory rituals. Comparatively, Islam finely combines spirituality and rituals. There is evidentiary documentation of rituals – obligatory and supererogatory – that can be directly traced to Prophet Muhammad ﷺ A good example is the five daily prayers, which collectively represent one of the five pillars of Islam. Interestingly, the five pillars of Islam can actually be identified in the Bible.

Five Pillars of Islam in the Bible: *Shahadah* (Testimony), *Salat* (Prayer), *Sawm* (Fasting), *Zakat* (Charity) and *Hajj* (Pilgrimage).

1. Shahadah: the first pillar of Islam is the primary testimony or declaration that there is no God but Allah; meaning that God is one. This declaration about the oneness of God can be found in some verses of the Bible. The oneness of God is mentioned in Deuteronomy:

Hear, O Israel: The Lord our God is one Lord –Deuteronomy 6:4.

In another section of the Bible, during a debate, a scribe questioned Jesus about the most important commandment:

"The most important one," answered Jesus, "is this: 'Hear, O Israel: The Lord our God, the Lord is one. – Mark 12:29

2. Salat: the second pillar of Islam is establishing prayer – worship. This involves physical rituals of prostration and putting the face to the ground. The Bible contains verses bearing similarities with the movements of Salat:

Abram bowed with his face to the ground– Genesis 17:3

Moses and Aaron went from the assembly to the entrance of the tent of meeting. Immediately, they bowed with their faces touching the ground
– Numbers 20:6

Immediately, Joshua bowed with his face touching the ground and worshiped.
– Joshua 5:14

Ezra praised the LORD, the great God; and all the people lifted their hands and responded, "Amen! Amen!" Then they bowed down and worshiped the LORD with their faces to the ground.
– Nehemiah 8:6

Jesus walked on a little way. Then he knelt with his face to the ground and prayed...
– Matthew 26:39

Note: ablution is a prerequisite before Salat is performed and it is a ritual purification that involves the cleansing of parts of the body, primarily with water. The Bible also contains verses depicting the process of ablution:

He placed the basin between the tent of meeting and the altar and put water in it for washing, and Moses and Aaron and his sons used it to wash their hands and feet. – Exodus 40:30-31

Ideally, when Salat is performed, apart from the satisfaction of worshipping the Only One worthy of worship, there should be a feeling of contentment that this mode of worship is not new and has been practiced by forerunners for an exceptionally long time.

3. Zakat: the third pillar of Islam is Zakat; which means charity. Charity donations can be in the form of money and can be given directly to the recipients, or to a religious body that will distribute accordingly. The Bible contains verses of charity and in a particular scenario, Jesus monitored the donations.

> *Jesus sat down near the collection box in the Temple and watched as the crowds dropped in their money. Many rich people put in large amounts.*
> – Mark 12:41

4. Sawm: The fourth pillar of Islam is Sawm; which means fasting. Specifically, it is the obligated fasting in Ramadan – the ninth month of the Islamic calendar:

(1) *Muharram* (2) *Safar* (3) *Rabi' al-Awwal* (4) *Rabi' al-Thani* (5) *Jumada al-Awwal* (6) *Jumada al-Thani* (7) *Rajab* (8) *Sha'ban* (9) *Ramadan* (10) *Shawwal* (11) *Dhu al-Qi'dah* (12) *Dhu al-Hijjah*

Though there are various Bible verses that mention fasting, there is, however, a particular verse that is fascinating, because it mentions fasting in the ninth month of the year.

> *In the ninth month of the fifth year of Jehoiakim son of Josiah king of Judah, a time of fasting before the LORD was proclaimed for all the people in Jerusalem and those who had come from the towns of Judah* –Jeremiah 36:9

5. Hajj: The fifth pillar of Islam is Hajj; which means pilgrimage. The Hajj involves a pilgrimage to Makkah (Mecca), and it is performed during the twelfth month of the Islamic calendar – Dhu al-Hijjah. The Hajj is one of the largest human gatherings and the structure of the Masjid al-Haram in Makkah is currently designed to accommodate four million people.[37]

The Bible has various verses describing the journey of pilgrims or the pilgrimage to a certain location. Also, there are certain Bible verses where the descriptions bear striking similarities with Makkah, like Isaiah 60:1-7:

> *Arise, shine, for your light has come, and the glory of the LORD rises upon you. See, darkness covers the earth and thick darkness is over the peoples, but the LORD rises upon you and his glory appears over you. Nations will come to your light, and kings to the brightness of your dawn. Lift up your eyes and look about you: All assemble and come to you; your sons come from afar, and your daughters are carried on the hip. Then you will look and be radiant, your heart will throb and swell with joy; the wealth on the seas will be brought to you, to you the riches of the nations will come. Herds of camels will cover your land, young camels of Midian and Ephah. And all from Sheba will come, bearing gold and incense and proclaiming the praise of the LORD. All Kedar's flocks will be gathered to you, the rams of Nebaioth will serve you; they will be accepted as offerings on my altar, and I will adorn my glorious temple – Isaiah 60:1-7*

In the Quran, one of the verses on Hajj (pilgrimage) to Makkah states:

> *And proclaim to mankind the Hajj (pilgrimage). They will come to you on foot and on every lean camel, they will come from every deep and distant (wide) mountain highway (to perform Hajj).*
> *– Quran 22:27*

Historically, Makkah used to be referred to as Bakkah, and are sometimes used synonymously. Whilst Bakkah is associated with the gatherings around the house of worship – Ka'bah, Makkah is associated with a geographical location – the city of Makkah al-Mukarramah.

It is important to note, at this juncture, that the Ka'bah built by Abraham and Ishmael was designated for the worship of Allah, but by the time the Prophet emerged in the Arabian Peninsula, the House of God – Ka'bah had been turned into a structure of idolism by the Arabs. Though the mission of Prophet Muhammad ﷺ was global, it started with the reminder to the Arabs to shun the worship of all forms of false deities and return to monotheism and restore the Ka'bah to its original designation. The Quran mentions the Ka'bah was built by Abraham and Ishmael:

> And (remember) when Ibrahim (Abraham) and (his son) Isma'il (Ishmael)
> were raising the foundations of the House (the Ka'bah at Makkah), (saying),
> "Our Lord! Accept (this service) from us. Verily! You are the All-Hearer, the
> All-Knower." – Quran 2:127

> And (remember) when We showed Ibrahim (Abraham) the site of the
> (Sacred) House (the Ka'bah at Makkah) (saying): "Associate not anything (in
> worship) with Me, [La ilaha ill-Allah (none has the right to be worshipped but
> Allah Islamic Monotheism], and sanctify My House for those who
> circumambulate it, and those who stand up for prayer, and those who bow
> (submit themselves with humility and obedience to Allah), and make
> prostration (in prayer, etc.); – Quran 22:26

Interestingly, both Bakkah and Makkah are mentioned in the Quran:

Indeed, the first House [of worship] established for mankind was that at Bakkah [i.e., Makkah] - blessed and a guidance for the worlds.
– Quran 3:96

And it is He who withheld their hands from you and your hands from them within [the area of] Makkah after He caused you to overcome them. And ever is Allah, of what you do, Seeing.
– Quran 48:24

From a biblical perspective, a section of the Bible also mentions pilgrimage and included a location named 'Baka' in Psalms 84:

How lovely is your dwelling place, LORD Almighty! My soul yearns, even faints, for the courts of the LORD; my heart and my flesh cry out for the living God. Even the sparrow has found a home, and the swallow a nest for herself, where she may have her young— a place near your altar, LORD Almighty, my King and my God. Blessed are those who dwell in your house; they are ever praising you. Blessed are those whose strength is in you, whose hearts are set on pilgrimage. As they pass through the Valley of Baka, they make it a place of springs; the autumn rains also cover it with pools. They go from strength to strength, till each appears before God in Zion. Hear my prayer, LORD God Almighty; listen to me, God of Jacob. Look on our shield, O God; look with favor on your anointed one. Better is one day in your courts than a thousand elsewhere; I would rather be a doorkeeper in the house of my God than dwell in the tents of the wicked. – Psalms 84:1-10

There have been theories about the correlation between the Quranic (Bakkah) and biblical (Baka) narratives, and discourse on the matter continues. Nonetheless, it is important to highlight that in Ibn Hisham's recension of Ibn

Ishaq's classic work about the life of Prophet Muhammad – Sirat Rasul Allah, 'Bakka' is mentioned in the story about the reconstruction of the Ka'bah. During the renovation of the Ka'bah, the Quraysh found a Syriac inscription that was undecipherable until a Jew translated thus:[38]

> *I am Allah the Lord of Bakka, I created it on the day I created heaven and earth and formed the sun and moon, and I surrounded it with seven pious angels. It will stand while its two mountains stand, a blessing to its people with milk and water*

ENJOINING GOOD AND FORBIDDING EVIL

A crucial aspect of being a balanced nation is the noble act of promoting what is good and forbidding what is evil. Those who claim to be Submitters – Muslims, should ideally be the best example for mankind.

> *You are the best nation produced [as an example] for mankind. You enjoin what is right and forbid what is wrong and believe in Allah. If only the People of the Scripture had believed, it would have been better for them. Among them are believers, but most of them are defiantly disobedient.* – Quran 3:110

The exceptional feat of Muslims being the ideal evolution of mankind is tied to enjoining righteousness and forbidding evil. The divine honour mankind has been bestowed is directly linked with the primary purpose of creation – to worship The Creator. Furthermore, the righteousness characteristic somewhat justifies the creation of man, because when Allah informed the angels, he was going to create man, the angels wondered why. However, in His ultimate wisdom and mercy, Allah responded by stating that He knows what they the angels do not know, because He is The All-Knowing.

Behold, thy Lord said to the angels: "I will create a vicegerent on earth." They said: "Wilt Thou place therein one who will make mischief therein and shed blood?- whilst we do celebrate Thy praises and glorify Thy holy (name)?" He said: "I know what ye know not."–Quran 2:30

Essentially, whenever Muslims are not enjoining good and forbidding evil, they are not fulfilling the purpose of their existence. The core of mankind's problems can be traced to the deliberate abandonment of the divine duty of enjoining good and forbidding evil. From a sociological viewpoint, forbidding evil is not exactly an easy feat. Being good is one thing, and enjoining good is another, but forbidding evil is more challenging, because people naturally do not like change – that's human nature. Obviously, enjoining good and forbidding evil must come from a place of love and humility. The motivation for such noble acts should be founded on love for fellow-creations, without haughtiness. Also, tact must be employed in such actions because forceful implementation would, in most cases, be counterproductive.

The composition of the human psyche is to resist change by default, and people tend to be naturally defiant. As a similitude, if people are told not to drink alcohol, some people will be defiant and more determined to drink alcohol, simply because there is a law that says alcohol consumption is not permitted. In contrast, if reverse psychology is applied to the situation and people are instructed that the nonconsumption of alcohol is illegal. In such a scenario, there are people who will not consume alcohol to establish their defiance. This similitude highlights the defiance some people have towards rules, especially divinely inspired laws or anything associated with God, and underpins their general aversion to religion. The usual mantra is 'nobody can tell me what to do' or 'I can live my life the way I want', and in the process, may decide to sing "I want to break free".

The societal manifestations of such parochial and often self-inimical scenarios, underscores why it is a wiser option to advice people via reminders of the benefits of righteousness. Nonetheless, the societal implications of not enjoining good and forbidding evil are felt by all member of the society. Unfortunately, the impact of crime on any society cannot be steered to affect a particular set of victims. For example, if a drunken person drives a car, and the consumed alcohol causes an error in judgement that leads to a fatal accident, the casualties could be far-reaching. In such a scenario, potential casualties of the fatal accident could be the inebriated driver or some innocent bystanders. In another example, a drug dealer sells hard drugs to a drug addict, and the effect of the drugs leads to the substance abuser attacking an innocent person on the street for no reason. As another example, a public servant tasked with the fixing of bad roads, decides to engage in graft – stealing – which leads to a ghastly accident, because the road was never fixed. The victims in the aforementioned instances can be traced to someone doing something terrible – an initial evil act that was committed, thereby triggering off a series of grievous events. In all the above citied scenarios, the friends and loved ones of all the parties involved are impacted by the manifestations of not forbidding evil. A Hadith succinctly highlights the detrimental effects of not enjoining good and forbidding evil with an analogy of a ship with two decks.

Narrated Al-Nu'man ibn Bashir: The Prophet ﷺ, said, "The parable of those who respect the limits of Allah and those who violate them is that of people who board a ship after casting lots, some of them residing in its upper deck and others in its lower deck. When those in the lower deck want water, they pass by the upper deck and say: If we tear a hole in the bottom of the ship, we will not harm those above us. If those in the upper deck let them do what they want, they will all be destroyed together. If they restrain them, they will all be saved together." – Sahih al-Bukhari 2361

A section of the Quran highlighting the distinctive positions of the Jews and Christians, and the reward for the sincere, specifically mentions the consequences of not enjoining good and forbidding evil by Children of Israel, and execrations during the eras of David and then Jesus.

> *Those among the Children of Israel who disbelieved were cursed by the tongue of Dawud (David) and 'Iesa (Jesus), son of Maryam (Mary). That was because they disobeyed (Allah and the Messengers) and were ever transgressing beyond bounds.*
>
> *They used not to forbid one another from the Munkar (wrong, evil-doing, sins, polytheism, disbelief, etc.) which they committed. Vile indeed was what they used to do.*
>
> *You see many of them taking the disbelievers as their Auliya' (protectors and helpers). Evil indeed is that which their ownselves have sent forward before them, for that (reason) Allah's Wrath fell upon them and in torment they will abide.*
>
> *And had they believed in Allah, and in the Prophet (Muhammad SAW) and in what has been revealed to him, never would they have taken them (the disbelievers) as Auliya' (protectors and helpers), but many of them are the Fasiqun (rebellious, disobedient to Allah).*
>
> *Verily, you will find the strongest among men in enmity to the believers (Muslims) the Jews and those who are Al-Mushrikun, and you will find the nearest in love to the believers (Muslims) those who say: "We are Christians." That is because amongst them are priests and monks, and they are not proud. And when they (who call themselves Christians) listen to what has been sent down to the Messenger (Muhammad SAW), you see their eyes overflowing with tears because of the truth they have recognised. They say: "Our Lord! We believe; so write us down among the witnesses.*
>
> *"And why should we not believe in Allah and in that which has come to us of*

the truth (Islamic Monotheism)? And we wish that our Lord will admit us (in Paradise on the Day of Resurrection) along with the righteous people (Prophet Muhammad SAW and his Companions)."

So because of what they said, Allah rewarded them Gardens under which rivers flow (in Paradise), they will abide therein forever. Such is the reward of good-doers. – Quran 5:78-85

The importance of forbidding evil is further emphasized in some Hadith:

Narrated Abu Sa'eed Al-Khudri: I heard the Messenger of Allah ﷺ say, "Whosoever of you sees an evil, let him change it with his hand; and if he is not able to do so, then [let him change it] with his tongue; and if he is not able to do so, then with his heart - and that is the weakest of faith." –Nawawi 34

Narrated Hudhaifah bin Al-Yaman: the Prophet ﷺ said, "By the One in Whose Hand is my soul! Either you command good and forbid evil, or Allah will soon send upon you a punishment from Him, then you will call upon Him, but He will not respond to you." – Jami at-Tirmidhi 2169, Book 33, Hadith 12

Narrated Umm Habibah: The Prophet, ﷺ said, "Every word of the son of Adam is against him, not for him, except for enjoining good, forbidding evil, or remembrance of Allah." – Sunan al-Tirmidhi 2412

BELIEF IN THE UNSEEN

Material obsession by some science proponents is actually a deceptive trajectory. The reality is that not every phenomenon is explainable by science. The constant preoccupation with subatomic particles, including neutrinos, electrons, protons, photons and other known and unknown particles, is not a guaranteed method of explaining all of life's mysteries. For instance, those who want to 'see God' as proof of His existence, are destined for an exercise in futility, primarily because of the flawed premise of their experiment.

> *And those who have no knowledge say: "Why does not Allah speak to us (face to face) or why does not a sign come to us?" So said the people before them words of similar import. Their hearts are alike, We have indeed made plain the signs for people who believe with certainty.* – Quran 2:118

From an Islamic position, the creation accepts that seeing the Creator is logically impossible, at least whilst existing as a creation on earth. Even if such a feat were possible, historical incidents have established, there are those would still reject the truth, even if such a special request is granted. Also, the illogicality of requesting to speak to The Creator cannot be overstated. The Computer Maker Analogy is just one example that highlights such illogicality. As a similitude, imagine a computer programmer entering a computer for purposes of revelation to a software code –it is simply absurd! Furthermore, the essentiality of being a believer is the ability to comprehend that a vital aspect of existence is belief in the unseen.

> *"This is the Scripture whereof there is no doubt, a guidance unto those who ward off (evil).*
> *Who believe in the Unseen, and establish worship, and spend of that We have bestowed upon them"*
> –Quran 2:2-3

This exceptional act of belief in the unseen is what makes believers unique. Belief in the unseen is the ultimate test. If humans could see God or visit the afterlife and return, then what would be the purpose for the test of life?

Life invariably becomes a meaningless endeavour and the criterion to ascertain belief is pointless! As a similitude, what will be the point of conducting examinations, if the questions and answers to the examination have been revealed prior to the examination? The basis of conducting the examination will be purposeless. Generally, tests or examinations are the accepted mediums to determine those who pass or fail – graduate to the next level or achieve success. Life can be appreciated from the perspective of being one big examination. Our very existence is evidence of enrolment in the examination. Most importantly, the creation is not in any position to determine how The Creator conducts examinations. In this regard, The Creator is the examiner, and the creation is the examinee.

PART THREE
THE MESSAGE

CHAPTER 19

THE MESSAGE AND MESSENGERS

The message can be appreciated from its perdurability and universality. The message has withstood the test of time and has been analysed scientifically, mathematically, linguistically, textually and contextually via historical and contemporary narratives. Contextually, there was nothing new in the message of Prophet Muhammad ﷺ; it is essentially a continuum of the same message preached by all the prophets and messengers that preceded him – the complete acknowledgment and declaration of the oneness of God: The Creator.

> *We never sent a messenger before you ʿO Prophetʾ without revealing to him: "There is no god ʿworthy of worshipʾ except Me, so worship Me ʿaloneʾ."*
> – Quran 21:25

From an historical viewpoint, events and documentation affirm that The Creator makes contact with His creation via various means. However, it is the handiwork of the creation that caused confusion and mischief globally, hence, the existence of religious multiplicity and strife.

The cruciality of Islam's message is that it is the only religion that connects all previous monotheistic prophets, and its position is authenticated with a perdurable scripture – the Quran. Also, a fundamental aspect of Islam is accepting all prophets and messengers completely. The Quran mentions those whose desire is to base their beliefs on cherry-picking.

> *Surely those who deny Allah and His messengers and wish to make a distinction between Allah and His messengers saying, "We believe in some and disbelieve in others," desiring to forge a compromise,* – Quran 4:150

Contemporary schisms and geopolitical machinations give a glimpse into why Islam, Prophet Muhammad ﷺ and previous messengers and prophets, the Quran and previous messages – scriptures, would have been rejected historically. The calumniation and propaganda against the message and messengers can be analysed from the prism of modern-day fake news. The recurring theme of rejection has been the preservation of selfish and parochial interests, at any cost. Like his predecessors, Prophet Muhammad ﷺ faced challenges and rejection by those he encountered, because change is challenging. Resistance to change explains why some humanly developed cultures that inculcate traditions, often clash with a divinely inspired religion, and get offended when reminded about their cultural deviations. Human beings tend to create an ethos that is definitely not the path ordained by God. Man left unchecked would literally manifest himself as a god on earth. The prevalence of human excesses is the primary reason prophets and messengers are sent to mankind as a reminder to be cognizant of their creator and ephemeral existence.

Islamic exegesis acknowledges there have been previous scriptures sent via messenger-prophets and five of them were mentioned in the Quran:

1. Suhuf – The Scrolls brought by Abraham (Ibrahim)

2. Taurat – The Torah brought by Moses (Musa)

3. Zabur – The Psalms brought by David (Dawud)

4. Injeel – The Gospel brought by Jesus (Isa)

5. Quran – The Criterion brought by Muhammad

The divine message is a continuum from the same source; dealing with mankind's issues as events necessitate and serving as an eschatological reminder. Also, there is a slight difference between a prophet and a messenger.

Generally, a prophet is meant to share divinely inspired knowledge with a specific audience, whilst a messenger usually brings a new scripture; which may contain instructions or legislation for a target audience. In other words, every messenger is a prophet, but not every prophet is a messenger. For example, Moses was both a prophet and messenger because he brought a new legislation – Torah. Prophet Muhammad ﷺ was both a Prophet and Messenger because he prophesied and brought a new scripture – legislation. Furthermore, research reveals variations in the numbers of prophets sent – possibly tens of thousands or hundreds of thousands, but no certain figure. However, the bottom line is that numerous prophets were sent by God to different parts of the world.

> *And We certainly sent into every nation a messenger, [saying], "Worship Allah and avoid ṭaghut." And among them were those whom Allah guided, and among them were those upon whom error was [deservedly] decreed. So proceed [i.e., travel] through the earth and observe how was the end of the deniers.* – Quran 16:36

The above-mentioned verse affirms every nation was indeed sent a Messenger, proclaiming the same authentic message about worshipping Allah and shunning evil. The contextual usage of nation represents a particular community or civilization at a specific period in history. This is a crucial message, especially to those who analyse Islam from a parochial prism. Abrahamic prophets – including the totality of Islamic prophets – sometimes come under criticism as foreign impositions on some cultures. From an Islamic viewpoint, some aspects of cultural traditions in any society across the globe are permissible, as long as it is not in contravention of monotheism. Basically, the excesses of any culture in the world should not undermine the supremacy of The Creator.

In addressing such criticism, elucidating on what constitutes prophethood in Islam becomes crucial. Human beings are meant to learn from the experiences of the numerous prophets sent at various points in history. Also, it is important to state that some groups of people in history may not have met prophets or messengers, or may have existed in between the coming of prophets, and what was left of their messages may have vanished. Obviously, those in this category are in an exceptional position and cannot be assessed on the same basis as those who received a prophet or messenger and a message. Their ultimate judgement and fate rests with The Most Merciful. However, this special category is not applicable to the current generation, and all those who came across a prophet or a message – such as the Taurat (Torah), Injeel (Gospel) or Quran. Based on scriptural evidence, there have been numerous prophets sent to every nation on the face of the earth. Nation, in this context can be analysed anthropologically, and with geographical manifestations, rather than contemporary nation states, especially postcolonial naming conventions. Furthermore, such criticisms are founded on a false equivalence premise because these particular monotheistic prophets cannot be equated to cultural traditions that deify and worship their respective autochthonous deities.

All prophets, without exception, were fundamentally and actively challenging the autochthonous deities that existed during their time. Importantly, whilst all prophets may be perceived as autochthonal – when analysed from their respective geographical abodes, their stories serve primarily as symbolic reminders. Of all the prophets sent in history, only a few are explicitly revealed. The reason for this is because the prophets are but conduits of a divine message. What is of utmost importance, are not the details of each prophet, but the actual message – consistent emphasis on the worship of God. Essentially, there is no concrete and indisputable evidence of any Islamic or Abrahamic prophet unequivocally claiming to be God, nor did anyone of them specifically request to be deified or worshipped.

In their respective missions across the globe, all the prophets, without exception, primarily professed the existence of an All-Powerful God, and the worship of that omnipotent God.

To further buttress the point that prophets were indeed sent to different parts of the globe, I will cite Africa as a geographical example. In the Quran, there is the story of Luqman The Wise – the eponymous character in Chapter 31 (Surah Luqman). Ethnographically, Luqman is reported to be African, in the contemporary geographical context of Africa, because the region that spans the African continent may have not been referred to as 'Africa' during Luqman's era. The mentioning of Luqman in the Quran is significant because only a few individuals are explicitly mentioned in the Quran. There are prophets mentioned and there are prophets who were not mentioned. Also, there are prophets and righteous characters not mentioned in their own stories – such as the prophet who anointed Talut as king and the three message-bearers of Surah Ya-Sin. In the case of Luqman, he was not only mentioned by name but has an entire Surah – Chapter 31 – dedicated to him. Islamic exegesis affirms Luqman was wise and righteous. The Quran states that Allah blessed Luqman with wisdom. Exceptionally, Luqman gave wise counsel to his son, and advised about the importance of maintaining strict Islamic monotheism and the dutiful worship of Allah without association of partners.

> *Indeed, We blessed Luqman with wisdom, ˹saying˺, "Be grateful to Allah, for whoever is grateful, it is only for their own good. And whoever is ungrateful, then surely Allah is Self-Sufficient, Praiseworthy. And (remember) when Luqman said to his son when he was advising him: "O my son! Join not in worship others with Allah. Verily! Joining others in worship with Allah is a great Zulm (wrong) indeed.*– Quran 31:12-13

The story of Luqman's establishes that not all the stories in the Quran are about Middle Easterners, or what is considered the Middle East region contemporarily. Interestingly, Prophet Muhammad ﷺ described Moses as dark-skinned (Black). The prophets that have traversed the earth were of different skin tones, and were specifically sent to regions, towns, communities and families, and at times, operated concurrently. It is vital to re-emphasize that not all the identities of prophets and messengers were revealed, and only some of them where explicitly mentioned. The Quran emphasizes this point:

> *Verily, We have sent the revelation to you (O Muhammad SAW) as We sent the revelation to Nuh (Noah) and the Prophets after him: We (also) sent the revelation to Ibrahim (Abraham), Ismail (Ishmael), Ishaq (Isaac), Yaqub (Jacob) and Al Asbat [the offspring of the twelve sons of Yaqub (Jacob)], Isa (Jesus), Ayyub (Job), Yunus (Jonah), Harun (Aaron), and Sulaiman (Solomon); and to Dawud (David) We gave the Zabur (Psalms). And Messengers We have mentioned to you before, and Messengers We have not mentioned to you- and to Musa (Moses) we spoke directly.*

– Quran 4:163-164

In this regard, the specific identities of the prophets and messengers are not necessary, what is of utmost importance is the consistency of the undiluted message. Admittedly, this does not discount the reality of the apotheosis that occurred historically and manifested contemporarily. Certain generations took it upon themselves to elevate monotheistic prophets to the status of deities. Possibly, some historic or revered figures, which are synonymous with particular geographical regions, may have been righteous beings during their lifetime, but their works somehow got corrupted, due to deliberate interpolations and false transmissions, over a protracted period.

I posit, that many of the revered figures, especially religious, in history, may have been sent to fulfil the purpose of the divine message across various geographical regions in the world. However, there is a possibility the purity or authenticity of their messages getting corrupted after their demise, and some people may have devised an un-sanctioned practice of worshipping these revered figures instead of the Only One worthy of worship – God The Creator. A classic example of a corrupted message is the worship of Jesus by contemporary Christians or how Jesus was equated to 'God'. Based on numerous verses in the Bible, being 'God' or 'Godhead' is a characteristic Jesus never attributed to himself directly. The attribution of God to Jesus was done by those who came after his era and is contradictory to the Bible. Two biblical examples are: Matthew 27:46 – "My God, my God, why have you forsaken me?", and John 5:30 – "By myself I can do nothing".

Another example of false worship was when Moses left his people for a period to visit the mountain for meditation and prayers to God. But, by the time Moses returned, they were inspired by a deviant amongst themselves, to start worshipping a hand-carved golden calf. This scenario is a typical example of how Satan influences mankind to go astray; Moses was gone for 40 days and was not even dead, and the people already broke their promise to Moses.

Whenever We sent a messenger or a prophet before you ˹O Prophet˺ and he recited ˹Our revelations˺, Satan would influence ˹people's understanding of˺ his recitation. But ˹eventually˺ Allah would eliminate Satan's influence. Then Allah would ˹firmly˺ establish His revelations. And Allah is All-Knowing, All-Wise.– Quran 22:52

PROPHETS' MIRACLES

God The Creator gave specific privileges and powers to prophets for the sake of their specific mission and in some instances for their personal conviction. These privileges are usually referred to as miracles – signs and wonders. Miracles are usually unexplainable feats beyond the metaphysical. From a sociological perspective, the societal ethos and prevailing form of knowledge, usually determines the type of miracle that the people will witness. The following are some examples of prophets' miracles mentioned in the Quran:

Salih (Saleh): Salih lived among the people of Thamud. The Thamud were a proud people blessed with architectural and technological advancements – building magnificent palaces and literally carving out houses from mountains. As Salih reminded his people about God and righteousness, he was compelled to perform a miracle to establish his prophethood. The miracle of Salih was bringing forth a pregnant she-camel from within a split mountain.

The story of Salih is mentioned in Quran 7:73-78, and below is an excerpt:

> *And to Thamud (people, We sent) their brother Salih (Saleh). He said: "O my people! Worship Allah! You have no other Ilah (God) but Him. (La ilaha ill-Allah: none has the right to be worshipped but Allah). Indeed there has come to you a clear sign (the miracle of the coming out of a huge she-camel from the midst of a rock) from your Lord. This she-camel of Allah is a sign unto you; so you leave her to graze in Allah's earth, and touch her not with harm, lest a painful torment should seize you.* – Quran 7:73

Ibrahim (Abraham): Allah honoured and chose Ibrahim as a 'friend' (Quran 4:125), and he is revered, especially among the Abrahamic faiths. One of the notable events in the life of Ibrahim includes his unscathed emergence from a blazing fire he was catapulted into, by the order of the king (Quran 2:258).

Ibrahim's survival of the fire was a spectacular miracle publicly witnessed by his people in the Mesopotamia region. Another notable miracle was Ibrahim's request for Allah to show him the process of resurrection. The conversation and the miracle that followed Ibrahim's request are detailed in the Quran:

> *And [mention] when Abraham said, "My Lord, show me how You give life to the dead." [Allah] said, "Have you not believed?" He said, "Yes, but [I ask] only that my heart may be satisfied." [Allah] said, "Take four birds and commit them to yourself.¹ Then [after slaughtering them] put on each hill a portion of them; then call them - they will come [flying] to you in haste. And know that Allah is Exalted in Might and Wise."* – Quran 2:260

Musa (Moses): Musa is the only one who had a direct conversation with Allah and the most mentioned personality in the entire Quran. The documented miracles of Musa in the Quran are as follows; his staff transmogrifying into a serpent (Quran 7:107), his staff striking the rock and produced twelve springs (Quran 7:160), the illuminating hand (Quran 7:108), the invocations of drought (Quran 7:130) and floods, locusts, lice, frog and blood (Quran 7:133), and the parting of the sea (Quran 26:63-68).

> *Then We inspired to Musa, 'Strike with your staff the sea,' and it parted, and each portion was like a great towering mountain.*
> *And We advanced thereto [i.e., the pursuers].*
> *And We saved Moses and those with him, all together.*
> *Then We drowned the others.*
> *Indeed in that is a sign, but most of them were not to be believers.*
> *And indeed, your Lord – He is the Exalted in Might, the Merciful.*
> – Quran 26:63-68

Musa was sent at a time where magic was the prevailing order and magic was rife in his society. The Pharaoh and his court magicians held sway, until Musa presented something that belittled their magic tricks; which they initially considered a superior form of 'magic' – though in reality, what they witnessed was a divine miracle from Allah. Interestingly, the Pharaoh's magicians turned against him, even after being threatened with crucifixion and death. However, the magicians did not care about the Pharaoh's threats, because through the miracles of Moses they had witnessed the truth from their Lord and were ready to be martyred.

So the magicians fell down in prostration, declaring, "We believe in the Lord of Aaron and Moses."

Pharaoh threatened, "How dare you believe in him before I give you permission? He must be your master who taught you magic. I will certainly cut off your hands and feet on opposite sides, and crucify you on the trunks of palm trees. You will really see whose punishment is more severe and more lasting."

They responded, "By the One Who created us! We will never prefer you over the clear proofs that have come to us. So do whatever you want! Your authority only covers the ˹fleeting˺ life of this world.

Indeed, we have believed in our Lord so He may forgive our sins and that magic you have forced us to practice. And Allah is far superior ˹in reward˺ and more lasting ˹in punishment˺."–Quran 20:70-73

Isa (Jesus):

During the time of Jesus, curative medicine was considered spectacular, and people were still yearning for miracles, especially as a criterion for acceptance of faith. Jesus' miraculous birth was Allah exposing the limitations of human knowledge and endeavour and exhibiting that He is The Creator, and He alone can alter the dynamics of nature. In the case of Jesus, Allah altered prevailing laws of nature, particularly in human reproduction, with just a word: "Be".

(Remember) when the angels said: "O Maryam (Mary)! Verily, Allah gives you the glad tidings of a Word ["Be!" - and he was! i.e. 'Iesa (Jesus) the son of Maryam (Mary)] from Him, his name will be the Messiah 'Iesa (Jesus), the son of Maryam (Mary), held in honour in this world and in the Hereafter, and will be one of those who are near to Allah." – Quran 3:45

Through that powerful word, creation exists and through that word, Mary the mother of Jesus conceived a child without the need for sexual intercourse. From the point of his birth, Jesus performed numerous miracles that gave hope to the masses and threatened the status quo. Jesus performed many miracles which he stated were by the permission of Allah; he spoke to mankind in his cradle (Quran 3:46); gave life to a bird created out of clay, healed the blind, cured the leper, raised the dead (Quran 3:49) and brought a table laden with food directly from heaven (Quran 5:112-114).

Behold! the disciples, said: "O Jesus the son of Mary! can thy Lord send down to us a table set (with viands) from heaven?" Said Jesus: "Fear Allah, if ye have faith."
They said: "We only wish to eat thereof and satisfy our hearts, and to know that thou hast indeed told us the truth; and that we ourselves may be witnesses to the miracle."
Said Jesus the son of Mary: "O Allah our Lord! Send us from heaven a table set (with viands), that there may be for us - for the first and the last of us - a solemn festival and a sign from thee; and provide for our sustenance, for thou art the best Sustainer (of our needs)." – Quran 5:112-114

In essence, everything Jesus did on earth, he acknowledged were by the permission of God; his Creator. Notably, after Jesus' departure, his divine message was corrupted; which eventually led to his deification and worship.

Muhammad ﷺ

Like his predecessors, Prophet Muhammad ﷺ had his documented miracles: exorcism, healing the sick and curing the blind, communication with trees, feeding multitudes of people with food and water, and many others. However, Muslims tend not to lay too much emphasis on the miracles of Muhammad ﷺ, and avoid the excesses of hagiography. The primary reason for this is because Muslims are aware miracles are done only by the permission of Allah. To buttress this point, during the Battle of Hunayn, Prophet Muhammad threw dust that blinded his adversaries. The incident at the Battle of Hunayn is mentioned in the Quran:

> *And you did not kill them, but it was Allah who killed them. And you threw not, [O Muhammad], when you threw, but it was Allah who threw that He might test the believers with a good test.Indeed, Allah is Hearing and Knowing.*
> – Quran 8:17

A couple of lessons can be derived from this incident. Firstly, it is by the permission of Allah anything is done. One of the tests for the believers who witnessed the effectiveness of the dust-throwing against adversaries, is not attributing the miracle to Prophet Muhammad ﷺ primarily, but to appreciate that the miracle was done by the permission of Allah. Clarity about such a climacteric situation is important because people without proper understanding may decide to excessively venerate the Prophet to the level of deification; thereby worshipping the creation (Prophet) instead of The Creator (Allah). Secondly, the Battle of Hunayn in particular, was a lesson for the believers to not be deceived by their size, as success comes from Allah. The Quran mentions how their multitudes, which they assumed advantageous, were of no consequence at all, until they were rescued by Allah.

> *Allah has already given you victory in many regions and [even] on the day of Hunayn, when your great number pleased you, but it did not avail you at all, and the earth was confining for you with [i.e., in spite of] its vastness; then you turned back, fleeing.* – Quran 9:25

Furthermore, another reason Muslims do not lay too much emphasis on the miracles of Muhammad ﷺ, is because of the cardinal reason – the greatest miracle of Muhammad ﷺ is actually the Quran.

> *And it was not [possible] for this Qur'ān to be produced by other than Allah, but [it is] a confirmation of what was before it and a detailed explanation of the [former] Scripture, about which there is no doubt, from the Lord of the worlds.* – Quran 10:37

Prophet Muhammad ﷺ came at a time of critical thinking, an era where human beings are challenged to think and encouraged to reason. Generally, humankind has evolved beyond the miracle epoch to an era of intellectualism, where science and books are the norm. In this regard, intellectual stimulation is the ethos, and the Quran is a book that surpasses all other books in existence, in every possible ramification, and shall remain so for eternity. Another notable point is that the region where Prophet Muhammad ﷺ emerged – Arabian Peninsula. The Arabs were a people moved by oratorical prowess – grandiloquence, beautifully spoken words and poetry.

When Prophet Muhammad ﷺ – who was not among the learned of society –

emerged with the Quran, they knew the authorship could not have been by an unlettered man like him and were completely astonished by its magnificence. Contemporarily, the Quran remains as magnificent as it was, since it was first revealed over fourteen centuries ago. In all the aforementioned instances of miracles performed by the prophets, there were still rejectors. Possibly, some of those who requested and witnessed these miracles did so for entertainment purposes. In this regard, rejection is very possible despite the witnessing of miracles, especially by those who requested the miracles from their respective prophets. In essence, what is of utmost importance, is not the region, ethnicity, tribe or skin colour of the prophets or messengers sent by God, because all the aforementioned societies where the prophets dwelled, are a microcosm of the wider world. Rather, what is of utmost importance is the consistency of the message from inception: the oneness of God The Creator.

[Be warned of] the Day when Allah will assemble the messengers and say, "What was the response you received?" They will say, "We have no knowledge. Indeed, it is You who is Knower of the unseen"

[The Day] when Allah will say, "O Jesus, Son of Mary, remember My favor upon you and upon your mother when I supported you with the Pure Spirit and you spoke to the people in the cradle and in maturity; and [remember] when I taught you writing and wisdom and the Torah and the Gospel; and when you designed from clay [what was] like the form of a bird with My permission, then you breathed into it, and it became a bird with My permission; and you healed the blind and the leper with My permission; and when you brought forth the dead with My permission; and when I restrained the Children of Israel from [killing] you when you came to them with clear proofs and those who disbelieved among them said, "This is not but obvious magic."

And [remember] when I inspired to the disciples, "Believe in Me and in My messenger Jesus." They said, "We have believed, so bear witness that indeed we are Muslims [in submission to Allah]."

[And remember] when the disciples said, "O Jesus, Son of Mary, can your Lord send down to us a table [spread with food] from the heaven? [Jesus] said, "Fear Allah, if you should be believers."

They said, "We wish to eat from it and let our hearts be reassured and know that you have been truthful to us and be among its witnesses."

Said Jesus, the son of Mary, "O Allah, our Lord, send down to us a table [spread with food] from the heaven to be for us a festival for the first of us and the last of us and a sign from You. And provide for us, and You are the best of providers."

Allah said, "Indeed, I will send it down to you, but whoever disbelieves afterwards from among you - then indeed will I punish him with a punishment by which I have not punished anyone among the worlds."

And [beware the Day] when Allah will say, "O Jesus, Son of Mary, did you say to the people, 'Take me and my mother as deities besides Allah?'" He will say, "Exalted are You! It was not for me to say that to which I have no right. If I had said it, You would have known it. You know what is within myself, and I do not know what is within Yourself. Indeed, it is You who is Knower of the unseen.

I said not to them except what You commanded me - to worship Allah, my Lord and your Lord. And I was a witness over them as long as I was among them; but when You took me up, You were the Observer over them, and You are, over all things, Witness.

If You should punish them - indeed they are Your servants; but if You forgive them - indeed it is You who is the Exalted in Might, the Wise."

Allah will say, "This is the Day when the truthful will benefit from their truthfulness." For them are gardens [in Paradise] beneath which rivers flow, wherein they will abide forever, Allah being pleased with them, and they with Him. That is the great attainment.

To Allah belongs the dominion of the heavens and the earth and whatever is within them. And He is over all things competent.

–Quran 5:109 –120

CHAPTER 20

THE PROPHET AND MESSENGER

And We have not sent you (O Muhammad SAW) except as a giver of glad tidings and a warner to all mankind, but most of men know not.
– Quran 34:28

Prophet Muhammad ﷺ is the quintessence of human aspiration. The attainment of Allah's love has righteousness as conditionality and the Prophet is the perfect paragon of that process. Evidently, Allah loves the righteous, and a guaranteed way of earning the love of Allah is by following Prophet Muhammad ﷺ – the embodiment of submission.

Say (O Muhammad SAW to mankind): "If you (really) love Allah then follow me (i.e. accept Islamic Monotheism, follow the Quran and the Sunnah), Allah will love you and forgive you of your sins. And Allah is Oft-Forgiving, Most Merciful."– Quran 3:31

Muhammad translates as 'praiseworthy' and is the most celebrated name across the globe. The name Muhammad, including cultural-oriented variations, has been popularized through adoption by hundreds of millions – past, present and future. Also, when the *Adhan* – call to prayer – is made five times daily, across all world time zones, the name Muhammad is repeated. There are many other instances that buttress the celebration of the name Muhammad globally. Beyond the naming convention, the character of Muhammad is an underlying factor for such naming choices. The Quran emphasizes the excellent character of Prophet Muhammad ﷺ:

And verily, you (O Muhammad SAW) are on an exalted standard of character. – Quran 68:4

The life of Muhammad was undoubtedly exemplary and worthy of emulation. The attributes of The Prophet transcended many facets of life and are applicable to the daily lives of humans across the globe. Furthermore, it is vital to emphasize The Prophet had possessed these oft-mentioned exemplary attributes before the beginning of his prophetic mission. For instance, before his prophetic mission, Makkah was highly idolatrous, and the city thrived on the tributes travellers paid to numerous idols contained within the city walls. Nevertheless, Muhammad was wise enough to realise that whoever created the universe could never be the idols that were being worshipped in his milieu. Also, there was impunity among the rulers and widespread corruption across the land. In order to avoid partaking in the societal ethos of idol worship and concomitant social activities, Muhammad chose to seclude himself from the city: retreating to a cave known as *Hira*. His periodic visits to the cave of *Hira* awarded him the opportunity to meditate and reflect on the world. Incidentally, it was during one of such meditative episodes Muhammad encountered Angel Jibreel and initiated his life-long prophetic mission of mercy. The Prophet was commanded to proclaim – read –recite:

Recite in the name of thy lord and cherisher Who created: Created man out of a clot of congealed blood. Recite! And thy lord is Most Bountiful, He who taught the use of pen; Taught man that which he knew not. – Quran 96:1-5

Crucially, it must be stated that Muhammad was not a learned man, and his natural response was to state the obvious – that he was not learned. The recital command given through Angel Jibreel and proclaimed by Muhammad was indeed miraculous and extraordinary. The peculiar encounter with Angel

Jibreel occurred when Muhammad turned forty and he spent the next twenty-three years of his life preaching the oneness of God. The prophetic mission of Prophet Muhammad ﷺ came with various trials and challenges; however, he was steadfast and optimistic, and never lost hope – whatever the situation. The ideal paradigm of steadfastness and optimism in the face of adversity was the major trial encountered on his mission to the *Banu Thaqif* in Taif. Following the privations endured during the boycott of the Hashemites by the Meccans, and the deaths of his uncle, Abu Talib and wife, Khadija, Makkah was not so hospitable for Muslims. Accompanied by Zayd ibn Harithah, Prophet Muhammad ﷺ decided to visit Taif to solicit support for his prophetic mission. Upon arrival in Taif, The Prophet had reached out to some notable and highly influential personalities and informed them about his mission. During his time in Taif, the Prophet preached that the people should abandon their idols and worship the one true God, but he was summarily rejected by the entire *Banu Thaqif* clan. On top of that, he was set upon by the louts and miscreants of Taif. The Taif misadventure was so terrible Prophet Muhammad ﷺ was bloodied from the various objects thrown at him. However, following his rejection and utter humiliation in Taif, his reaction was something very remarkable and almost angelic – he made a special prayer:

O Allah! I complain to You of my weakness, my scarcity of resources and the humiliation I have been subjected to by the people. O Most Merciful of those who are merciful. O Lord of the weak and my Lord too. To whom have you entrusted me? To a distant person who receives me with hostility? Or to an enemy to whom you have granted authority over my affair? So long as You are not angry with me, I do not care. Your favor is of a more expansive relief to me. I seek refuge in the light of Your Face by which all darkness is dispelled and every affair of this world and the next is set right, lest Your anger or Your displeasure descends upon me. I desire Your pleasure and satisfaction until You are pleased. There is no power and no might except by You.

That special prayer was indeed answered manifold, because the descendents of those who abused and stoned Prophet Muhammad ﷺ in Taif became Muslims and have largely remained Muslims till this very day. The Taif encounter remains a remarkable story with many lessons, particularly in an era of rising Islamophobia, prevalence of hate speech and attacks on Muslims. Such exemplar traits of displaying courage, humility and steadfastness, whilst facing adversity, are what Muslims must learn to inculcate and practice in dealing with antagonists of Islam and Muslims. A widespread emulation of such unique attributes will surely assist in the quest for peaceful coexistence and the promotion of world peace.

THE PROPHET'S CHARACTER

By all authentic accounts, Prophet Muhammad ﷺ can be described as an easy-going man that exuded uncommon calmness. The Prophet was a man of integrity and it was because of his exceptional moral rectitude he was nicknamed "*Al-Amin*"; which translates as trustworthy - meaning "the trustworthy one". Long before Muhammad's call to prophethood, he dealt with everyone fairly and kindly, and this continued after his prophethood. An example of his peaceful mien was witnessed during a fateful incident involving a man who came to urinate in the *Masjid* (place of worship) whilst The Prophet was present. The companions of The Prophet were understandably livid by what they witnessed and were eager to react. However, as they were rushing towards the man in the Masjid, The Prophet instructed the man should not be interrupted and be allowed to finish urinating. Afterwards, The Prophet instructed the companions to pour a bucketful of water on the affected area for cleansing and stated:

Verily, you were sent only to make maters easy, and you were not sent to make matters difficult. – Sahih al-Bukhari Volume 8, Book 73, Number 150

The Masjid incident highlights the gentle nature of Prophet Muhammad ﷺ, as he did not react angrily when a man eased himself in the Masjid. Imagine if such an incident occurred in our contemporary world – someone easing himself in the Masjid! I daresay, what certain Muslims would do to the man, can only be imagined. The Quran states Prophet Muhammad ﷺ was sent as a mercy to the worlds:

"And We have not sent you, [O Muhammad], except as a mercy to the worlds."–Quran 21:107

Certainly, Prophet Muhammad ﷺ was of impeccable character and such was his nature well before his prophethood. Based on various historical narrations, Muhammad was respected in the Arabian society, including the ruling class. According to Ibn Ishaq, there was a particular incident during the reconstruction of the Kabah in Makkah. After the tribes of Quraysh gathered all the stones and built the Kabah up to the point of placing the black stone, there arose a dispute over which tribe would place the black stone in its position. The situation was so intense the tribes had formed alliances and were ready to go to battle. Following some days of the stalemate the Quraysh gathered around the Kabah to find a solution to the impasse, and then the oldest among them suggested the first man through the gate be the arbitrator on the matter. Those present agreed with this suggestion and the first man through the gates was Muhammad, and they acknowledged him by his name and called him by his nickname Al-Amin – "the trustworthy one". After Muhammad was briefed about the matter, he requested a cloak and placed the black stone in it, then told all the tribes to hold onto the cloak.

Following Muhammad's instruction, all the tribes carried the cloak with the black stone to the point where it was to be placed, and Muhammad placed the black stone in its rightful position.[39]

Prophet Muhammad ﷺ was known for his good-neighbourliness and always endeavoured to treat everyone with kindness and respect, regardless of how he was treated. The Prophet encountered incidents of different people who made it a habit of irritating him and deliberately trying to make his life difficult. Rather than react angrily, the Prophet chose the path of nobility and clemency, and remained resolute with his objectives.

The Prophet once helped an old lady with her heavy load and she was so grateful for his kindness that she decided to repay him with some valuable advice; which was to stay away from a man named Muhammad, because the man was dividing the community with his preaching about the oneness of God. The old lady told him that this man's preaching of one God was against the traditions of their ancestors and was causing disharmony in the land. Eventually, the old lady was shocked to discover the kind man who had helped her was none other than the man she had been admonishing. It is reported the old lady in question became a Muslim because of this incident.

The aforementioned scenarios are just some of many examples in a long list of how the Prophet impacted society. Prophet Muhammad ﷺ had societal impact because he wore many hats and fulfilled various roles, which included husband, father, companion, friend, ally, kind neighbour, honest trader, trusted banker, arbiter, reformer, statesman, prophet and messenger. From a sociological perspective, there are many other roles the Prophet played and some of those roles will be elucidated accordingly.

Convivial Character

Prophet Muhammad ﷺ was known for his conviviality and despite his jovial encounters with others, his honesty was unwavering. There were many instances of the Prophet joking with others. For instance, there was a period the Prophet challenged his wife Aisha to a race and lost, afterwards, when Aisha had gained some weight, he challenged her to a race again, but this time, the Prophet won the race and joked with Aisha about it.

Once an old lady came to the Prophet to pray for her admittance into paradise and the Prophet responded by saying, there will be no old ladies in paradise. This response made the woman sad, but the Prophet cheered her up by explaining that there will be no old age in paradise generally, because everyone will be young in paradise.

The cordial nature of Prophet Muhammad ﷺ was witnessed in the story about the man who came to report himself for having sex with his wife on a day during fasting in Ramadan. To expiate for his mistake, he was given the option of manumission of a slave, or fasting for two consecutive months, or feeding sixty poor people, and his response was "No" to each option. Whilst the man waited, a basket of dates was brought to the Prophet and the man was told to give the dates in charity. The man stated that he could not be charitable with the dates because he was in need of the charity, that no family was poorer than his, and the Prophet agreed to his request smiling. Such was the nature of a loving man who understood the plight of others.

The Prophet and the Prankster: Al-Nuayman ibn Amr was a companion of Prophet Muhammad ﷺ, and a reputed prankster. He played various pranks on The Prophet and fellow companions, which people had a good laugh about. On one occasion, Nuayman went to the marketplace and noticed some sumptuous-looking food. So, Nuayman decided to order some of the food as a gift to Prophet Muhammad ﷺ. Upon receiving the food gift, the Prophet shared the meal with his family. Afterwards, the food vendor requested payment of the purchased food from Nuayman, and the vendor was informed that the food was actually for the Prophet. And on to the Prophet they went. Upon reaching the Prophet, the vendor requested payment for the consumed food. The Prophet asked Nuayman to confirm if the food was a gift? Nuayman stated that yes indeed it was a gift. He further explained that when he saw the food, he thought the Prophet would like it and was eager to present it as a gift; however, he had no money to pay for the food. After his explanation, Nuayman told the Prophet to pay the vendor! The Prophet laughed at the incident and paid the vendor for the food. There are other pranks by Abu Nuayman which the Prophet found amusing.

Trusted Banker

Prophet Muhammad was referred to as Al-Amin (the trustworthy one) and this trust was extended to safekeeping. As a result, various people, including travellers passing through Makkah trusted Muhammad to keep their valuable possessions. Ironically, even after becoming a prophet and the persecution from the Quraysh ensued, Prophet Muhammad ﷺ was still entrusted with their valuables. So, in spite of their religious differences, the Quraysh were still very comfortable keeping their valuables with the Prophet, whilst he resided in Makkah. Eventually, when the Prophet decided to migrate to Madinah, he instructed Ali to return all the stored valuables to their respective owners.

Honest Merchant

As a teenager, Muhammad gained valuable experience from accompanying his uncle, Abu Talib, on commercial trade trips outside Makkah. In time, his reputation as an honest merchant grew and caught the attention of a wealthy merchant from an aristocrat family named Khadija bint Khuwaylid. From a successful trade alliance emerged a powerful love story and fruitful marriage.

Family Man

Muhammad was a loving family man who kissed his grandchildren and carried them on his back for kiddie games. He was a loving husband, and it is impossible to discuss the life of Muhammad without acknowledging his first wife, Khadija bint Khuwaylid. Khadija was his human pillar and foundational backbone; she was the support he needed when confronted with the humongous task of prophethood. Following Muhammad's first encounter with Angel Jibreel, Muhammad was perturbed, but Khadija allayed his worries and reassured him. Khadija took Muhammad to her cousin Waraqah ibn Nawfal – a known monotheist and scholar who refused to participate in the idolatry prevalent in Makkah. Based on his knowledge of previous scriptures, Waraqah ibn Nawfal confirmed Muhammad's prophethood.

Their love story was extraordinary, considering their initial acquaintance was business oriented. Khadija was a wealthy merchant from a prominent family. As a single successful woman, she was not lacking in suitors. However, she indirectly sent overtures to Muhammad through a close friend. Khadija's friend discussed marriage aspirations with Muhammad until it was revealed that Khadija was the potential bride. Though, there may have been other factors for Khadija's interest in Muhammad, but from a logical viewpoint, no sensible woman would pass on the golden opportunity to marry an honest man. Moreover, Muhammad was a business associate who had increased the fortunes of her trading enterprise.

Based on the chronological analysis of historical events, the ages of Khadija and Muhammad at the time of their marriage were 40 and 25, respectively. They were monogamously married for 25 solid years until Khadija died and Muhammad had polygamous marriages afterwards.

In other words, Muhammad spent a significant portion of his life in a monogamous marriage, because he died just over a decade after Khadija.

Also, it is noteworthy to mention that all the other wives came after prophethood. Considering the socio-political dynamics of that period, various people wanted to associate with the Prophet to form alliances, and marriages were one of the means of achieving such an important affiliation.

Of all the other women the Prophet married, Aisha bint Abu Bakr is probably the most known for many reasons. Aisha was the daughter of Abu Bakr – the closest friend of Prophet Muhammad ﷺ. Also, Aisha was a scholar in her own right and collector of thousands of Hadith. However, Aisha's prominence stems from the discussions about her alleged age at the time of marriage – due to the story of her being 6 or 9. Whilst Aisha's age is not the crux of this discourse, it cannot be overemphasized that a lot of extensive research has gone into this subject matter. Based on research, the minimum age Aisha could have been at the time of consummating her marriage was her mid-to-late teens – sixteen (16) to nineteen (19) years old. The approximation is based on various chorological analyses of historical events and other related factors; Aisha's acceptance of Islam, previous betrothal to Jubair ibn Mutim, the period between the death of Khadija bint Khuwaylid, the Prophet's marriage to Sawdah bint Zam'ah and the migration (Hijrah) to Madinah, the age and time death of Aisha's older sister Asma bint Abu Bakr, Aisha's role at the Battle of Uhud, Aisha's scholarly contributions, time of Aisha's death and other irrefutable historical facts. Another crucial point is that the Prophet faced constant criticism from traducers and opponents of Islam, and every aspect of his life was scrutinized and often derided. Yet, there is no document in recorded history mentioning the age of Aisha as one of the topical bases of criticism. For purposes of clarification, the absence of evidence is not because it was the ethos, rather, it was because those who existed at the time had an idea about Aisha's actual age. Furthermore, it was not customary at the time of the Prophet, nor is there any evidence to support the notion, that anyone in 7th century Arabian society, especially the companions, practiced child marriage. Although customs evolve over different periods, there is still no historical evidence of a pervading practice in the Arabian society of that particular era. More importantly, the Quran does not mention it, neither did the Prophet specifically mention nor sanction such a practice. The Quran actually stipulates a level of physical and mental maturity – intellectual capability and sound mental judgement before marriage. It is crucial to emphasize the actual Islamic position on such matters, so some deluded people would not hide under the cloak of religion to perpetrate crimes against the girl-child. Sexual perversion comes in various shades, and religion must never be associated with, nor used as an excuse for committing such abominable perversions.

Finally, those who claim to be followers of Islam are meant to follow the example of Prophet Muhammad ﷺ. The life of the Prophet can be an exemplary marriage model for men. The choice of wife does not always have to be younger. Similarly, women should not shy away from marrying younger men. Rather than concentrate on the pursuit of younger girls, there are many societies with single older women, especially widowed, who require marriage. After all, a majority of the Prophet's wives were widows – food for thought!

CHAPTER 21

THE PROPHET-SERVANT

Prophet Muhammad ﷺ was not a prophet-king like Solomon and David respectively, even though he had the opportunity to be a king and establish a monarchy. Rather, the Prophet humbly chose to be a "prophet –servant", and in another narration, a "servant-messenger".

THE PROPHET'S ACTIVISM

Activism can be described as social or political action with change being an intended objective. Prophet Muhammad ﷺ brought about change that impacted his milieu, region and the world. The socio-political actions taken by the Prophet and ensuing manifestations are a testament to his activism credentials, especially when analysed from a contemporary perspective.

The following are some examples of the Prophet's roles, exemplified with relatable latter-day explications.

The Statesman

Prophet Muhammad ﷺ was Head of State – President and Commander-in-Chief in the contemporary parlance, and he governed with a constitution. Notably, following the return of Prophet Muhammad ﷺ from exile, he took control and magnanimously granted amnesty to everyone who had killed and persecuted his followers for years.

Despite various domestic commitments, Prophet Muhammad ﷺ amicably handled foreign and international relations. As the Head-of-State and Commander –in- Chief, he established diplomatic ties with other countries and sent emissaries to other world leaders. Some notable emissary missions include the Negus of Abyssinia, Heraclius the Caesar of Byzantium, Muqawqis of Egypt and Khosrow II of Persia. The Prophet employed diplomacy in dealing with international and domestic issues, particularly municipal and regional matters. Some notable events that occurred include the first migration of Muslim contingents to Abyssinia, the mission to Taif, the Pledges of al-Aqabah, the Constitution of Madinah and the Treaty of Hudaybiyyah. Prophet Muhammad ﷺ maintained his nobility in all his political engagements. The statesmanship of Prophet Muhammad ﷺ sets an ideal template for how nation states could be governed, and his unique leadership style serves as an admonition to all those who practice tyranny under the guise of governance.

We are most knowing of what they say, and you are not over them a tyrant. But remind by the Qur'an whoever fears My threat. – Quran 50:45

The Emancipationist

The relationship between Prophet Muhammad ﷺ and Zayd ibn Harithah affirm the prophet's emancipationist credentials. A very young Zayd ibn Harithah was on a trip with his mother when he was captured by raiders from another Arab tribe. Zayd's family tried in vain to find him, but he had been sold into slavery. Hakim ibn Hizam was the man who bought Zayd, and he gifted Zayd to his aunt named Khadija bint Khuwaylid. When Khadija later married Muhammad (before prophethood), she presented Zayd to him as a wedding present. The bond between Muhammad and Zayd grew stronger from the point of their initial meeting.

On a particular occasion, Zayd encountered his kinsmen who had travelled to Makkah, and he decided to send a message home to allay their grief regarding his unfortunate kidnap years before. Upon receiving the message from the travellers, Zayd's father and uncle travelled to Makkah with the intention of rescuing Zayd, no matter the cost of manumission.

When Zayd's family located Muhammad, they offered him any amount for Zayd's freedom. However, the Prophet stated he was not interested in the payment for Zayd's freedom but preferred to defer to Zayd for his position on the matter. Remarkably, Zayd informed his father and uncle that he had observed something extraordinary about the man known as Muhammad and he would not leave his company for anyone. Following Zayd's decision, Muhammad proceeded to do something extraordinary and publicly adopted Zayd as a son, legally. At the time, such an act of manumission and adoption was unprecedented.

From an historical viewpoint, the slavery enterprise was a global practice linked with the commoditization of human beings, and the cheapest means of accessing labour. Empires, nations and societies needed cheap and often exploitative labour to achieve their socioeconomic objectives. Sadly, labour supply involved the kidnapping of random people and was basically a survival of the fittest matter. Just as it was in many societies, the strong preyed on the weak and the Arabs were no exception. The modus operandi of Arab slave traders was to capture anyone, regardless of skin colour or ethnicity. In comparison to the Western slave traders; who primarily concentrated on Africans, particularly during the transatlantic slave trade, Arabs captured anyone, even among themselves. Arabs were of different shades – from darker to lighter skin tones, so all groups were susceptible to Arab slavers. Susceptibility to slavery was why lineage and tribal association were integral to Arab culture. Without any affiliation with a strong family or tribe, people were susceptible to being enslaved.

Another interesting point to note is that it was not in the best economic interest for the Arab slave traders to convey the message of Islam to captives. The situation is pathetically ironic, because if the Arab slavers were truly Islamic and understood the teachings of Islam, they would not have any involvement in the slavery enterprise. This situation can be described as an oxymoronic complexity that seemingly attempts to justify slavery by the weighing of available options. Ideally, such a decision should not just consider the options of not teaching Islam to captives or not enslaving non-Muslims, rather, the decision should focus on Islam being antithetical to the practice of slavery. Furthermore, the concept of slavery in Western societies is divergent from slavery in Eastern societies, particularly after Islam was revived in the Arabian Peninsula under Prophet Muhammad ﷺ. During that era, there were various reasons people were in captivity; either through being the kidnapped victims of marauding slavers or as prisoners of war. Regardless of how people came into captivity, Islam generally encouraged manumission of the captives – freeing of slaves. This, however, does not mean everyone in the Arabian region adhered to the teachings of Islam, especially after the era of the Prophet. Nonetheless, it is crucial to emphasize what Islam stipulates, and highlight the systematic approach of Prophet Muhammad ﷺ towards the eradication of slavery – a process that came to be known as abolitionism many centuries later.

Prophet Muhammad ﷺ advocated utmost compassion in the treatment of servants:

> *Your slaves are your brothers and Allah has put them under your command. So whoever has a brother under his command should feed him of what he eats and dress him of what he wears. Do not ask them (slaves) to do things beyond their capacity (power) and if you do so, then help them.*

As it was with other societal reforms, the approach was phased. For instance, those who insisted on maintaining their bondsmen, either for domestic work or whatever reasons; the caveat was to treat all those under their authority with dignity and have a clear path to manumission, especially if freedom was requested by the bonded. Also, the terms of slavery were not intergenerational

– children were freeborn. From a sociological position, such a well-planned and instituted framework facilitated upward mobility. On one occasion Prophet Muhammad ﷺ counselled the people about the importance of obeying their leadership, and specifically cited the scenario of a slave becoming the leader – whoever it is, must be obeyed.

> *I counsel you to have taqwa (fear) of Allah, and to listen and obey [your leader], even if a slave were to become your Ameer.*
> – Prophet Muhammad ﷺ

The Prophet's compassionate position was one of the main reasons, slaves and those in servitude trooped into Islam; because Islam propagated equality of all human beings. Conversely, one of the major reasons the upper echelons of the Arabian society detested Prophet Muhammad ﷺ was because the message of Islam was affecting the status quo and giving ideas to those in the lower classes. Equality of human beings was a revolutionary concept the elite of the Arabian society were not willing to accept, hence their going to war against Islam. At that point in history, slavery was embedded in many societies, including the Arabs, and Islam came with a message that encouraged manumission and highlighted the benefits. There are various verses in the Quran that mention the freeing of human captives; Quran 2:177, Quran 4:92, Quran 5:89, Quran 9:60, Quran 90:13, etc.

From a linguistic perspective, a distinction between *Raqabah* and *Abd* must be highlighted. Generally, *Raqabah* and its variations, such as *Raqab* and *Riqab*, are the words used to describe those in servitude to others in the Quran. The literal translation is "the neck" – freeing the neck of the enslaved. Contextually, the ideal translation for Raqabah should be servant, though some translators of the Quran often opted for translating Raqab as slave.

Abd and its variations, like *Abid*, mean "slave", though in the context of worship. Ideally, Abd (slave) should only be in the context of slave of Allah. Below are a few examples in the Abd contextuality in the Quran:

> *[Jesus] said, "Indeed, I am the servant of Allah. He has given me the Scripture and made me a prophet.* – Quran 19:30

> *There is none in the heavens and the earth but comes unto the Most Beneficent (Allah) as a slave.* –Quran 19:93

> *And among people and moving creatures and grazing livestock are various colors similarly. Only those fear Allah, from among His servants, who have knowledge. Indeed, Allah is Exalted in Might and Forgiving.*
> – Quran 35:28

Furthermore, there are instances where Prophet Muhammad advised against utilizing the "slave" phraseology for human and interpersonal interaction.

> *Do not refer to anyone as 'my slave,' for all of you are the slaves of Allah. Rather, you should refer to him as 'my young man.' The slave should not refer to anyone as 'my lord,' but rather he should refer to him as 'my master.'*
> – Sahih al-Bukhari2414

In this regard, Abd is the ideal translation for slave and should only be used in the context of referring to a slave of Allah. Also, nobody can be an Abd to anyone. For example, the name Abdullah – portmanteau of Abd and Allah (Abd-Allah) – is a common theophoric name which means "slave of Allah". Essentially, even though certain human factors manifested the utilization of existing social classifications, only Allah is entitled the majestic honour of owning slaves. The actions of Prophet Muhammad ﷺ towards the slavery institution were unprecedented and revolutionary, especially for his time, hence, the reason why the message of Islam is emancipatory.

The Anti-Racist

From an historical perspective, Prophet Muhammad ﷺ is probably the first person in history to unequivocally condemn racism publicly. The Prophet's public declaration was not only physically witnessed by a momentous crowd but documented for later generations to read and acknowledge. Racial equality is a crucial aspect of Prophet Muhammad's Farewell Sermon; as it emphasized nobody is superior to anyone else. An excerpt from the translation goes thus:

> *O people, your Lord is one and your father Adam is one. There is no superiority of an Arab over a non-Arab, nor a non-Arab over an Arab, and neither white skin over black skin, nor black skin over white skin, except by righteousness.* – Musnad Ahmad 23489

The Prophet's public asseveration directly addressed the issue of racism and the promotion of racial equality. From that epochal moment onwards, many generations have been inspired by the stance of Prophet Muhammad ﷺ on racism and racial equality. A befitting example is the life of El-Hajj Malik El-Shabazz aka Malcolm X; as he was one of the prominent personalities in the struggle against racism. It is essential to emphasize that Malcolm X grew up in a deeply segregated United States, and the milieu shaped his disposition. However, a paradigm shift that challenged his preconceived notions on race occurred during Malcolm's pilgrimage (Hajj) to Mecca in 1964. The journey had a profound effect on Malcolm X and completely changed his worldview. Malcolm X's epiphanic realization was contained in the famous letter he wrote from Mecca. The following are excerpts from Malcolm X's Mecca letter: [40]

"I have never before witnessed such sincere hospitality and the practice of true brotherhood as I have seen it here in Arabia. In fact, what I have seen and experienced on this pilgrimage has forced me to 'rearrange' much of my own thought-pattern, and to toss aside some of my previous conclusions. This "adjustment to reality" wasn't too difficult for me to undergo, because despite my firm conviction in whatever I believe, I have always tried to keep an open mind, which is absolutely necessary to reflect the flexibility that must go hand in hand with anyone with intelligent quest for truth never comes to an end."

"There are Muslims of all colors and ranks here in Mecca from all parts of this earth, During the past seven days of this holy pilgrimage, while undergoing the rituals of the hajj [pilgrimage], I have eaten from the same plate, drank from the same glass, slept on the same bed or rug, while praying to the same God—not only with some of this earth's most powerful kings, cabinet members, potentates and other forms of political and religious rulers —but also with fellow-Muslims whose skin was the whitest of white, whose eyes were the bluest of blue, and whose hair was the blondest of blond—yet it was the first time in my life that I didn't see them as 'white' men. I could look into their faces and see that these didn't regard themselves as 'white.'"

"Their belief in the Oneness of God (Allah) had actually removed the 'white' from their minds"

"If white Americans could accept the religion of Islam, if they could accept the Oneness of God (Allah) they too could then sincerely accept the Oneness of Men, and cease to measure others always in terms of their "difference in color". And with racism now plaguing in America like an incurable cancer all thinking Americans should be more respective to Islam as an already proven solution to the race problem."

"But as America's insane obsession with racism leads her up the suicidal path, nearer and nearer to the precipice that leads to the bottomless pits below, I do

believe that whites of the younger generation, in the colleges and universities, through their own young, less hampered intellect, will see the 'handwriting on the wall' and turn for spiritual salvation to the religion of Islam and force the older generation of American whites to turn with them…this is the only way white America can worn off the inevitable disaster that racism always leads to, and Hitler's Nazi Germany was best proof of this."

Notably, it is symbolic that it was during the pilgrimage (Hajj) that Prophet Muhammad ﷺ gave his farewell sermon that espoused racial equality – condemned racism and accentuated the universality of Islam. And it was during the pilgrimage (Hajj) that Malcolm X experienced an ignited consciousness about how the universality of Islam can tackle racism.

Sadly, racism is still a major issue in the United States and other parts of the world. Racism and racial inequality are prevalent in many societies, and the so-called 'Muslim' dominated countries are not exempt from this destructive disease. Racism is a societal problem globally. To address the racism menace, the teachings of Prophet Muhammad ﷺ can be inculcated to attain racial equality. From a spiritual perspective, racism is a manifestation of arrogance within – a disease of the heart. Islamic exegesis affirms the first racist was Iblis (Satan) – who boasted about being better than Adam. In other words, racists have a lot in common with Satan – they are satanic. Prophet Muhammad ﷺ is the perfect role model not Satan, so the racial equality message is crucial to humanity. Furthermore, a critical derivative from the Farewell Sermon is the essential difference between anti-racism and non-racism. Whilst non-racists may not overtly exhibit discriminatory views, they also do not work against racism. Progressively, non-racists can up the ante to the level of anti-racists and emulate the anti-racism stance of Prophet Muhammad ﷺ; who publicly declared the importance of racial equality and worked towards the eradication of systemic racism. In view of contemporary realities, Islam is the ideal panacea to all forms of racism – individualized and systemic.

The Environmentalist

Prophet Muhammad ﷺ was environmentally conscious and in one of his sayings, he stated; "removing a harmful object from the road is a charity". The Prophet showed compassion to every living thing, including plants and animals. Prophet Muhammad said in a Hadith: "In every living being there is a reward for charity." Humans and other creations such as animals, plants and other organisms exist as part of an environment – an intricately woven and well-balanced ecosystem. There are interactions and interrelationships between creations and the existence of different types of symbiosis – mutualistic, commensalistic and parasitic. Whatever the complexity of the existing relationships within the ecosystem, all creatures have a fundamental right to exist. The Quran mentions the existence of communities among all living creatures and analogizes their existence to human communities:

> *And there is no creature on [or within] the earth or bird that flies with its wings except [that they are] communities like you. We have not neglected in the Register a thing. Then unto their Lord they will be gathered.* – Quran 6:38

Animals: Various animals are mentioned in the Quran, and there are numerous teachings of Prophet Muhammad ﷺ that emphasize the importance of being compassionate to animals. There is a famous Hadith about a prostitute being forgiven by Allah of her sins, because she quenched the thirst of a dog.

> *Allah had once forgiven a prostitute. She passed by a dog panting near a well. Seeing that thirst had nearly killed him, she took off her shoe, tied it to her*

scarf, and drew up some water. Allah forgave her for that.

– Sahih al-Bukhari 3143

There is a narration by Prophet Muhammad ﷺ about an incident, which involved an ant and a prophet from another age that highlights the rights of tiny creatures. As the story goes, there was a prophet from a previous era resting under a tree and an ant bit him, so in reaction, that prophet decided to burn the ant's dwelling place – formicary. That prophet's excessive reaction necessitated an admonition from Allah:

> *Narrated Abu Huraira: The Messenger of Allah, PBUH), said, "An ant bit a prophet among the prophets, so he ordered for the colony of ants to be burned. Allah revealed to him: One ant has bitten you and you destroy a nation among the nations that praise Allah?"* – Sahih Muslim 2241

Prophet Muhammad ﷺ generally warned against animal cruelty and in some instances, rebuked the killing of animals for sport and recreation:

> *Narrated Hisham bin Zaid: Anas and I went to Al-Hakam bin Aiyub. Anas saw some boys shooting at a tied hen. Anas said, "The Prophet has forbidden the shooting of tied or confined animals."*
> –Sahih al-Bukhari 5513

In a related Hadith, Prophet Muhammad stated:

> *Narrated Abdullah ibn Umar: The Messenger of Allah, ﷺ, said, "If someone kills so much as a sparrow, or anything larger, without a just cause, Allah Almighty will ask him about it on the Day of Resurrection." It was said, "O Messenger of Allah, what is a just cause?" The Prophet said, "A*

just cause is that you slaughter it for food, but you should not cut off its head and throw it aside."– Sunan al-Nasai 4445

Narrated Abdullah: We were on a journey with the Messenger of Allah, ﷺ, *and he went out to relieve himself. We saw a red sparrow that had two chicks with her and we took her chicks, so the sparrow started to flap her wings. The Prophet came to us and he said, "Who has upset her by taking her children? Give her children back to her."*– Sunan Abi Dawud 5268

Narrated Abdullah ibn Ja'far: The Prophet, ﷺ, *entered a garden among the Ansar. When a camel saw the Prophet, it started weeping and making sounds as its tears flowed. The Prophet came to it and patted it on the head, so it became silent. The Prophet said: Who is the master of this camel? To whom does it belong? Do you not fear Allah regarding this animal that Allah has put in your possession? Verily, she has complained to me that you keep her hungry and tired.* – Sunan Abi Dawud 2549

Water: Water is the essence of life and is one of the many blessings from Allah. The Quran mentions water and watering of the earth as a blessing in various verses and one of such verses connects the role of water (rain) to foods grown for human consumption:

And He is the One Who sends down rain from the sky—causing all kinds of plants to grow—producing green stalks from which We bring forth clustered grain. And from palm trees come clusters of dates hanging within reach. ⸢There are⸣ also gardens of grapevines, olives, and pomegranates, similar ⸢in shape⸣ but dissimilar ⸢in taste⸣. Look at their fruit as it yields and ripens! Indeed, in these are signs for people who believe.– Quran 6:99

Water is an essential natural resource. Generally, conservation protects the environment through the responsible use of natural resources, and preservation protects the environment from the abuse effectuated by harmful human activities. Prophet Muhammad ﷺ was concerned about the conservation and preservation of water and warned against wastage.

> *Narrated Abdullah ibn Amr: The Messenger of Allah, peace and blessings be upon him, passed by Sa'd while he was performing ablution. The Prophet said, "What is this excess?" Sa'd said, "Is there excess with water in ablution?" The Prophet said, "Yes, even if you were on the banks of a flowing river."* – Sunan Ibn Majah 425

Food: Food is directly linked to water because water is required for food production. In this regard, food, like water, is also a blessing from Allah. The Quran states:

> *O believers! Eat from the good things We have provided for you. And give thanks to Allah if you ˹truly˺ worship Him ˹alone˺.*– Quran 2:172

Furthermore, the Quran cautions against being wasteful:

> *O Children of Adam! Dress properly whenever you are at worship. Eat and drink, but do not waste. Surely He does not like the wasteful.*
> – Quran 7:31

> *Surely the wasteful are ˹like˺ brothers to the devils. And the Devil is ever ungrateful to his Lord.*
> – Quran 17:27

In a Hadith, Prophet Muhammad ﷺ cautioned against food wastage and gluttony:

> *Narrated Jabir: The Messenger of Allah* ﷺ*, said, "The food of one person is enough for two, the food of two is enough for four, and the food of four is enough for eight." –* Saḥiḥ Muslim 2059

In a related Hadith:

> *The son of Adam cannot fill a vessel worse than his stomach, as it is enough for him to take a few bites to straighten his back. If he cannot do it, then he may fill it with a third of his food, a third of his drink, and a third of his breath. –* Sunan al-Tirmidh 2380

From an ecological perspective, everything human beings consume has its implication on the environment and leaves an ecological footprint. Eco-footprint is the proportion of land and water required to support anyone's overall consumption levels, and the reabsorption process of the waste generated. For instance, research endeavours in the area of water footprint, reveal that the average amount of water required to produce a 150-gram apple is 125 litres.[41] In order words, throwing away one apple is like wasting 125 litres of water. A 200-gram banana equals 160 litres of water and a kilogram of beef is 15400 litres of water on average. Wasting a hamburger is the equivalent to wasting about 2500 litres of water.

The highlighted examples underscore the environmental implications of wastage. Manifestly, there are environmental implications of wastage, including physiological implications of overeating, especially obesity.

Purification: Environmental purification is essential for the survival of humans and other species. Mankind must prevent environmental degradation, and care for their environment and the habitat of other living organisms. Prophet Muhammad ﷺ emphasized the importance of not just self-purification, but environmental purification. In a Hadith, the Prophet said, "removing a harmful object from the road is a charity". Also, the Prophet warned against irresponsibility and abuse of the environment:

> *Beware of the three acts that cause you to be cursed: relieving yourselves in shaded places (that people utilize), in a walkway or in a watering place.*

Prophet Muhammad ﷺ encouraged the plating of trees, and he highlighted the environmental benefits generally, and the spiritual benefits specifically:

> *There is none amongst the Muslims who plants a tree or sows seeds, and then a bird, or a person or an animal eats from it, but is regarded as a charitable gift for him.* – Sahih al-Bukhari 2320

Evidently, tree planting has numerous environmental benefits, particularly in the absorption of carbon dioxide (CO_2) emissions. Trees purify the air through the absorption of air pollutants and particulates. Human beings must use the earth's natural resources responsibly and be cognizant of the harmonious relationship between livings things and the environment.

> *Have you not seen that Allah has subjected for you whatever is in the heavens and whatever is on the earth, and has lavished His favours upon you, both seen and unseen? ˹Still˺ there are some who dispute about Allah without knowledge, or guidance, or an enlightening scripture.* – Quran 31:20

CHAPTER 22

THE PROPHETIC MISSION

Prophet Muhammad ﷺ came to complete the same message of his predecessors – Noah, Abraham, Moses, Jesus and thousands of others who have traversed the earth that are unknown – unrevealed to human beings.

> *And We have already sent messengers before you. Among them are those [whose stories] We have related to you, and among them are those [whose stories] We have not related to you. And it was not for any messenger to bring a sign [or verse] except by permission of Allah. So when the command of Allah comes, it will be concluded [i.e., judged] in truth, and the falsifiers will thereupon lose [all].* – Quran 40:78

The prophetic mission of Prophet Muhammad ﷺ can be appreciated as a continuation of the same message about the oneness of God. Islam is not founded on starting an entirely new religion, but the completion of a precedent religious system. Prophet Muhammad ﷺ acknowledged mankind as one family and that all previous prophets were his brothers and were sent from the same source. Furthermore, the prophets may have been of different skin colours, ethnicities and nations, but shared a bond. This unique bond is stated in a Hadith:

> *Narrated Abu Huraira: Allah's Apostle said, "Both in this world and in the Hereafter, I am the nearest of all the people to Jesus, the son of Mary. The prophets are paternal brothers; their mothers are different, but their religion is one."* – Sahih al-Bukhari 3443, Book 60, Hadith 113

Islam is as old as time and the meaning remain unchanged. Islam simply means "The Submission" and those who 'submit' to God or the 'submitters' are Muslims. There is no ambiguity of definition or clarity required for the meaning. The concept of submission applies to all Prophets and Messengers from God. The prophets' regions, nations, skin colour, languages and tongues may have been different, but the meaning of Islam remained the same in their respective dialects –To Submit. The message of Islam is a unifying call that does not exclude anyone on any basis and emphasises equality of all humans. Islam is antipodal to the superiority doctrine that some other ideologies and religions profess. Before the revivification of Islam under Prophet Muhammad ﷺ, the previous prophets sent to all nations across the globe, spoke various languages, other than Arabic. During the time of their prophetic mission, predecessor prophets presented Islam (submission) in their respective dialects and mother tongues; however, that did not affect the authenticity of the message. Arabic was the prevailing language where Prophet Muhammad ﷺ emerged and was necessary of its immediate recipients. The Arabs, just like the other initial recipients of the message from their respective prophets and messengers, are a microcosm of the wider world. The message of Islam can be delivered in any language, so Arabic and Islam should not be conflated – these are two separate entities.

Islam's transformative message impacted billions of lives globally. The transformation was initiated by the Prophet and the initial impact was felt by the companions. For instance, the second Caliph of Islam, Umar ibn Al-Khattab acknowledged how humiliated they used to be until Islam gave them honour. Historically, there exists no documented record of a book – message (Quran), transforming a bunch of nobodies and catapulting them into global prominence. The Arabs were not an advanced civilization nor were they considered among the superpowers of their era, but Islam transformed literal nonentities into globally renowned propagators and upholders of peace, justice and harmony. Essentially, there is no natural explanation as to how one man – Muhammad – changed the entire world, except by divinity.

GLOBAL IMPACT

The prophetic mission of Prophet Muhammad ﷺ has had global impact. The message of an unlettered man from the deserts of the Arabian Peninsula transformed a backward people to a great civilization. The Prophet achieved a stratospheric rise within a relatively short period – 23 years. In 23 years, the Prophet was forced to migrate from his land of birth and was sanctioned, but he returned victorious as ruler and granted amnesty to all, including traducers and persecutors. There is hardly anywhere in the world where Islam and the name of the Prophet Muhammad is not known. There are almost 2 billion Muslims on the planet and Islam is set to be the dominant world religion in a couple of decades. Certainly, no sword or army made Islam the fastest growing religion in the contemporary world. The growth of Islam has been largely organic and is not solely due to the Muslim efforts – it is divine intervention.

It is He who has sent His Messenger with guidance and the religion of truth to manifest it over all religion, although they who associate others with Allah dislike it. – Quran 9:33

The life of Prophet Muhammad ﷺ can be appreciated from the perspectives of the everyday man with regular interhuman relations, daily routines and generally dealing with life's various challenges. Portraying the different roles and situations from the Prophet's life, underscores the importance of finding the right balance between spirituality and dealing with the realities of our daily lives. The Prophet did not live as a recluse or in perpetual seclusion but balanced his spirituality with the challenges of living and survival.

Largely, the issues the Prophet addressed will manifest in our lives, one way or another. The issues could be personal, interpersonal and communal. Human beings have been guided with the proper etiquette on how to deal with every aspect of existence: hygiene, sex, family, neighbours, community, economy, politics, international relations, etc. Every aspect of life was covered! The Quran describes Prophet Muhammad 🕌 as an excellent example:

> *Indeed, in the Messenger of Allah you have an excellent example for whoever has hope in Allah and the Last Day, and remembers Allah often.*
> –Quran 33:21

SELECTED OPINIONS

Harvard Law School commissioned a "Words of Justice" exhibition circa 2012.[42] The gallery was situated on some faculty walls and it featured 33 quotations – culled from 350 submitted – about law and justice in history. In recognition of Prophet Muhammad 🕌, one of the quotes displayed during the exhibition was an excerpt from a Quran verse (Quran 4:135):

> *"O ye who believe! stand out firmly for justice, as witnesses to Allah, even as against yourselves, or your parents, or your kin, and whether it be (against) rich or poor: for Allah can best protect both…"*

Michael H. Hart, an American astrophysicist, published a book in 1978 titled "The 100: A Ranking of the Most Influential Persons in History".[43] The book is based on a compiled list of exceptional human beings who had the most influence on human history. Following the research, various criteria and categories of selection, the person who earned the top position on the list was Prophet Muhammad 🕌. In "The 100" book, Michael H. Hart stated:

My choice of Muhammad to lead the list of the world's most influential persons may surprise some readers and may be questioned by others, but he was the only man in history who was supremely successful on both the religious and secular level. – Michael H. Hart

James Albert Michener, an American writer and author, who wrote a piece titled "Islam: The Misunderstood Religion" in the May 1955 issue of Reader's Digest, stated: [44]

No other religion in history spread so rapidly as Islam. The West has widely believed that this surge of religion was made possible by the sword. But no modern scholar accepts this idea, and the Qur'an is explicit in the support of the freedom of conscience.– James Albert Michener

William Montgomery Watt, a Scottish Orientalist, historian, writer and priest, in his 1953 book titled "Muhammad at Mecca", stated:[45]

His readiness to undergo persecutions for his beliefs, the high moral character of the men who believed in him and looked up to him as leader, and the greatness of his ultimate achievement - all argue his fundamental integrity. To suppose Muhammad an impostor raises more problems than it solves. Moreover, none of the great figures of history is so poorly appreciated in the West as Muhammad. – William Montgomery Watt

Annie Besant, a British writer, orator, women's rights activist, theosophist and educationist, in her 1932 publication titled The Life and Teachings of Muhammad, stated:[46]

It is impossible for anyone who studies the life and character of the great Prophet

of Arabia, who knows how he taught and how he lived, to feel anything but reverence for that mighty Prophet, one of the great messengers of the Supreme. And although in what I put to you I shall say many things which may be familiar to many, yet I myself feel whenever I re-read them, a new way of admiration, a new sense of reverence for that mighty Arabian teacher. – Annie Besant

Laura Veccia Vaglieri, an Italian Orientalist, author and Professor at University of Naples "L'Orientale", in her 1925 book titled "An Interpretation of Islam", stated:[47]

Muhammad as a preacher of the religion of God was gentle and merciful, even towards his personal enemies. In him were blended justice and mercy two of the noblest qualities which the human mind can conceive. – Laura Veccia Vaglieri

Mahatma Gandhi was an Indian anti-colonial nationalist and nonviolent resistance advocate. An excerpt from his Young India publication, circa 1924 stated:[48]

I became more than ever convinced that it was not the sword that won a place for Islam in those days in the scheme of life. It was the rigid simplicity, the utter self-effacement of the Prophet, the scrupulous regard for his pledges, his intense devotion to his friends and followers, his intrepidity, his fearlessness, his absolute trust in God and in his own mission. These and not the sword carried everything before them and surmounted every trouble. – Mahatma Gandhi

De Lacy Evans O'Leary, a British Orientalist, stated in his 1923 book titled "Islam at the Cross Roads: A Brief Survey of the Present Position and Problems of the World of Islam": [49]

History makes it clear, however, that the legend of fanatical Muslims, sweeping through the world and forcing Islam at the point of the sword upon conquered races is one of the most fanatically absurd myths that historians have ever repeated–De Lacy Evans O'Leary

Herbert George Wells was an English writer, and in his 1920 book titled "Outline of History", he described the tremendous impact of the Prophet's Farewell Sermon, thus:[50]

The reader will note that the first paragraph sweeps away all plunder and blood feuds among the followers of Islam. The last makes the believing Negro the equal of the Caliph. They may not be sublime words, as certain utterances of Jesus of Nazareth are sublime; but they established in the world a great tradition of dignified fair dealing, they breathe a spirit of generosity, and they are human and workable. They created a society more free from widespread cruelty and social oppression than any society had ever been in the world before. – H.G. Wells

Washington Irving, an American writer, historian and diplomat, in his 1920 book titled "Life of Mahomet", stated:[51]

In his private dealings he was just. He treated friends and strangers, the rich and poor, the powerful and the weak, with equity, and was beloved by the common people for the affability with which he received them, and listened to their complaints. – Washington Irving

Marcus Dods, a Scottish author and biblical scholar, in his 1905 book titled "Mohammed, Buddha, and Christ: Four Lectures on Natural and Revealed Religion", stated:[52]

He saw truth about God which his fellow-men did not see, and he had an irresistible inward impulse to publish the truth. In respect to this later qualification Mohammed may stand comparison with the most courageous of the heroic prophets of Israel. For the truth's sake he risked his life, he suffered daily persecution for years, and eventually banishment, the loss of property, of the goodwill of his fellow-citizens, and of the confidence of his friends — he suffered, in short, as much as any man can suffer short of death, which he only escaped by flight, and yet he unflinchingly proclaimed his message. No bribe, threat or inducement, could silence him. — Marcus Dods

Thomas Carlyle, a Scottish essayist, philosopher, mathematician, translator and historian, in his 1884 book titled "On Heroes, Hero-Worship, and The Heroic in History", stated:[53]

Our current hypothesis about Mahomet, that he was a scheming Impostor, a Falsehood incarnate, that his religion is a mere mass of quackery and fatuity, begins really to be now untenable to any one. The lies, which well-meaning zeal has heaped round this man, are disgraceful to ourselves only. — Thomas Carlyle

Stanley Lane-Poole, a British writer and Orientalist, in his 1882 book titled "The Speeches & Table-talk of the Prophet Mohammad: Chosen and Translated, With Introduction and Notes", stated:[54]

The day of Mohammad's greatest triumph over his enemies was also the day of his grandest victory over himself. He freely forgave the Koreysh all the years of sorrow and cruel scorn in which they had afflicted him and gave an amnesty to the whole population of Mekka. Four criminals whom justice condemned made up Mohammad's proscription list when he entered as a conqueror to the city of his bitterest enemies. The army followed his example, and entered quietly and peacefully; no house was robbed, no women insulted. One thing alone suffered destruction. Going to the Kaaba, Mohammad stood before each of the three hundred and sixty idols, and pointed to it with his staff, saying, "Truth is come and falsehood is fled away"; and at these words his attendants hewed them down, and all the idols and household gods of Mekka and round about were destroyed. It was thus that Mohammad entered again his native city. Through all the annals of conquest there is no triumphant entry comparable to this one.

– Stanley Lane-Poole

Reginald Bosworth Smith, an English author, Harrow schoolmaster and fellow of Trinity College Oxford, in his 1874 book titled "Mohammed and Mohammedanism: Lectures Delivered at the Royal Institution of Great Britain in February and March 1874", stated:[55]

Head of the State as well as of the Church, he was Caesar and Pope in one; but he was Pope without Pope's pretensions, Caesar without the legions of Caesar. Without a standing army, without a bodyguard, without a palace, without a fixed revenue, if ever any man had the right to say that he ruled by a right Divine, it was Mohammed; for he had all the power without its instruments and without its supports.– Reginald Bosworth Smith

Alphonse de Lamartine, a French author and Statesman, described Prophet Muhammad ﷺ as philosopher, orator, apostle, legislator and warrior in his 1854 book titled "Histoire de la Turquie" (History of Turkey).[56]
The following excerpt is from the aforementioned book:

If greatness of purpose, smallness of means, and astounding results are the three criteria of human genius, who could dare compare any great man in modern history with Muhammad? The most famous men created arms, laws, and empires

only. They founded, if anything at all, no more than material powers which often away before their eyes. This man moved not only armies, legislations, empires, peoples and rumbled dynasties, but millions of men in one-third of the then inhabited world; and more than that he moved the altars, the gods, the religions, the ideas, the beliefs and souls. On the basis of a Book, every letter of which has become law, he created a spiritual nationality which blended together peoples of every tongue and of every race. – Alphonse de Lamartine

Finally, a historic and profound statement that typifies the essence of the prophetic mission was made by Abu Bakr – the first Caliph of Islam. The message came at an epochal period in history; right after the death of Prophet Muhammad ﷺ.

No doubt! Whoever worshipped Muhammad, then Muhammad is dead, but whoever worshipped Allah, then Allah is Alive and shall never die.
– Abu Bakr

Despite the oppositions and machinations, Islam flourished and has continued to grow since the death of the Prophet, primarily because Allah is ever-living. Prophet Muhammad ﷺ died circa 632 and his impact has been long-lasting, particularly because of his greatest and time-transcending miracle: The Quran.

Muhammad is no more than a messenger; other messengers have gone before him. If he were to die or to be killed, would you regress into disbelief? Those who do so will not harm Allah whatsoever. And Allah will reward those who are grateful. – Quran 3:144

CHAPTER 23

QURAN

Had We sent down this Quran upon a mountain, you would have certainly seen it humbled and torn apart in awe of Allah. We set forth such comparisons for people, ˹so˺ perhaps they may reflect.
– Quran 59:21

The Quran is clearly an extraordinary book in a class by itself: a captivating compendium with unprecedented inimitability and incomparable originality, which has maintained its pristine form since its revelation. The Quran has a transcendental essence; whereby the same verses can be interpreted historically for contextuality and reinterpreted contemporarily for topical relevance. The Quran can be defined as "The Recital". Some other names by which the Quran can be referred include Book, Revelation, Criterion, Admonition, Reminder, Light, Guidance, Healing, Mercy, etc. The Quran is the pinnacle of miracles under the prophethood of Prophet Muhammad ﷺ. From an historical perspective, the miracles that are meant to have taken place were never witnessed by those who were not present at the time of the miracle. So those who came afterwards may choose to believe or doubt if the miracle ever occurred. Also, people may doubt or question if the main character associated with a particular miracle, ever existed. Based on the presupposition of scepticism, if anyone doubts whether Prophet Muhammad ﷺ ever existed, the existence of the Quran summarily nullifies such a notion.

The exceptionality of the Quran is because it is the only existing miracle on earth, and it is readily accessible for authentication and examination, via any procedure, most especially the scientific method. Furthermore, notable people in history are usually assessed by their contributions to the cause of humanity. All great men in history, who made their indelible contributions to mankind, are assessed by their greatest work – *magnum opus*. The greatest work of Prophet Muhammad ﷺ is the Quran. The matter of Prophet Muhammad ﷺ becomes more intriguing, because there is no historical record about his literacy, however, he marvelled the great intellectuals of his time and successive generations. At the core of the puzzle was, how could someone without any formal education, create such a spectacular book.

> *Your companion [i.e., Muhammad] has not strayed, nor has he erred,*
> *Nor does he speak from [his own] inclination.*
> *It is not but a revelation revealed,*
> *Taught to him by one intense in strength [i.e., Gabriel] -*
> *One of soundness. And he rose to [his] true form*
> – Quran 53:2-6

The story about the revelation process of the Quran, through Angel Jibreel (Gabriel) to Prophet Muhammad ﷺ, established he was unlettered. The first word to be revealed was *"Iqra"*, which means "Read". During the encounter, Angel Jibreel thrice instructed Muhammad "Read!" And thrice Muhammad replied, "I cannot read". Contextually, the instruction to read also serves as an encouragement to strive for enlightenment.

> *Read, in the Name of your Lord Who created—*
> *created humans from a clinging clot.*
> *Read! And your Lord is the Most Generous,*
> *Who taught by the pen—*
> *taught humanity what they knew not.*
> – Quran 96:1-5

A comparative analysis with other religious scriptures affirms the Quran stands out for its uniqueness, transmission and syntax. The sequence and rhythmic structure, characterized by the assonance at the end of the verses, is a rarity, and is incomparable to any other book. Audaciously, the Quran is the only book in history, with an open challenge to mankind; direct from God The Creator. Since the Quran was revealed, Mankind has been openly challenged to produce just a verse that is similar to any of what is contained in the Quran. A few verses in the Quran emphasizing its indisputable uniqueness include:

Say, ˹O Prophet,˺ "If ˹all˺ humans and jinn were to come together to produce the equivalent of this Quran, they could not produce its equal, no matter how they supported each other." – Quran 17:88

Or do they say, "He has fabricated it?" Say, "Then produce ten surahs like it, fabricated, and call upon whomever you can apart from Allah, if you are truthful. – Quran 11:13

Do they say that the Messenger has himself composed the Qur'an? Say: 'In that case bring forth just one surah like it and call on all whom you can, except Allah, to help you if you are truthful. – Quran 10:38

QURAN FEATURES

The following are some of the features that make the Quran exceptional.

Divine Connectivity

One of the unique features of the Quran is the direct relation of the words without any intermediaries. The Quran is literally the word of God.

There are numerous sections of the Quran that instruct the reader – reciter to "Say". In particular, there is an *Ayah* (verse) where Allah responds directly to a prospective question to emphasize His accessibility.

> *And when My servants ask you about Me—indeed, I am near; I respond to the call of the caller when he calls upon Me. So let them respond to Me and let them have faith in Me, that they may become prudent.* – Quran 2:186

From a grammatical perspective, the verse (Quran 2:186) can be analysed as a conversation that involves three discussants: first-person, second-person and third-person. For illustrative purposes only, the 'first-person' in this scenario is Allah, the second-person is The Prophet and the third-person represents His creation (servants). Ideally, the conversational structure should keep all the discussants, actively engaged from beginning to end; instruction from the first-person to the second-person regarding a prospective question by third-person: "when My servants ask you about Me". Following the same conversational structure; instruction from first-person to the second-person regarding a response to a prospective question by the third-person, it should be: "tell them I am near". Based on human logic, the conversation should have gone thus: "when My servants ask you about Me – tell them I am near." Rather, in the Quran, the second-person is bypassed and the first-person responds to the third-person directly: "indeed I am near". Thus: "when My servants ask you about Me – indeed, I am near".

Essentially, this verse (Quran 2:186), is emphasizing that no intermediaries are required to communicate with God The Creator, as is the case with some religions, religious traditions and cultures. In Islam, Muslims are meant to communicate with God directly and not through anyone; clergymen nor supposed saints and especially not through Prophet Muhammad ﷺ.

Accordingly, anyone who wants to sincerely establish a relationship with their Creator, can communicate directly, and shall be guided aright. This direct communication process can be likened to some type of superfast quantum frequency connectivity. Contextually, the verse (Quran 2:186) also explicates another verse about the closeness of Allah to His creation.

And We have already created man and know what his soul whispers to him, and We are closer to him than [his] jugular vein – Quran 50:16

Basically, if Allah is that close to His creation (closer than the jugular vein), when you call upon Him, He is indeed near, and can answer you directly.

Protected Scripture

The Quran's revelation came embedded with protection and preservation accompaniments. The Quran's capabilities against all forms of corruption are not primarily because of human effort, but a divine declaration. The Quran emphasizes this point in the following verse:

Verily We: It is We Who have sent down the Dhikr (i.e. the Quran) and surely, We will guard it (from corruption). –Quran 15:9

The emphasis on protecting the Quran from corruption is necessary, because of what happened to previous scriptures, particularly from a Judeo-Christian perspective. The closest chronological Holy Scripture to the Quran is the Bible. For an historical viewpoint, Islamic exegesis asserts there were Holy Scriptures that preceded the Quran, which include the Injeel (Original Gospel of Jesus), Zabur (Psalms of David), Taurat (Torah of Moses) and Suhuf (Scrolls of Abraham). However, previous scriptures – particularly the Gospel, was to a great degree, corrupted, after Jesus departed.

We have revealed to you ⌐O Prophet⌐ this Book with the truth, as a confirmation of previous Scriptures and a supreme authority on them.– Quran 5:48

At this juncture, it must be emphatically stated that, this discourse is in no way meant to ridicule or offend Christians, as these highlighted facts are well-documented within Christendom. The primary objective of this exposition is to underpin the necessity of the Quran's preservation from corruption, apropos the aforementioned verse (Quran 15:9).

As a researcher and student of comparative religion, I have owned Bibles for decades, and examined more than one version. Many years ago, I made a peculiar discovery in one of the Bible versions – the Revised Standard Version. What I discovered in the Preface section of the RSV Bible was a statement – caveat somewhat – that literally condemned the King James Version of the Bible: "The King James Version has grave defects and that these defects are so many and so serious as to call for revision."

The debates about the Bible being the actual word of God continue. Generally, Muslims are the ones that make the audacious claim that their religious scripture (Quran) is divine – directly from God – literally the word of God. And one of the reasons for that recurring assertion is the protection accompanies the Quran. The crux of the discourse is to emphasize that, if the Quran was not guarded from corruption, various people would have written their own versions, as it has been done with the Bible. Sadly, people have become so daring, they write anything they like and label it 'Bible' – a couple of examples are the so-called "Devil's Bible" aka *Codex Gigas* (Giant Book) from the 13th century and the 20th century Satanic Bible.

The preceding points highlight human tendencies and excesses and underline the necessity of protecting the Quran from all forms of corruption. Generally, anything that can be written, especially by human beings, can be corrupted.

Language Rationale

And We did not send any messenger except [speaking] in the language of his people to state clearly for them, and Allah sends astray [thereby] whom He wills and guides whom He wills. And He is the Exalted in Might, the Wise.
— Quran 14:4

Why was the Quran revealed in Arabic? To this common question, I could easily respond with: 'Allah in His infinite wisdom knows why or that Allah does what He wills'. However, analysing from a sociological position, the revelation of the Quran in Arabic can be appreciated as a wise decision. Assuming the Quran could have been revealed in any language, the logical and most effective option was the language of the receiving prophet's milieu. In the case of the Quran, the messenger-prophet was domiciled in the Arabian Peninsula, so it was crucial those in his immediate environment understood the message before it was translated and transmitted to others globally. Though a global message, the Quraysh – Arabs, can be appreciated as a microcosmic representation of any society across the globe. Whatever the language of revelation, there would still have been people pettifogging on such nugacities. For example, I have encountered people who complained that the Quran was not revealed in their native language. Such narcissistic reasoning is provincial and inimical to intellectualism. Analysing from a linguistic perspective, there are at least 7000 languages spoken in the world. Let us assume the Quran could either be revealed via two mediums: in one language or multiple languages. Does the medium the Quran was revealed alter the essentiality of the message? Messages can indeed be translated to various languages.

The Vaccination Analogy: A scientist, who happens to be Arab, discovers the cure for some infectious disease such as HIV, Ebola or Coronavirus.

Whilst developing the vaccine, the scientist conducted the research in Arabia and documented the findings and medical manuscripts in Arabic. In practical terms, the language in which the research was conducted has no correlation with the efficacy of the vaccine. Similarly, the ethnic identity of the scientist does not affect the potency of the vaccine. In such a hypothetical scenario, what is of crucial importance to humanity is that the scientist successfully developed a vaccine, and the process of making the research replicable, and producible to various languages for global benefit.

Based on this scenario, it would be absurd to reject the vaccine for flimsy reasons, such as the language and ethnic orientation of the scientist. The scenario highlighting the absurdity of those being fixated on the scientist being Arab, is the ideal similitude for those being obsessed with the language of revelation being Arabic and the ethnic identity of the prophet being Arab.

In this regard, it does not matter what language the Quran was revealed or whether Prophet Muhammad ﷺ came from the Arabian Peninsula, what is of utmost importance is the message! Essentially, the medium of conveyance is not as important as the actual message.

Preservation

In the case of the Quran, the language of revelation also serves as a mode of preservation. Apart from the Quran's divine protection guarantee, preserving the language of revelation serves as a means of authentication. In the event of any issue with the translation process, the original language of revelation can be referred to for authenticity. As a comparative example, Jesus spoke the Galilean dialect of Aramaic during his mission and his initial message would have been in the same language. The message of Jesus has been translated to many languages ever since and in the process; the authenticity of the message has been lost in translation. Contemporarily, Aramaic is endangered and may soon go extinct because it is not a widely used language. As a result, Aramaic cannot be referenced as a form of authentication for the many translations of the Bible that exist today. The Quran does not suffer from this limitation because it has been preserved in its original language of revelation.

It cannot be proven false from any angle. ˈIt isˈ a revelation from the ˈOne Who isˈ All-Wise, Praiseworthy. – Quran 41:42

Memorization

A remarkable feature of the Quran is its ease of memorization. Actually, there is no other book in the world, especially of that volume, that can be easily memorized. The message of the Quran is easy to memorize and understand, at least for those who have not abandoned their God-gifted reasoning faculties. People may not be conversant with the Arabic language but can recite and memorize the Quran. Also, this exceptional memorization characteristic serves as means of preservation. Hypothetically, if all the copies of the Quran were gathered and destroyed, the entire Quran can be reproduced immediately. Because the Quran is a book committed to memory, to salvage such a hypothetical situation, different *Hafiz* – memorizers of the Quran – can be gathered from any part of the world to recite the Quran and it will be documented. In fact, this was how the Quran was first revealed to Prophet Muhammad ﷺ; it was initially memorized and subsequently documented.

And We have certainly made the Quran easy to remember. So is there anyone who will be mindful? – Quran 54:17

Spiritual Concordance

Though people can pray in any language, when Muslims perform their daily obligatory prayer – the Salat, it is observed in the language the Quran was originally revealed. The wisdom behind this is for the attainment of concordance. For instance, it would be chaotic if different people with various languages and dialects gathered to worship – perform Salat. However, by adopting a uniform mode, people of various languages across the world, who may not have been able to communicate with one another, can worship together concertedly.

Hypothetically, without understanding the respective languages of one another, an Australian, Bosnian, Cape Verdean, Danish, English, Fijian, Gambian, Honduran, Italian, Jamaican, Korean, Liberian, Malaysian, Norwegian, Omani, Pakistani, Qatari, Russian, Samoan, Tahitian, Ugandan, Vietnamese and Yemeni, can congregate for Salat (worship)in unison.

Additionally, the spread of the Arabic language is a spiritual by-product. The Arabic language was spread because people wanted to understand and appreciate the Quran, not because Arabs wanted their language globalized. The meaning of the message of the Quran supersedes the Arabic language itself. Of what use is it to one's soul or physical well-being if one can recite the Quran, but the meanings of those words have no impact on one's life?

Though understanding Arabic is advised to appreciate its beauty and uniqueness, the primary objective is in the meaning of the words, and not just the words. Even to ethnic Arabs and Arab speakers, the Quran is unique because of its rarity. The language is considered classical Arabic, which is slightly different from standard Arabic. It is important to emphasize that the Arabic language is not meant to extirpate our primary languages and cultures but complement what we already have in our possession. Also, it is not compulsory to have Arabic names when accepting Islam. Any name, in any language, is suitable, as long as the meaning of that name does not negate the fundamentals of monotheism – either through the deification of human beings or the glorification of autochthonous deities. This naming condition applies to Arabs as well. Human names should not glorify helpless deities.

From an historical viewpoint, as the Arabic language spread, it became an internationally acceptable standard of communication at some point in history, just as the English language is contemporarily. As I often quip, people speaking English contemporarily would probably have been speaking Arabic if they existed in the era of the 'Islamic Golden Age'. Historically, Arabic was once the dominant language of scholarship, knowledge acquisition and the sciences. Essentially, non-Muslims who studied Arabic were primarily motivated by knowledge – science, and Muslims who studied Arabic were primarily motivated by Religion – Islam.

A comparative historical analysis highlights the probability that the Western world realised the linguistic possibilities attained with Arabic's global success at the time, and adopted the same model with their languages, especially English. Though such a strategy would be more material oriented than spiritually motivated. In sooth, the Arabs were not exactly preoccupied with the dominance of the Arabic language. The language becoming widespread is a consequence of Islamic propagation by Muslims generally, and not primarily a devised strategy by the Arabs.

Systematic Revelation

The Quran's revelation is an unprecedented and unusual pattern that can only be attributed to the divine. Superficially, the revelation process appears unsystematic; however, a holistic analysis of the Quran reveals the intricate arrangement of a deliberately designed system. Furthermore, the entire revelation process becomes more puzzling considering the Quran was dictated and memorized over a period of two decades (23 years).

Incidentally, it was the aftermath of the tragic loss of 70 Hafiz (memorizers of Quran) during a campaign under Caliph Abu Bakr, that Umar Ibn al-Khattab suggested the material documentation of the Quran. To fulfil this objective, a committee was inaugurated, and the members gathered all the Hafiz and transcripts from the era the verses were initially revealed.

The original transcripts there were written on various materials such as bone fragments, cloth, leather and paper were all collated. Providentially, the transcendence and magnificence of the Quran fully manifested after it was formally documented as a complete book.

Book Writing Analogy: Typically, book authorship adheres to a structured process that includes, but not limited to, planning, outline, chapterization, sequencing, proofreading, editing, etc. So, imagine an author decides to write a book without any plan, structure or format, but with random compilations of words. Also, the author does not follow any sequence or chronological order. On top of that, there is no proofreading or editing process before publication. Such a book writing process would certainly emerge a literary disaster.

Thus is the verisimilitude of the Quran's revelation. The verses of the Quran were revealed based on putatively random societal incidents, which included questions, interrogations and challenges from believers, non-believers and adversaries, respectively. During the revelation process, there were various interspersions that were not chronological. For example, some verses may be for chapter 100 and another set were for chapter 20. Then the next set of verses may be for chapters 70, 3 and 45. So, the revelation of the Quran did not follow a sequential pattern of chapters – 1, 2, 3, 4, 5, etc.

Following this phenomenal revelation process, somehow everything comes together systemically, like it was chronologically planned. Furthermore, the Prophet was illiterate, and the revelation was not written, but recited and committed to memory. I will reiterate, when the Quran was initially revealed, it was not written down, but memorized by the Prophet.

Essentially, a book that was compiled from recitations, which were generally based on circumstantial events, unwritten and unedited, but eventually materialized systematically structured – that is supernatural! The Quran contains 144 Surahs (Chapters) and 6, 236 Ayahs (verses), and its revelation process is indubitably preternaturally phenomenal.

> *Do they not then consider the Quran carefully? Had it been from other than*
> *Allah, they would surely have found therein much contradictions.*
> – Quran 4:82

CHAPTER 24

BOOK OF SIGNS

We will show them Our Signs in the universe, and in their ownselves, until it becomes manifest to them that this (the Quran) is the truth. Is it not sufficient in regard to your Lord that He is a Witness over all things? – Quran 41:53

The Quran is often referred to as a book of signs (*Ayah*) because of its content. The Arabic word *Ayah* is usually translated as 'verse' in the English language, though this does not do justice to the meaning of the word. From a Quranic position, Ayah contextually means signs, evidence or miracle. The arrangement, the mathematical accuracy and consistency was what marvelled the literary geniuses, academics and poets since it birthed, and the Quran still marvels the contemporary world. The Quran is a science and an eternal phenomenon, where researchers unravel and update empirical findings continually. The Quran is an interdisciplinary knowledge base that transcends the science of time and numbers, and contains scientific and numeric miracles and prophecies, among many other discoveries. Based on personal research, I have counted well over one hundred discoveries in the Quran, and the discoveries are ongoing. This discourse will expatiate on a few discoveries.

LINGUISTIC DISCOVERIES

Symmetrical Structure

The most powerful Ayah in the Quran is Ayat al-Kursi aka Ayatul Kursi and is commonly translated as Verse of The Throne. Though allegorical, it is more linguistically accurate to translate as Verse of The Footstool; where Kursi represents 'Footstool' instead of 'Throne' – which literally means *Arsh*. Ayatul Kursi is embedded within Surah Baqarah; which is the longest Surah of the entire Quran – Chapter 2 (The Cow). Baqarah has 286 verses, and the verse of the throne is verse 255.

Allah! There is no god ˹worthy of worship˺ except Him, the Ever-Living, All-Sustaining. Neither drowsiness nor sleep overtakes Him. To Him belongs whatever is in the heavens and whatever is on the earth. Who could possibly intercede with Him without His permission? He ˹fully˺ knows what is ahead of them and what is behind them, but no one can grasp any of His knowledge—except what He wills ˹to reveal˺. His Seat encompasses the heavens and the earth, and the preservation of both does not tire Him. For He is the Most High, the Greatest. – Quran 2:255

Thematic Analysis: A thematic analysis of Ayat al-Kursi reveals nine interrelated sections.

1. The Ever-Living, The Sustainer (Unparalleled Power)
2. No Drowsiness, No Sleep (Constant Advertence)
3. The Owner of Heaven and Earth (Absolute Authority)
4. The Granter of Intercession (Divine Permission)
5. Total Awareness (Knowledge of Future and Past; Prevenient and Subsequent; Ahead and Behind)
6. The Granter of Knowledge (Divine Permission)
7. The King of Heaven and Earth (Absolute Authority)
8. No Tiredness as The Preserver (Constant Advertence)
9. The Most High, The Greatest (Unparalleled Power)

Theme 1: Unparalleled Power (1 and 9)

Theme 2: Constant Advertence (2 and 8)

Theme 3: Absolute Authority (3 and 7)

Theme 4: Divine Permission (4 and 6)

Theme 5: Total Awareness (5)

Explanation: Theme 5 doubles as Section 5 and is strategically placed at the centre to represent an awareness of sections 1- 4 and sections 6-9 (knowledge of what is ahead and behind)

Illustrative Depiction: An illustration of the symmetrical phenomenon.

Verse of The Footstool–Ayat al-Kursi

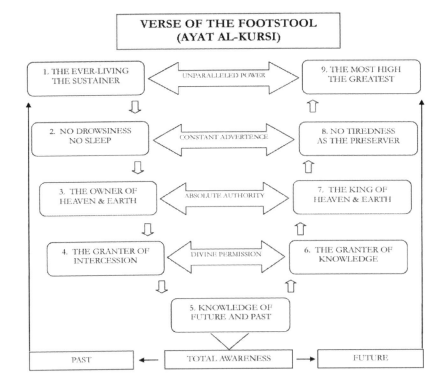

From a linguistic perspective, the thematic structure in the Verse of the Footstool (Ayatul Kursi) is unique and impossible to execute, whilst maintaining its contextuality in relation to its location. The execution becomes more remarkable, considering the Quran was not initially written down but recited during revelation.

Specificity – Kings and Pharaohs

A remarkable discovery in the Quran involves the historical accuracy of the title of ancient Egyptian kings and the exactitude of phraseology vis-à-vis Egyptology and the antiquated languages. From an historical perspective, Hieroglyphic had gradually become extinct in Egypt around the fourth century C.E. Research into Egyptian hieroglyphs was somewhat revived following the 1799 discovery of a slab with inscriptions at Rosetta (Rashid) in the Nile Delta, east of Alexandria, Egypt. Historical analyses of events in Egypt reveal that during the time of Joseph and the era of Moses, there were distinctive terminologies for the rulers of Egypt. Pharaoh was not the formal title for Egypt's king. In describing the Pharaoh epithet, the Encyclopedia Britannica states the following:[57]

> Pharaoh, (from Egyptian per 'aa, "great house"), originally, the royal palace in ancient Egypt. The word came to be used metonymically for the Egyptian king under the New Kingdom (starting in the 18th dynasty, 1539–1292 BCE), and by the 22nd dynasty (c. 945–c. 730 BCE) it had been adopted as an epithet of respect. It was never the king's formal title, though, and its modern use as a generic name for all Egyptian kings is based on the usage of the Hebrew Bible.

Essentially, the Bible popularized the usage of the Pharaoh title for all Egyptian kings in history. However, further research has revealed this position is not historically accurate.

The biblical narrative of 'Abram' and 'Sarai' in Egypt refers to the king as Pharaoh throughout the story. Genesis 12:15 is just one those instances:

> *And when the princes of Pharaoh saw her, they praised her to Pharaoh. And the woman was taken into Pharaoh's house.* – Genesis 12:15

Another biblical narrative involves Joseph and the Pharaoh's dream:

> *When two full years had passed, Pharaoh had a dream: He was standing by the Nile,* – Genesis 41:1

A biblical narration of Moses and the Pharaoh goes thus:

> *Then the LORD said to Moses, "Go to Pharaoh and say to him, 'This is what the LORD says: Let my people go, so that they may worship me.* – Exodus 8:1

The history of ancient Egypt is usually divided into periods that include the Old Kingdom (c. 2686-2181 BCE), First Intermediate (c. 2181-2055 BCE), the Middle Kingdom (c. 2055-1650 BCE), Second Intermediate (c. 1650-1550 BCE) and the New Kingdom (c. 1550-1069 BCE).

Historical research has narrowed down the era Joseph existed to within the Middle Kingdom and Second Intermediate periods. Similarly, the era Moses existed has been identified as the New Kingdom period. Furthermore, during the time of Joseph, the title of King was used and during the time of Moses, the Pharaoh title had become normalized. Historically, Pharaoh (per-aa – "great house") was a symbolic representation of an intermediary between the people and their gods. Seemingly, a structural representation transubstantiated into a form of human totemism.

The Egyptians came to believe the Pharaoh would attain divinity upon his death. Especially, the Pharaoh (Ramses II) Moses encountered during his mission, was probably the most prominent in Egyptian history, because he thought himself to be a god and unilaterally ascribed divinity upon himself. The Quran mentions the Pharaoh's delusions of grandeur:

> *Then he gathered his people and cried aloud*
> *Saying: "I am your lord, most high"*
> — Quran 79:23-24

Crucially, the Quran makes the astonishing distinction between the era of Joseph and Moses in numerous verses. In all the stories relating to Joseph, the title 'King' (*Malik*) is used and in all the narrations relating to Moses, the epithet 'Pharaoh' is used. The title, 'Malik' means King when translated from Arabic to English. An example of the specificity of the ruler during the time of Joseph; King of Egypt:

> *And the king (of Egypt) said: "Verily, I saw (in a dream) seven fat cows,*
> *whom seven lean ones were devouring - and of seven green ears of corn, and*
> *(seven) others dry. O notables! Explain to me my dream, if it be that you can*
> *interpret dreams."* – Quran 12:43

And an example of the specificity of the ruler during the time of Moses; Pharaoh of Egypt:

> *And Moses said, "O Pharaoh! I am truly a messenger from the Lord of all*
> *worlds,* – Quran 7:104

These aforementioned verses confirm the Quran's historical precision.

Also, from a biblical perspective, this discovery highlights anachronism in the Bible, especially pertaining to the story of the Pharaoh and other notable historic figures – Abraham, Joseph and Moses. More importantly, this discovery puts paid to unfounded theories of plagiarism. There are dozens of examples where the Quran is distinctive from any other scripture. So, all those who mischievously spread the unfounded plagiarism fable against Prophet Muhammad ﷺ have obviously not done their research. Generally, these types of revelations call to question the historicity of the biblical narratives, particularly from a chronological prism.

Specificity – Middle Nation

One of the Quran's unique features is its specificity with the situation or positioning of words.

A good example of the Quran's specificity is the "Middle Nation" phrase mentioned in the longest Surah of the Quran – Baqarah (Chapter 2: The Cow). Baqarah has 286 Ayahs and if the Surah is divided by 2 [286/2 =143], the Ayah of 143 contains the "Middle Nation" – a middle identification embedded within the middle verse.

Thus We have appointed you a middle nation– Quran 2:143

Contextual Distinction – Location

Historically, Madinah used to be known as Yathrib; however, there is a distinction between the two. Whilst Prophet Muhammad ﷺ lived in Makkah, the city was referred to as Yathrib, but after the Hijrah – the migration to the city, the named changed to Madinah: *Madinat un-Nabi* (City of The Prophet). The Quran mentions Madinah on numerous occasions but Yathrib once. The only instance of the Quran using Yathrib was to highlight the mindset of the hypocrites during a siege by the enemies of Islam on Madinah.

The hypocrites were not committed to the changes that came with the arrival of the Prophet. From a linguistic position, 'Yathrib' was utilized as an implicature to convey a message of the pre-Muhammad era; when they oversaw the city's leadership. The Quran's only instance of Yathrib goes thus:

> And ⌐remember¬ when a group of them said, "O people of Yathrib! There is no point in you staying ⌐here¬, so retreat!" Another group of them asked the Prophet's permission ⌐to leave¬, saying, "Our homes are vulnerable," while ⌐in fact¬ they were not vulnerable. They only wished to flee.
> – Quran 33:13

Contextual Distinction – Addressees

Though Moses and Jesus were sent to the Israelites, they both addressed their respective audiences distinctively. This distinction is highlighted in two proximate Ayahs in the Quran –Quran 61:5 and Quran 61:6:

When Moses addresses the people he says, "O my People":

> And (remember) when Moses said unto his people: O my people!

When Jesus addresses the people he says, "O Children of Israel":

> And remember, Jesus, the son of Mary, said: O Children of Israel!

The reason for this distinction is because nations are determined by the father, especially in Semitic traditions. For example, mankind is referred to as Children of Adam, and not Eve. Other examples are Children of Abraham and Children of Jacob. However, in the case of Jesus he technically has no biological father, because he was miraculously conceived by his virgin mother Mary, through the permission of Allah. So, Jesus does not use the same terminology as Moses – whose father is from among his people.

SCIENTIFIC DISCOVERIES

Frontal Lobe – Lie Detection

The brain is the main organ of the human nervous system and consists of the cerebrum, brainstem and cerebellum. The cerebrum is the largest part of the human brain and is divided into two cerebral hemispheres. The cerebral hemisphere can be further divided into four lobes – the frontal lobe, temporal lobe, parietal lobe, and occipital lobe. Recent scientific research in neuroanatomy and neuroscience have revealed the section of the brain responsible for wilful deceit – lying – falsehood, is the frontal lobe.

By creative art standards, one may expect the noses of liars to grow in accordance with their lies, just like Pinocchio. Such an observable process would have been very convenient for human beings because conspicuous nose extensions would make a liar easily identifiable. Alas! The identification of prevaricators is not as apparent, and some experienced liars may actually be able to pull a poker face or may have mastered the art of beating the lie detector test – polygraph or functional magnetic resonance imaging (fMRI).

According to Islamic exegesis there is an analogous reference to a known liar who routinely antagonized the Prophet, though he is a symbolic representation of all forms of falsifiers. All those who conceal, suppress and deny the truth fall into the same falsehood category. In fact, the literal meaning of the Arabic word *Kafir* – which usually denotes denier or disbeliever – is 'to cover', i.e., the one who conceals the truth. In this regard, liars may not be easily detectable to human beings, but The Creator of all creation, including human beings, is surely aware of all the internal workings of His entire creation.

The Quran specifically mentioned where lies are detected in the brain:

> *But no! If he does not desist, We will certainly drag him by the forelock—a lying, sinful forelock.* – Quran 96:15-16

Reproduction: Human Fertilization and Embryology

Human sexual reproduction is a complex system and became more intriguing after a fortuitous discovery of spermatozoa by Antoni van Leeuwenhoek circa 1677. The process of human embryogenesis, cell ingestion and differentiation – differentiated cells and undifferentiated cells, was described in the Quran:

> *O mankind, if you are in doubt about the Resurrection—We have indeed created you from dust, then from a drop of semen, then from a clinging form, then from a lump of flesh, (partly) differentiated and (partly) undifferentiated, in order to clarify things for you. And We settle in the wombs whatever We will for a stated term, and then We bring you out as infants until you attain your full strength. And of you is one who is taken (at death), and of you is one who is returned to the most abject age, so that he may not know anything after having known. And you see the land still, but when We send down water on it, it shakes and swells and germinates all kinds of lovely plant.*–Quran 22:5

Another Quran Ayah describes the human embryonic development thus:

> *Man We did create from a quintessence (of clay);*
> *Then We placed him as (a drop of) sperm in a place of rest, firmly fixed;*
> *Then We made the sperm into a clot of congealed blood; then of that clot We made a (foetus) lump; then we made out of that lump bones and clothed the bones with flesh; then we developed out of it another creature. So blessed be Allah, the best to create!* –Quran 23:12-14

Reproduction: Plant Sexuality (Pairs)

From a botanical perspective, the reproductive capabilities of plants are in pairs – male (stamen) and female (carpel). Further reproductive categorizations include the dioecious; individualized separation of male (stamen) and female (carpel) organs, and monoecious: possessing both male (stamen) and female (carpel) organs. Dioecious fruit trees include aspen, currant, ginkgo, holly, juniper, persimmon and winterberry. Monoecious fruit trees include almond, apricot, cherry, nectarine, peach, plum, prune, oak and walnut. Historically, taxonomical and botanical research birthed experiments in plant sexuality – pollination and fertilization (allogamy and autogamy) by Rudolph Camerarius, circa 17th century. Miraculously, the Quran mentioned the inherent reproductive capabilities in plants fourteen centuries ago:

> *and of all fruits He placed therein two spouses (male and female)*
> –Quran 13:3

Sea Barrier

Recent studies in oceanography reveal that each of the seas has their respective characteristics that include density, temperature and salinity. Also, a pellucid barrier system has been observed in the region where the two seas converge. Whilst a seemingly homogenization process occurs around the barrier, the two seas remain distinctive. A practical demonstration of this phenomenon can be observed in Egypt – where the River Nile intersects with the Mediterranean Sea and at the Strait of Gibraltar – where the Mediterranean Sea and Atlantic Ocean converge. The Quran mentions these phenomena in some Ayahs:

> *He has let free the two bodies of flowing water, meeting together:*
> *Between them is a Barrier which they do not transgress:* –Quran 59:19-20

And He is the One Who merges the two bodies of water: one fresh and palatable and the other salty and bitter, placing between them a barrier they cannot cross.—Quran 25:53

Seawater and Rain

The Quran wants mankind to be reflective on water. An analogy is derived from the potential dangers of seawater or salty water as rain, and why mankind should be grateful for water:

> *Have you considered the water you drink?*
> *Is it you who bring it down from the clouds, or is it We Who do so?*
> *If We willed, We could make it salty. Will you not then give thanks?*
> – Quran 56:68-70

The Quran's salty rain analogy is worthy of reflection and will be appreciated through an explication of the rain and salt production process. Rainwater is like fresh water from the sky, however when it rains, the water mixes with atmospheric carbon dioxide and becomes slightly acidic. As some of the rain travels through land, it comes into contact with rocks and the acidic content of the water initiates the weathering of rocks. The salt and minerals from the rocks mixes with water as it journeys through lakes, streams and rivers, and eventually at sea. In addition, hydrothermal vents from the ocean floor release other minerals including sodium chloride that mix with water. Following geomorphic processes, seawater becomes saline. To put the salt concentration in perspective, seawater has a salinity of about 35,000 ppm, which is equivalent to 35 grams of salt per one litre of water.

The ingestion of seawater or high concentration of sodium can cause hypernatremia – excess sodium in the body causes intestinal issues that may trigger diarrhoea and dehydration.

Severe hypernatremia can lead to permanent brain damage in some instances, and causes delirium, muscle spasms or twitching, seizures, coma and death. This explains why seawater consumption could be lethal and underpins why mankind ought to be grateful the water that rains from the sky is not salty.

> *And He is the One Who sends the winds ushering in His mercy, and We send down pure rain from the sky,* – Quran 25:48

Deep-Sea

The deep-sea can be described as the deeper parts of the sea or ocean. Research studies in oceanography have categorised the ocean into various depth levels. The ocean can be divided into five layers. (1) Sunlight Zone: Epipelagic, Euphotic) (2) Twilight Zone: Mesopelagic, Dysphotic (3) Midnight Zone: Bathypelagic, Aphotic (4) Abyss Zone: Abyssopelagic (5) Trench Zone: Hadalpelagic. More specifically, in relation to sunlight penetrating ocean levels, the ocean is divided into three zones – the first three zones: Euphotic, Dysphotic and Aphotic.In terms of sunlight travel distance, the Euphotic zone is from the sea level to 200 meters (656 feet); the Dysphotic zone is between 200 meters (656 feet) and 1,000 meters (3,280 feet); and the Aphotic zone is anything beyond 1,000 meters (3,280 feet).

The reason for this particular classification is because 'photic' pertains to light and after the aphotic zone, sunlight cannot penetrate, and the entire region is enshrouded in darkness. Oceanography studies are relatively recent – circa 19th century; following the seminal Challenger expedition (1872-1876). However, about thirteen centuries earlier, the Quran mentioned the varying levels of sea and associative darkness, to describe the situation of those who disbelieve:

Or [the state of a disbeliever] is like the darkness in a vast deep sea,
overwhelmed with a great wave topped by a great wave, topped by dark clouds,
darkness, one above another, if a man stretches out his hand, he can hardly see
it! And he for whom Allah has not appointed light, for him there is no light.
– Quran 24:40

Ant Communication

Science has discovered that ants communicate with each other, via various techniques that include an advanced system of pheromones (secretions), stridulation (sound), body language (signals) and touch. The Quran mentions the story of an ant warning other ants about the impending danger of Solomon and his contingents:

And there were gathered before Sulaiman (Solomon) his hosts of jinns and
men, and birds, and they all were set in battle order (marching forwards).
Till, when they came to the valley of the ants, one of the ants said: "O ants!
Enter your dwellings, lest Sulaiman (Solomon) and his hosts crush you, while
they perceive not."
So he [Sulaiman (Solomon)] smiled, amused at her speech and said: "My
Lord! Inspire and bestow upon me the power and ability that I may be grateful
for Your Favours which You have bestowed on me and on my parents, and that
I may do righteous good deeds that will please You, and admit me by Your
Mercy among Your righteous slaves." – Quran 27:17-19

Notably, the Quran specifically mentions the gender of the ant that warned the colony as female. Studies in myrmecology have revealed the importance of female ants. Interestingly, the female ants' career path either culminates as the queen or be designated as part of the workers. Female ants literally run the colony! The queen ant is the colony founder and is tasked with laying eggs.

The female workers are invariably tasked with the harmonious running of the colony, and part of their duties includes protecting the colony from harm. Based on these classifications, the female ant mentioned in the Quran could either have been a queen ant or a member of the female workers regiment.

Celestial and Orbital Order

Since the pre-Socratic era, there has been obsession with celestial bodies and their movements in space. Philosophers such as Plato and Aristotle propounded the geocentric astronomical model. Geocentrism was the prevailing astronomical postulation, and the theory was based on the Earth being orbited by the Sun, Moon, stars and planets. A popular proponent from the geocentric era was Ptolemy and the Ptolemaic system was that the Earth was at the centre of the universe and other celestial bodies – planets, stars, and the Sun – revolved around Earth. Notably, around the 13th century, some astronomers critiqued the Ptolemaic astronomical model, and they were mainly from the Maragheh Observatory in Persia. Prominent among the astronomers were Nasir Al-Din al-Tusi and Al-Urdi. This research phase effectively buried the geocentric astronomical model and laid the foundation for what was to be known as the heliocentric astronomical model around the 16th century.

Heliocentrism postulates the Earth and planets revolving around a centric Sun. There have been various proponents of the heliocentric-oriented model, such as Nicholas Copernicus, Giordano Bruno, and Galileo Galilei. Whilst Copernicus popularized Heliocentrism through his heliocentric theory of planetary motion during his era, Bruno and Galileo literally paid with their lives for espousing related cosmological theories in their respective eras. In the case of Bruno, the Church – Roman Inquisition – accused him of heresy and was executed by burning at the stake. On his part, the Roman Inquisition sentenced Galileo to house imprisonment until his death in 1677.

Hypothetically, some exposure to Islamic exegeses in the West, particularly the clergy, could have saved the lives of some brilliant minds. The Quran mentions a related concept of rotational celestial bodies. Celestial bodies are mentioned as moving in their respective orbit, based on an established celestial order:

> *It is not for the sun to catch up with the moon, nor does the night outrun the day. Each is travelling in an orbit of their own.* – Quran 36:40

The Earth's rotational speed varies and is dependent on some factors such as its molten core, oceans, atmosphere and other celestial bodies. The time Earth takes to rotate on its axis is 24 hours and to revolve around the sun it takes 364.25 days. Also, the Earth rotates once in about 24 hours in relation to the Sun. The Sun rotates around its axis in 27 days, though this calculation is dependent on latitude. Whilst the average rotation is 27 days, around the sun's equatorial regions, the rotation takes about 25 days and 38 days at the poles. The moon's orbital movements are not visible from Earth because synchronized rotation makes it appear static. The moon orbits the Earth via an elliptical path – lunar perigee and apogee. The moon rotates around its axis and completes a revolution around the Earth in about 27 days. Also, it takes the moon 29.5 days to complete a full lunar cycle. The moon completes a cycle every month, whilst the sun completes a cycle in a year. The Quran mentions the rotation of the sun and the moon in relation to the Earth's rotation – alternation of night and day:

> *He wraps the night around the day, and wraps the day around the night. And He has subjected the sun and the moon, each orbiting for an appointed term.* – Quran 39:5

Contextually, the 'wraps' in the above Ayah represents a rotational movement.

In practical terms, when you wrap two items around each other, a rotational motion is produced. Also, in some translations of the Quran, the word wrap 'is substituted with other words, such as 'roll' and 'overlap', which are all signifying various forms of rotation.

> *And He is the One Who created the day and the night, the sun and the moon—each travelling in an orbit.* – Quran 21:33

Expanding Universe

In 1925, American astronomer Edwin Hubble was the first contemporary scientist to prove the universe is expanding. Hubble proved the direct relationship between the speeds of distant galaxies and their distances from Earth – this is known as Hubble's Law. Also worthy of mention is that the Hubble Space Telescope was named after Edwin Hubble. The Quran already mentioned this relatively recent discovery of an expanding universe:

> *We built the universe with ˹great˺ might, and We are certainly expanding ˹it˺* – Quran 51:47

The aforementioned examples are just a few of many discoveries in the Quran. These presented discoveries are to establish the originality of The Quran. The authenticity of the Quran is indisputable, and the origins can only be attributed to divinity.

> *Alif-Lam-Ra. ˹This is˺ a Book whose verses are well perfected and then fully explained. ˹It is˺ from the One ˹Who is˺ All-Wise, All-Aware.*
> – Quran 11:1

CHAPTER 25

PROPHECIES

Generally, prophecies can be classified into fulfilled and expected categories. The Quran contains prophecies that are distinctive from the prophecies contained in the Hadith of Prophet Muhammad ﷺ. Some Quran and Hadith prophecies are highlighted below.

QURAN PROPHECIES

Pharaoh's Cadaver Discovery

When tourists travel to Egypt, one of the excursions on offer is to visit the tomb of Pharaoh. The tomb of Ramses II is on display in the Royal Mummies Room at the Egyptian Museum. Pharaoh Ramses II was an arrogant tyrant who was deluded by his self-ascribed divinity and was the principal antagonist during the prophethood of Moses. Ramses II existed about 3000 years ago and his cadaver was only discovered in the 19th century (1881).

Remarkably, about 13 centuries earlier, the Quran mentioned the discovery of the Pharaoh's (Ramses II) corpse:

> *And We took the Children of Israel across the sea, and Fir'aun (Pharaoh) with his hosts followed them in oppression and enmity, till when drowning overtook him, he said: "I believe that La ilaha illa (Huwa): (none has the right to be worshipped but) He, in Whom the Children of Israel believe, and I am one of the Muslims (those who submit to Allah's Will)."*
> *Now (you believe) while you refused to believe before and you were one of the Mufsidun (evil-doers, corrupts, etc.).*

So this day We shall deliver your (dead) body (out from the sea) that you may be a sign to those who come after you! And verily, many among mankind are heedless of Our Ayat (proofs, evidences, verses, lessons, signs, revelations, etc.).
–Quran 10:90-92

Notably, there have been many discovered mummies in the region that were mummified before burial. Since the first discovery, there has been extensive archaeological research on mummies, including the discourse on the corpse of Ramses II containing traces of salt and the distinction between sea salt and Natron. Natron comprises sodium carbonate decahydrate, sodium bicarbonate, sodium chloride and sodium sulphate, and it was used as a desiccant for mummification in ancient Egypt. Furthermore, according to archaeologists, the mummy of Ramses II was one of the very few pharaohs whose body "survived largely intact".[58]However, the case of Ramses II is unique because the Quran specifically mentions that he drowned at sea and his corpse was rescued – on a particular day. So, the actual emphasis is on the day the Pharaoh's dead body was saved from the sea after drowning. Technically, the corpse of Pharaoh Ramses II could have been left to decompose at sea and it could have disintegrated beyond recognition by the time it was discovered or may never have been discovered. However, his body was discovered – possibly washed ashore – and preserved for not only identification purposes, but for the veracity of Moses' divine mission.

Plastic Surgery

Plastic surgery is a surgical procedure that involves the restoration, reconstruction or alteration of parts of the human body. Surgeries can be divided into two main categories: reconstructive surgery and cosmetic surgery. Whilst reconstructive surgery focuses on the functionality of human parts, cosmetic surgery focuses on aesthetics and subjective standards of beauty.

Cosmetic surgery is a multibillion-dollar industry, and it keeps growing. According to the American Society of Plastic Surgeons, Americans spent more than $16.5 billion on cosmetic surgery in 2018, and that is just in the United States alone.[59] The reality is that there are people addicted to surgeries and they will never be contented with their appearance or whatever they possess. This lack of contentment is an ailment, which sometimes leads to death – during or after the surgery, and in some cases suicide.

The Quran mentions the altering of creation as one of the ways Satan will mislead mankind:

> *I will certainly mislead them and delude them with empty hopes. Also, I will order them and they will slit the ears of cattle and alter Allah's creation." And whoever takes Satan as a guardian instead of Allah has certainly suffered a tremendous loss.* – Quran 4:119

In addition, the above verse has been associated with some aspects of genetic engineering, particularly attempts at cloning humans and animals.

Fingerprint Recognition

A fingerprint is a unique identifier and can be likened to a personalised code. No two individuals share the same fingerprints, not even twins. The use of fingerprinting has been prevalent in forensics since the 19th century. Advanced fingerprint technology is now part of our daily lives; election thumbprints, biometrics for immigration and travelling, building access and various forms of authentication. In affirming the eventuation of human resurrection, the Quran mentions fingerprints as an example of procedural precision:

> *Yes ˹indeed˺! We are ˹most˺ capable of restoring ˹even˺ their very fingertips.*
> – Quran 75:4

Also, there are a couple of related verses that can be interpreted as being in concordance with this unique identification technology. There is an Ayah about people literally arguing with their own skin for testifying against them:

> *They will ask their skin ʿfuriouslyʾ, "Why have you testified against us?" It will say, "We have been made to speak by Allah, Who causes all things to speak. He ʿis the One Whoʾ created you the first time, and to Him you were bound to return.* – Quran 41:21

In another verse, hands will be commanded to give testimony:

> *That day, We will seal over their mouths, and their hands will speak to Us, and their feet will testify about what they used to earn.* – Quran 36:65

Sun Termination

Theoretically, the Earth's Sun is going to die! Scientific research postulates that the sun has a lifespan. Through an internal nuclear fusion process, a combination of light elements like hydrogen into heavier elements like helium and then lithium, oxygen, carbon till iron, produces a large amount of energy within the Sun. The Sun consumes about 5 billion kilograms of its "nuclear hydrogen fuel" per second.[60] A star like the Sun will burn for a period of about 10 billion years. The current estimate of the Sun's age is about 4.6 billion years. So, the Sun is almost at the halfway point of its lifespan. Based on this calculation, the Sun has about 5 billion years left, before its extinction. The Sun's extinction process involves the red giant phase and the depletion of its hydrogen and helium supply, and the sun's eventual collapse into a white dwarf.

The Quran mentions that the Sun will run its fixed course for an appointed term – until its termination:

> *And the sun runs on its fixed course for a term (appointed). That is the Decree of the All-Mighty, the All-Knowing.* – Quran 36:38

In a related verse, the Quran mentions the sun alongside the moon and that both will independently orbit for an appointed term:

> *He has subjected the sun and the moon, each orbiting for an appointed term.* – Quran 13:2

Universe Transformation

The Quran literally describes the rolling up of the heavens like a scroll. Following a type of reproduction process that is yet to occur, the procedure is likened to the creation of the first creation. This phenomenon can be interpreted as a new type of world – the afterlife.

> *On that Day We will roll up the heavens like a scroll of writings. Just as We produced the first creation, ⸢so⸣ shall We reproduce it. That is a promise binding on Us. We truly uphold ⸢Our promises⸣!* – Quran 21:104

Gog and Magog

The Gog and Magog story are part of the fascinating travels of Dhul Qarnain. During his journey Dhul Qarnain encountered a people who had perennial issues with marauding creatures. Through divine wisdom, Dhul Qarnain invented a special type of iron-copper blend to help seal up the giants at a location between two mountain-cliffs, and by divine decree the giants are unable to escape – Quran 18: 93-99. There have been many speculations about where the creatures are sealed, but all are conjectural, without any certainty. According to the Quran, the giants will be let loose again before the last day:

> *And on that Day [i.e. the Day Ya'juj and Ma'juj (Gog and Magog) will come out], We shall leave them to surge like waves on one another, and the Trumpet will be blown, and We shall collect them all together.*– Quran 18:99

In some related Ayahs, the Quran gives an elaborative description of the Gog and Magog recrudescence, and regret that ultimately will befall the deniers:

> *Until, when Ya'juj and Ma'juj (Gog and Magog) are let loose (from their barrier), and they swiftly swarm from every mound.*
> *And the true promise (Day of Resurrection) shall draw near (of fulfillment). Then (when mankind is resurrected from their graves), you shall see the eyes of the disbelievers fixedly stare in horror. (They will say): "Woe to us! We were indeed heedless of this; nay, but we were Zalimun (polytheists and wrong-doers, etc.)."*
> – Quran 21:96-97

Furthermore, it is important to emphasize that research reveals that about 65% of the earth remains largely unexplored.[61] There are new plant and animal species that are discovered in remote or generally inaccessible locations regularly. Through anthropological research, human habitats that were hitherto unknown have been discovered; like the dozens of isolated tribes that have emerged from the Amazon.[62] Also, from a cartographical perspective, the world technically remains unmapped, even with the aid of latest technologies and best efforts of Google Maps.[63] The Earth has locations that can be considered relatively recent discoveries, including the uninhabited, sparsely inhabited, largely unexplored or not fully explored and some of them include,

The Namib Desert in Southern Namibia, Cape Melville in Australia, Vale do Javari in Brazil, Devon Island in Canada, North Sentinel Island is an archipelago in the Bay of Bengal, the Gangkhar Puensum in Bhutan, which is the world's tallest unclimbed mountain and Star Mountains in Papua New Guinea, which has the Hindenburg Wall – a plateau network of limestone over a mile in height. The crux of the cited examples is to establish there are many parts of Earth that are newly discovered and remain undiscovered, so there is a possibility Gog and Magog are still dwelling somewhere on Earth.

The Beast

The Quran mentions the advent of a beast from the earth as one of the signs of The Hour. The beast will distinctively mention those who failed to take heed and refused to believe in the various signs – Prophets, Messengers, Miracles, Scriptures, etc. A logical interpretation of that is, at that point in time, even if people denied previous signs, for whatever reason, they cannot deny the beast in their very presence. And at that point, it may be too late.

> *And when the decree ⌐of the Hour¬ comes to pass against them, We will bring forth for them a beast from the earth, telling them that the people had no sure faith in Our revelations.*– Quran 27:82

The Trumpet

The Quran mentions the blowing of The Trumpet to signal the end of life as we know it and a pivotal herald for the next dispensation – eternal life.

> *The Trumpet will be blown and all those in the heavens and all those on the earth will fall dead, except those Allah wills ⌐to spare¬. Then it will be blown again and they will rise up at once, looking on ⌐in anticipation¬.* – Quran 39:68

HADITH PROPHECIES

The Hadith prophecies are extracted from the life and sayings of Prophet Muhammad ﷺ. The prophecies of Prophet Muhammad ﷺ can be termed eschatological, because his coming signalled the end times. There are dozens of prophecies that have been fulfilled and are also ongoing; which include the prevalence of open sexual immorality, fornication, adultery, excessive alcohol consumption and women dressed but actually naked. A night out in some cities across the globe will confirm some of these prophecies. Furthermore, technology has made pornography accessibility much easier, via various gadgets. Fornication as long been hiding under the guise of dating or casual relationships and adultery has been relabelled an affair. Alcohol is one of the deadliest drugs in the world; it is readily available and has led to various deaths – accidents, suicide, alcohol-related disease, alcohol poising and alcoholism.

There are some prophecies that were fulfilled during the prophet's time and some prophecies occurred centuries afterwards, whilst some prophecies have not yet occurred. Some of the fulfilled prophecies have since puzzled researchers, and naysayers who may have previously doubted and dismissed these events as coincidental, are now analysing other prophecies.

Clairvoyance

On a particular occasion, the Prophet literally gave, what can be described as a clairvoyant live commentary of an event occurring in real-time, hundreds of miles away. This phenomenon occurred during a battle in Jordan and when the expedition returnees got to Madinah, they confirmed the accuracy of what the Prophet had informed the companions present.

From a contemporary perspective, such a feat can be visualized with the use of satellite or drone technology at a location and the viewer screen at another position. Surely, a futuristic type of technology could not have been deployed in the desert fourteen centuries ago. So, it is safe to conclude it was paranormal – miraculous. The Hadith about the incident states:

> *Narrated Anas: The Prophet ☒had informed the people of the martyrdom of Zaid, Ja`far and Ibn Rawaha before the news of their death reached. The Prophet* 🕌 *said, "Zaid took the flag (as the commander of the army) and was martyred, then Ja`far took it and was martyred, and then Ibn Rawaha took it and was martyred." At that time the Prophet's eyes were shedding tears. He added, "Then the flag was taken by a Sword amongst the Swords of Allah (i.e. Khalid) and Allah made them (i.e. the Muslims) victorious."* – Sahih al-Bukhari 4262

Pre-emptive Interlocution

The Prophet was gifted with the ability of an awareness of questions even before the questioner asked him the question. A Hadith about one of such instances states:

> *Narrated Wabisah ibn Ma'bad: The Messenger of Allah* 🕌 *said to me, "Have you come to ask about righteousness and sin?" I said yes. The Prophet clenched his fist and struck his chest, saying:*
> *"Consult your soul, consult your heart, O Wabisah. Righteousness is what reassures your soul and your heart, and sin is what wavers in your soul and puts tension in your chest, even if people approve it in their judgments again and again."* – Sunan al-Darimi 2533

Greening of the Desert (Arabia)

> *Narrated Abu Huraira: The Messenger of Allah* 🕌 *said: "The Hour will not begin until the land of the Arabs once again becomes meadows and rivers."*
> –Sahih Muslim 157

The above cited Hadith not only confirms the Arabian region's frondescent past, but the certainty of reverting to that state verdure. This phenomenon was confirmed via satellite imagery conducted by NASA in 2012, titled "NASA Sees Fields of Green Spring up in Saudi Arabia".[64] Since then, there has been various observation of greenery spring up in different parts of Arabia. Also, in 2014, a research team from Oxford University discovered a giant, 325,000-year-old tusk belonging to an extinct species of elephant known as "Palaeoloxodon". Archaeologists involved in the research stated the discovery is testament that giant creatures once roamed lush and fertile plains of the Nafud Desert and estimate there are over "7000 [dried-up] lake beds on the peninsula", mostly in Saudi Arabia.[65]

Arabs Construction Competition

When the shepherds of black camels start boasting and competing with others in the construction of higher buildings. And the Hour is one of five things which nobody knows except Allah. – Sahih al-Bukhari 50

Contextually, shepherds of camel refer to desert dwellers – Bedouins –Arabs. Currently, there are various tall buildings in Arab lands that are solely-funded by Arabs. For example, the current tallest building in the world is the Burj Khalifa in Dubai, which has a height of 828 metres (2, 717 ft).

Another example is the Abraj Al-Bait aka the Clock Tower in Makkah, which has a height of 601 metres (1, 971 ft), and is currently the third tallest building in the world. Interestingly, there is another building under construction named the Jeddah Tower and is expected to be at least 1000 metres when it is completed. Also, if completed, the Jeddah Tower would be the first building that is 1 kilometre (3, 280 ft) in height.

Crucially, despite the evidence of various tall physical structures, the crux of the message (prophecy by Prophet Muhammad ﷺ) should focus on the detriments of excessive material competition. Moreover, the prioritization of materialism over spiritualism, would certainly lead to disharmony and other shortcomings – which are contemporarily evident.

Usury Prevalence

> *Narrated Abu Huraira: The Messenger of Allah* ﷺ *said, "A time will come upon people in which they will consume usury." It was said, "All of the people?" The Prophet said, "Whoever does not consume it will be affected by its dust."*
> – Musnad Aḥmad 10191

The archaic definition of usury is described as interest charged or paid on a loan. The present-day definition of usury usually involves the charging of excessive, extortionist or illegally high rate of interest on borrowed money. Contemporarily, usury has been institutionalised and re-branded as interest. The entire global financial system is literally built on usury (interest) and it has permeated all segments of society. Usury has become the unavoidable sin that stares you in the face daily, because almost all money related transactions are directly and indirectly tied to interest. The banking system was built on usury. Banks can literally create money ex-nihilo and grant loans that are not asset-backed. A major pitfall of the system is the reliance on paper money, at the expense of real assets like gold. Also, due to regulation laxity and lack of punitive deterrents for reckless shadow banking activities, the interest-laden system motivates financial speculation that eventually cause financial crisis. Particularly, the 2008 global financial crisis called into question, the veracity of supposedly sound economic theories. The detrimental socioeconomic effects of the financial crisis – economic recession, cut across every societal stratum.

Family units and individuals were gravely affected, especially through hardship, broken homes and suicides. Such usury-preponderant and casino-styled financial models perpetuate economic disparity and a widening of existing chasms. With the 2008 global financial crisis came the associative 'credit crunch' parlance, and subsequent trend of events have confirmed that episode would not be the last financial disaster; as more boom-bust cycles are expected. From an Islamic perspective, the term for usury in the Quran is *Riba*, which is meant to cover all forms of interest. The Quran warns about the implication of usury in this world and the hereafter:

Those who devour usury will not stand except as stands one whom the Evil one by his touch hath driven to madness. That is because they say "Trade is like usury," but Allah hath permitted trade and forbidden usury. Those who after receiving direction from their Lord desist, shall be pardoned for the past; their case is for Allah (to judge); but those who repeat the offense are companions of the Fire: they will abide therein (for ever)

Allah will deprive usury of all blessing, but will give increase for deeds of charity; for He loveth not creatures ungrateful and wicked."

–Quran 2:275-276

Communications Technology

Narrated Abu Sa'id al-Khudri: The Prophet ﷺ said, "By the One in Whose Hand is my soul! The Hour will not be established until predators speak to people and until the tip of a man's whip and the straps on his sandal speak to him, and his thigh informs him of what occurred with his family after him."

– Jami at-Tirmidhi 2181, Book 33, Hadith 24

The aforementioned Hadith deals with communication – interaction and information sharing. This Hadith can be categorized into; predators, whip, straps, and thigh, and can be appreciated as various forms of interactive technology. Specifically, the 'predators' represents a form of translation technology, whilst the 'whip' and 'straps' represent different types of wearable technology, and the 'thigh' represents mobile technology.

Predators: "predators speak to people". This can be interpreted as human and animal interaction. At this juncture, one may be thinking of Prophet Solomon and his ability to communicate with animals or in the world of fiction, Dr. Dolittle. Whilst those examples may be good starting points for an extended reverie, a technological interpretation will be explicated. For some years, there have been research endeavours in neuroscience, artificial intelligence and machine learning, focused on making animals' vocalizations, facial expressions and body language more understandable.[66] For example, BowLingual is a dog bark translator collar that launched in Japan since 2002 and has been making technological strides ever since.[67] For purposes of visualization, a good cinematic reference is the special dog collar in the 2009 Pixar Movie, Up – a proper tearjerker. Anyway, there have been other developments in the human-animal communication sector, which are not primarily technology dependent.

Whip: "tip of man's whip". This can be interpreted as the buckle of a man's belt. Contextually, for the benefit of a 7th century desert audience, 'whip' is probably an ideal analogy for a futuristic belt that would be prevalent in future fashion. For example, in 2016, a Samsung affiliated company launched a smart named WELT – which is a portmanteau coined from wellness and belt.[68] The WELT is special belt and can be appreciated as wearable technology. The WELT is fitted with a sensor, pedometer and Bluetooth within the buckle, to monitor activities, and it also has a port for charging and interoperability.[69][70]

Straps: "straps on his sandals speak". More specifically, sandal straps. This can be interpreted as interactive wearable technology. Contemporarily, the health and fitness industry have various gadgets to monitor activities – walking and running. With technology, the journey or route of a runner can be seen through a computer or phone screen and can be heard via the activation of the voice mode feature. There are so many running apps available with inbuilt audio and voice features. Also, there are smart bands that give the option to wear on the wrist or clip onto shoes – sandals and trainers.

Thigh: "his thigh informs him" This can be interpreted as mobile technology. Mobile devices are usually kept around the thigh region of the body – in the pocket. Also, the emphasis was on men, because women may wear clothing without pockets or may not be able store their devices in the thigh area of their attire. The technology here may be the use of mobile phones to communicate and get information about one's family whilst way from home. Also, the technology may be interpreted as the installation of cameras, or the paring of two camera phones at any location, which can be conveniently monitored via a mobile app from anywhere. These are tech products that are readily available and can be purchased for immediate use.

Spread of Islam

> *Narrated Tamim al-Dari: The Messenger of Allah* 🕋 *said, "This matter will certainly reach every place touched by the night and day. Allah will not leave a house or residence but that Allah will cause this religion to enter it, by which the honorable will be honored and the disgraceful will be disgraced. Allah will honor the honorable with Islam and he will disgrace the disgraceful with unbelief."*
> – Musnad Aḥmad 16957

Islam is generally considered the fastest growing religion in the world and has been forecast to be largest religion in the world. According to a 2017Pew Research Center report, the growth projection for the global Muslim population in the coming decades would be 32%. Also, the number of Muslims is expected to increase by 70% – from 1.8 billion in 2015 to about 3 billion in 2060. Essentially, in 2015, Muslims were 24.1% of the global population and by 2060 they are projected to be about one-in-three of the world's populations (31.1%).[71]

Though high birth rates are usually mentioned as a growth factor; however, that does not cover the reason for the growing numbers of coverts to Islam. I am of the opinion technology has played a crucial role in Islam's rapid development, at least from a contemporary viewpoint. Despite coordinated and protracted attacks on Islam, especially by media, the accessibility to information via various technology platforms aids independent research. People can watch, read and listen to information through their devices and come to their own conclusions about Islam. No other religion has been so vehemently attacked, yet somehow, Islam manages to turn negativity to positivity and keeps spreading. In a related Ayah, the Quran emphatically states the perdurability and perfection of Islam. Evidently, the spread of Islam is not primarily because of the effort of Muslims, but because of Allah.

The proclamation in the Quran states:

> *They want to extinguish the light of Allah with their mouths, but Allah will perfect His light, although the disbelievers dislike it.* – Quran 61:8

Following the discourse on prophecies, it is necessary to emphasize that knowledge acquisition and discoveries are an ongoing endeavour. Scientists make discoveries regularly, and the advent of technology paraphernalia has assisted science immeasurably.

There are research and discoveries that are currently possible that were not possible decades or centuries ago. Essentially, at the core of all these elaborated discoveries in the Quran is transcendentalism. When analysed, there should be no incongruity between the Quran and established scientific facts. The intellectual puzzle and challenge has consistently been that these postulated discoveries were already contained in a book (Quran) over fourteen centuries ago.

More importantly, the presenter (Muhammad ﷺ) of the book, was not known to be vast in such intellectual matters. From a geopolitical perspective, the emergence of this book and prophet was from a region that was generally considered inconsequential. Also, at that point in history, the Arabs were so backward that even world leaders of that era were not desirous of conquering them. The Arabs were quite literally, the lowest of the low.

> *We were the most humiliated people on earth and God gave us honour through Islam. If we ever seek honour through anything else, God will humiliate us again.* — Umar ibn Al-Khattab

Furthermore, the Quran was recited and memorised in an interspersed format over a twenty-three-year period, to an illiterate man fourteen centuries ago. The only logical explanation as to why all these discoveries are contained in the Quran is divinity; which affirms that Allah revealed the Quran to Prophet Muhammad ﷺ.

> *You ⌜O Prophet⌝ could not read any writing ⌜even⌝ before this ⌜revelation⌝, nor could you write at all. Otherwise, the people of falsehood would have been suspicious.* – Quran 29:48

CHAPTER 26

CLIMACTERIC CONSIDERATIONS

SALMAN THE PERSIAN EXEMPLUM

Salman The Persian (Salam al-Farsi) is acknowledged as the first Persian to accept Islam. The spiritual peregrination of Salam al-Farsi is worthy of emulation because of his dedication and sincerity. The extraordinary life of Salman al-Farsi is a lesson in perseverance in the quest and acceptance of the truth. As it is one thing to seek the truth and another thing entirely, to accept the truth. All truth-seekers can learn from the remarkable life of Salman. The exceptionality of Salman's life stems from the fact that his spiritual peregrination traverses three religions – Zoroastrianism, Christianity and Islam. Salman was born with the name Roozbeh in Jayyan near Isfahan and his family were originally from Ram-Hurmuz. Salman's family were Magians (Zoroastrians), and his father was a prominent *Dihqan* (land-owning chief) who happened to be the wealthiest person in town. His father's overprotectiveness and love led to Salman being constantly kept within the confines of their house. Salman was occupied with living as a priest-in-training would, to potentially become a Magus, and he became the custodian of the fire at the temple. Salman's primary duty was tending to the fire constantly and ensuring the flames of fire did not burn out. Logically, Salman was aware that he was responsible for keeping the fire burning, so he probably had doubts about the religion his father chose to adopt for himself and family.

On a particular day, his father was busy with some duties, so he instructed Salman to go and deal with one of the affairs of his vast estate. On the way to his father's land, Salman passed by a Nestorian Christian group in a church and was attracted by the emanating sounds – psalms and canticles.

Salman was pleasantly surprised to see a different form of worship and devotion by the people he had noticed. He was so impressed by their religious method, that Salman decided to stay with the people until it was sunset, and he forgot all about his primary assignment of tending to his father's property. Salman's father had obviously been worried and had sent out a search party to look for him. On returning home, he narrated his meeting with the Christian group to his father, and this led to an argument about religion. Salman was of the opinion that what the Christian group practiced was better than their religion, and his father got upset and stated that their religion is the religion of their forefathers, so it is the better religion. Not wanting a repeat of the incident, and to prevent his proselytizing to a new religion, Salman's father took the drastic measure of imprisoning him at home, with chains.

During Salman's brief engagement with the people of the church, he was informed that the origins of the religion were in the Levant – Jordan, Lebanon, Palestine, Syria, also referred to as Bilad al-Sham. So, whilst he was incarcerated at home by his father, Salman sent a message to the church that he wanted information about the itinerary of Christian merchants who were returning to Syria. Once he was aware of the time of travel, he escaped from his manacles and joined the Christian merchants on their return journey to Syria. Upon arrival in Syria, Salman requested for the best person in the practice of the Christian religion, and he was directed to the highest bishop in the church. Salman told the bishop he wanted to be a follower of the religion and be of service to the church, and the bishop obliged.

After some time, Salman noticed that the bishop was not truly a righteous man; because he hoarded the charity the people were donating and refused to distribute the wealth to the needy. Salman deeply despised the bishop for his greed and selfishness. So, when the bishop died, Salman showed the people the wealth he had exhorted from them; amassed in seven chests of gold and silver.

The people were astonished by this discovery, and instead of giving the bishop a befitting burial, he was crucified. Another bishop was appointed for the church and Salman observed he was truly pious. Sadly, the bishop died, but before passing away, he informed Salman about the existence of another righteous man in Mosul that Salman should seek.

Salman journeyed to Mosul to find the pious man and once in his company, Salman informed him about the bishop that instructed him to come and live a righteous life in his company. After some time, the righteous man informed Salman about the only other righteous man he knew in Nusaybin (Nisibis), before passing away. Salman travelled to Nusaybin to find the described righteous servant of God. Upon meeting the righteous man, Salman narrated his story, and he was allowed to stay. After spending some time with the righteous man, he too gave Salman advice to seek out a righteous man in Amuriyah (Amorium), before dying.

Salman travelled to Amuriyah and met a righteous man whom he narrated his story to as well, and he was allowed to stay and practice the same religion as all the previous righteous men he had met. Once again, Salman was confronted with the dying advice of the righteous man he had been worshipping with. However, in a shift from the usual advice he received from all the clergymen he had previously engaged, Salman was informed that there was no other known righteous principal for recommendation. However, the dying man told Salman that the time had come for the emergence of a prophet who will revive the religion of Abraham (Ibrahim) and revealed some signs for the prophet's identification. The prophesied prophet was expected to emerge from the Arabian Peninsula, and he would migrate to a land with lots of date palm trees in-between two volcanic rocks. The prophet was described as an honest man who will accept gifts, but not charity, and he would have a mark – Seal of Prophethood – somewhere between his shoulder blades. Salman noted all the signs of this expected prophet.

After the righteous man died, Salman waited a bit at Amuriyah. During his time there, he had acquired some wealth in the form of livestock – cattle and sheep. With his acquired resources, Salman met and negotiated with some Kalbite merchants – from Banu Kalb – to take him on their journey to the Arab lands. Sadly, when they got to Wadi al-Qura, the travellers reneged on their contract and sold Salman into slavery. Salman was purchased by a Jewish man who later sold him to his relative from the Banu Qurayzah tribe, and he ended up in the land of palm trees –Yathrib (Madinah). One day, Salman busied himself with the work of his new master as usual and was on top of a palm tree, when his master's cousin came cursing the Banu Qayla (Arab tribe) who were gathered in the town of Quba, and ecstatic to welcome a man from Makkah they believe to be a prophet. Salman was so excited to hear the news of the prophet's arrival in Quba that he thought he would fall on his master beneath the tree. Though Salman managed to climb down from the tree, his excitement made him forget himself and he boldly asked the bearer of the news to repeat what he had just stated. Following Salman's audacity of questioning his master's guest, his master got angry and rebuked him for interfering in matters beyond his concern. Salman got struck by his master and was told to get back to his work, but that did not matter to an excited Salman.

Later in the night, Salman happily gathered some of his belongings and went to visit the Prophet in Quba; which was in the outskirts of Madinah.

The mission of Salman was to meet the Prophet and affirm his authenticity through the signs he had been provided by the righteous man he had last engaged. At this point, two of the signs had been fulfilled: emergence from Arabia and migration to a land of palm trees – though the Prophet was still in Quba, en route to Madinah. The outstanding signs were three: the prophet will not consume anything from charity and will only accept a gift, and he had a mark on his back that signified the Seal of Prophethood.

Upon meeting the Prophet, Salman informed him that he learned that he is an honest man, and his entourage were strangers in this land who had travelled from another place and were needy, and he wanted to give them a deserving charity as his way of expressing hospitality. So, Salman presented some food as charity to the Prophet, and the Prophet gathered some companions to eat from the dates but did not partake in eating himself. Salman took note of what had happened and departed.

Days later, Salman gathered more of his belongings and went to visit the Prophet again, but this time in Madinah. When he met the Prophet, Salman said that he noticed that the Prophet did not partake in eating from the charity he gave the last time, and that he had brought gifts this time around. Salman presented some food, but, unlike their previous meeting, the Prophet and his companions ate the gifted food. With these two separate incidents, two of the three outstanding signs, given to the People of the Book about the coming of a prophet, had been fulfilled. Salman then thought of how he would fulfil the outstanding sign of the Seal of Prophethood, because it is meant to be in a somewhat obscure place that is not easily accessible – the Prophet's back. On a particular day, there was a burial of the Prophet's companion at Al-Baqi, so Salman noticed the Prophet was wearing two shawls to cover his top and bottom – like the ihram worn by Hajj pilgrims. Salman went behind the Prophet and kept trying to observe the Prophet's back, in the hope that the upper garment will reveal the seal. The Prophet noticed Salman's constant movements behind him, so he lowered his upper garment and made it easy for the seal to be revealed. Once Salman saw the Seal of Prophethood on the back of Prophet Muhammad, he exclaimed, fell on his knees, embraced the Prophet and began to cry. The Prophet knew this was an epiphanic experience for Salman, considering the People of the Book had been given signs of a coming prophet. Following Salman's emotional expression, the Prophet asked Salman to narrate his story to everyone.

Though Salman entered the fold of Islam and became a Muslim, he remained enslaved to the Jewish man. Salman's slavery situation hindered him from practising Islam as he wanted to, and he notably missed the battles of Badr and Uhud, respectively. Prophet Muhammad ﷺ implored Salman to draw up a manumission contract to negotiate his freedom from his master. However, Salman's master was not reasonable with his demand, and he requested 300 growing date palms and money (40 *uqiyah* of silver). Once the terms of the manumission were clear, Prophet Muhammad ﷺ instructed the companions to assist their brother – Salman. The companions collaborated to fulfil the 300 date palms request and Prophet Muhammad ﷺ emphasized that he wanted to personally plant all the trees, after all the holes had been dug.

As for the outstanding money, Prophet Muhammad ﷺ gave Salman a gold nugget, which miraculously weighed the exact amount required to fulfil the terms of manumission, and Salman became free. Afterwards, Salman participated in major campaigns and his ingenuity played a prominent role in the success of Battle of the Trench (Kandhaq). Salman was the only companion who was not a blood relative or member of the Prophet's household, who Prophet Muhammad ﷺ honoured as *Ahl al-Bayt* (People of the Household). Amongst other notable feats, Salman translated the Quran to the Persian language, and he maintained his ascetic lifestyle even after becoming the governor of Al-Mada'in (Ctesiphon region). Essentially, Salman journeyed from Persia, through Syria, Mosul, Nusaybin (Nisibis) and Amuriyah (Amorium) to Madinah, all in the quest for truth.

Thus was the story of the pious man who stated about his ancestry:

"I am Salman, the son of Islam from the children of Adam."

MUHAMMAD: THE SUCCESSOR TO JESUS

Narrated Abu Huraira: I heard Allah's Messenger 🕌 *saying, "I am the nearest of all the people to the son of Mary, and all the prophets are paternal brothers, and there has been no prophet between me and him (ie Jesus).*
— Sahih al-Bukhari 3442, Book 60, Hadith 112

A critical analysis of the story about the life of Salman the Persian – from Zoroastrianism to Christianity and then Islam – affirms that Prophet Muhammad 🕌 was foretold in earlier scriptures, before the deliberate adulteration, corruption and alteration that occurred over centuries. This rejection stems from arrogance – spiritual arrogance and typifies the delusion and desperation of those who reject the truth. The rejectors enmeshed themselves in unabashed forgeries and insensate alteration of their scriptures to suit their parochial socio-religious and socio-political agendas. Evidently, the institutionalization of the schism to discredit Prophet Muhammad 🕌 as the natural successor to Jesus had long been established and has existed ever since. It is indeed the greatest schism! The systemic delegitimization of Prophet Muhammad 🕌 has been a lifelong mission for those not satisfied with his emergence. From a biblical narrative, there was a successor to come – "the Prophet". According to the Bible, when John the Baptist emerged, he was questioned about his identity:

> *Now this was John's testimony when the Jewish leaders in Jerusalem sent priests and Levites to ask him who he was.*
> *He did not fail to confess, but confessed freely, "I am not the Messiah."*
> *They asked him, "Then who are you? Are you Elijah?" He said, "I am not."*
> *"Are you the Prophet?" He answered, "No."* – John 1:19-21

Based on these biblical verses (John 1:19-21), it is evident, there are four characters identified in the conversation between John the Baptist and the delegation. Apart from the main subject (John); the first identity is the first person of enquiry (Jesus – "I am not the Messiah"); the second identity is the second person of enquiry (Elijah – "I am not"), third identity is the third person of enquiry ("the Prophet" – "No"). Since John had identified himself, and confirmed he is neither Jesus nor Elijah, then who is the Prophet? The contextual meaning of "Are you the Prophet" is, are you the Prophet (Muhammad) that was foretold in our scriptures?

Historically, the Jews and Christians were expecting a prophet to emerge from the Arabian Peninsula. The Jews in particular, were strategically settled in Arabia and expectant of the prophesied prophet and were generally excited about the prospects. However, when the Prophet emerged, they radically rejected him, even though the Prophet fulfilled all the criteria. The Quran states that they recognised the Prophet like they recognised their own sons, but for ungodly reasons, rejected Prophet Muhammad ﷺ:

> *Those to whom We have given the Scripture (Jews and Christians) recognize him (i.e. Muhammad SAW as a Messenger of Allah, and they also know that there is no Ilah (God) but Allah and Islam is Allah's Religion), as they recognize their own sons. Those who destroy themselves will not believe.* – Quran 6:20

It is worth mentioning that the much disputed and often debated Gospel of Barnabas, is one of the books usually referenced when discussing the matter of Jesus' successor, however the book does not need be cited in this discourse. The Quran is substantial enough as evidence, and does not need any reinforcement or validation, and specifically addresses the issue:

And [mention] when Jesus, the son of Mary, said, "O Children of Israel, indeed I am the messenger of Allah to you confirming what came before me of the Torah and bringing good tidings of a messenger to come after me, whose name is Ahmad" But when he came to them with clear evidences, they said, "This is obvious magic."– Quran 61:6

Prophecy Foretold

A detailed analysis of Abraham's life reveals that the emergence of a prophet in the Arabian Peninsula was a prophecy fulfilled. Though Quran 14:37 mentions the story of how Abraham's family – Hajar and Ishmael ended up in the Arabian region, the Bible actually mentions how that historic episode was a prophecy fulfilled. The Bible states:

When Isaac grew up and was about to be weaned, Abraham prepared a huge feast to celebrate the occasion.

But Sarah saw Ishmael—the son of Abraham and her Egyptian servant Hagar—making fun of her son, Isaac.

So she turned to Abraham and demanded, "Get rid of that slave woman and her son. He is not going to share the inheritance with my son, Isaac. I won't have it!"

This upset Abraham very much because Ishmael was his son.

But God told Abraham, "Do not be upset over the boy and your servant. Do whatever Sarah tells you, for Isaac is the son through whom your descendants will be counted.

But I will also make a nation of the descendants of Hagar's son because he is your son, too."

So Abraham got up early the next morning, prepared food and a container of water, and strapped them on Hagar's shoulders. Then he sent her away with their son, and she wandered aimlessly in the wilderness of Beersheba.

When the water was gone, she put the boy in the shade of a bush.

Then she went and sat down by herself about a hundred yards away. "I don't

want to watch the boy die," she said, as she burst into tears.

But God heard the boy crying, and the angel of God called to Hagar from

heaven, "Hagar, what's wrong? Do not be afraid! God has heard the boy crying

as he lies there.

Go to him and comfort him, for I will make a great nation from his

descendants."

– Genesis 21:8-18

Prophetically, a great nation did manifest with the emergence of Prophet Muhammad ﷺ. Also, the Bible mentions another prophecy with the parable of the cornerstone:

Jesus said to them, "Have you never read in the Scriptures: 'the stone that the

builders rejected has become the cornerstone; this was the Lord's doing, and it is

marvellous in our eyes'? Therefore I tell you, the kingdom of God will be taken

away from you and given to a people producing its fruits

– Matthew 21:42-43

Essentially, the transfer of power from the descendants of Ishaq (Isaac) to the descendants of Ishmael was prophesied in the Bible.

Those to whom We gave the Scripture know him [i.e., Prophet Muhammad ﷺ]

as they know their own sons. But indeed, a party of them conceal the truth while

they know [it].– Quran 2:146

In awaiting the fulfilment of this prophecy of a prophet, some of those knowledgeable in the scriptures were already living in Arab lands, particularly

Jewish tribes. At this juncture, the logical trajectory is to question why there was a large concentration of Jews living in the Arabian Peninsula, before the arrival of the prophesied prophet. The main Jewish tribes in old Arabia were the Banu Nadir, Banu Qainuqa, and Banu Qurayza. Based on exegeses of historical accounts about their relationship with the Arabs, the Jews usually taunted the Arabs by alluding to the coming of their prophet. So, the Jews were proud and expectant of a special prophet to come. The Quran affirms their scriptures stated the coming of a prophet:

> *"⸢They are⸣ the ones who follow the Messenger, the unlettered Prophet, whose description they find in their Torah and the Gospel. He commands them to do good and forbids them from evil, permits for them what is lawful and forbids to them what is impure, and relieves them from their burdens and the shackles that bound them. ⸢Only⸣ those who believe in him, honour and support him, and follow the light sent down to him will be successful."* – Quran 7:157

Despite overwhelming evidence, as contained in their scriptures, the truth about the Prophet was too bitter a pill to swallow. Interestingly, there is a narration from Islamic exegesis, which highlights the length of deception and height of arrogance by some rejectors of the truth. Prophet Muhammad ﷺ had a Jewish wife named Safiyya bint Huyayy, who was the daughter of Huyayy ibn Akhtab. Safiyya bin Huyayy narrated a remarkable story that transpired within her family, about the identity of the Prophet:

> *I was the favourite child of my father and my uncle Abu Yasir. When I was present they took no notice of their other children. When the apostle was staying Quba with B. 'Amr b. 'Auf, the two went to see him before daybreak and did not return until after nightfall, weary, worn out, drooping and feeble. I went up to*

them in childish pleasure as I always did, and they were so sunk in gloom that they took no notice of me. I heard my uncle say to my father, "Is he is? Do you recognize him, and can you be sure?" "Yes" "And what do you feel about him?" "By God I shall be his enemy as long as I live"

Huyayy was vehement in his excoriation and became an inveterate enemy of the Prophet, and by extension Islam. The conversion of a prominent Jew named Abdullah ibn Salam probably exacerbated his hatred and hostility. The opposition of Huyayy was not an isolated incident. Based on historical accounts, the Jews of Arabia were expectant of a prophet as described in their scriptures, but their expectancy turned to antagonism because the prophet they were expecting was not Jewish. Hypothetically, if the prophet they were expecting was Jewish, they would not have any qualms with the development. In other words, there was a conditionality attached to their faith and acceptance of truth. Evidently, their faith was not sincere.

And if only they had acted according to the Taurat (Torah), the Injeel (Gospel), and what has (now) been sent down to them from their Lord (the Quran), they would surely have gotten provision from above them and from underneath their feet. There are from among them people who are on the right course (i.e. they act on the revelation and believe in Prophet Muhammad ﷺ like 'Abdullah bin Salam), but many of them do evil deeds. – Quran 5:66

The rejection displayed by Huyayy ibn Akhtab, gives an insight into the mindset of those who reject the truth. Such arrogance has driven many generations of human beings, and those who rejected the truth of yore can be likened to the prideful actions of a much earlier era; when Iblis (Satan) rejected the commandment of The Creator to prostrate to Adam.

And (remember) when We said to the angels; "Prostrate to Adam." So they prostrated except Iblis (Satan). He was one of the jinns; he disobeyed the Command of his Lord. Will you then take him (Iblis) and his offspring as protectors and helpers rather than Me while they are enemies to you? What an evil is the exchange for the Zalimun (polytheists, and wrong-doers, etc).

– Quran 18:50

Certainly, arrogance has disastrous consequences and those that reject the truth for whatever reason, are towing the path of the accursed. In this regard, the People of the Book (Jews and Christians), in particular, have been cautioned about the implications of their position.

And there is none of the people of the Scripture (Jews and Christians), but must believe in him ['Iesa (Jesus), son of Maryam (Mary), as only a Messenger of Allah and a human being], before his ['Iesa (Jesus) or a Jew's or a Christian's] death (at the time of the appearance of the angel of death). And on the Day of Resurrection, he ['Iesa (Jesus)] will be a witness against them. – Quran 4:159

Ultimately, everyone's fate is determined by the mercy of The Creator. In summary, there is no documentary evidence, even via biblical sources, that prove Christianity was established as a religion by Jesus. What occurred centuries after the departure of Jesus, was syncretism – the coalescence of collective practices that were somehow labelled 'Christianity'. Clearly, those who follow the remaining aspects of the authentic message of Jesus will find certain features of Christianity spiritually beneficial. However, based on research, I am intellectually inclined to posit Christianity a spiritual transition agency. I am convinced, that, what came to be known as Christianity was actually meant to be a transitional mode of worship until the emergence of the next prophet (the last prophet), with a new set of divine instructions about the

formal institutionalization of the primal and only divinely ordained religion –
The Submission (Islam).

> *And indeed now We have conveyed the Word (this Quran in which is the news of*
> *everything to them), in order that they may remember (or receive admonition).*
> *Those to whom We gave the Scripture [i.e. the Taurat (Torah) and the Injeel*
> *(Gospel), etc.] before it, - they believe in it (the Quran). And when it is recited to*
> *them, they say: "We believe in it. Verily, it is the truth from our Lord. Indeed*
> *even before it we have been from those who submit themselves to Allah in Islam as*
> *Muslims (like 'Abdullah bin Salam and Salman Al-Farisi, etc.).*
> *These will be given their reward twice over, because they are patient, and repel evil*
> *with good, and spend (in charity) out of what We have provided them.*
> – Quran 28:51-54

The Quran categorically mentions a double reward for those from among the
receivers of previous scripture (Torah and Gospel), who were sincere in their
belief when they became aware of the truth, and accepted Islam. This is the
noble path for the 'People of The Book.

From an historical position, contemporary Christians; those who claim to be
Christ-like, followers of Jesus or the adherents of Christianity, cannot be
outrightly blamed for the deception, distortions of scripture, history
revisionism and schisms that occurred within Christendom, for thousands of
years. The leaders of Christendom of centuries past will bear the brunt for the
deception they established and the manifestations that emanated therefrom.

> *(O Muslims) do you still fancy that they will believe you, although a group of*
> *them used to hear the word of Allah, and then, having understood it, used to*
> *distort it knowingly?* – Quran 2:75

Regardless of what occurred with deliberate distortions historically, once the truth is presented to contemporary Christians for example, the onus is on them to be sincere and not follow the path of the deceptors of yore. This sincere advice is equally relevant to the Jews because their progenitors cannot be exculpated from the historical schisms and the deliberate rejection of revealed truth, and the manifestations that have occurred ever since.

> *They have taken their rabbis and monks as well as the Messiah, son of Mary, as lords besides Allah, even though they were commanded to worship none but One God. There is no god ⸢worthy of worship⸣ except Him. Glorified is He above what they associate ⸢with Him⸣!* – Quran 9:31

Thus, it is important to explicitly state that any advice given is nothing but guidance and should not be misconstrued as passing judgement. Judgmental condemnation is beyond the scope of this discourse. Such crucial decisions are exclusive to The Creator and ultimately rest with The Judge. The primary purpose of these revelations is to share the truth. Verily, the truth is incontrovertible, and facts cannot be obnubilated forever. Discovering the truth is innate; human beings have a natural disposition to verity. Once discovered, the truth is undeniable.

> *And you will know the truth, and the truth will set you free.* – John 8:32

> *And say, "Truth has come, and falsehood has departed. Indeed is falsehood, [by nature], ever bound to depart."* – Quran 17:81

CHAPTER 27

REJECTIONISM:
PROVINCIALISM AND CONSEQUENTIALISM

THE ARABISM MATTER

Arabs and some Muslims in particular, are sometimes guilty of presenting the universal message of Islam via a cultural prism – provincialism. Consequently, this provincial approach manifested as a problem. For instance, a common theme associated with rejecting Islam and Prophet Muhammad ﷺ is the obsession with his Arab ancestry. To address such issues, Islam must be extricated from Arabism. Historically, Arabs had their cultural orientation before the enlightenment of Islam. After the Prophet's era, some Arabs may have been implicitly guilty of being preoccupied with Arabism, possibly at the expense of Islam. When the rapid spread of Islam beyond the Arabia is taken in cognizance, the plausibility of an Arab agenda cannot be easily discounted. Considering Islam is what made the Arabs prominent, some Arabs may have felt threatened by the involvement of everyone, particularly non-Arabs, from across the globe – which ironically, is what Islam prescribes. Though, Prophet Muhammad ﷺ specifically stated in his last sermon that everyone is equal, and an Arab has no superiority over a non-Arab, some ancient and contemporary Arabs failed to inculcate this integral message of Islam. Also, there is a possibility the actions of some Arabs may not have been a deliberate attempt at diluting the message of Islam, but their actions may have inexplicably achieved the objective of promoting Arabism. Analysing from historical and contemporary perspectives, Arabs cannot be exculpated from undermining the core message of Islam, whatever their intentions.

Importantly, it is crucial to emphasize that Arabism serves a symbolic objective in this discourse, because the problem is not exclusive to Arabs. In reality, any ethnic group in the world can be potentially complicit in such provincialism. No ethnic group should impose their culture on others, especially under the guise of Islam. The ideal paradigm is to put Islam first always. Cultural excesses and overzealousness tend to complicate an uncomplicated religion; thereby masking the beautiful and universal message of Islam.

Islamic exegesis details non-Arabs who increased their sphere of influence over time. The Abbasid Caliphate had Persian influence and the Ottoman Empire was Turkish. For instance, the *Imazighen* (Berbers) played significant roles during the Iberian Peninsula campaign and were led by a Berber, Tariq ibn Zayd – after whom the Rock of Gibraltar (Jabel-al-Tariq) is named.

Historically, religion was hijacked for provincial socio-political agendas, and calls to question the supposed religiosity or spirituality of those wielding power. Good cases in point were the Ottoman Interregnum and the ensuing fratricide that consumed the empire. A classic example was the fratricide committed during the reign of Mehmed III. After his accession to power, Mehmed III murdered 19 of his brothers in one night. Comparatively, except for the variation in casualties, there is no difference between Mehmed III's massacre and the legend of the Indian emperor of the Mauryan dynasty Ashoka – who allegedly murdered 99 of his brothers.

In the Islamic context, where exactly does Islam fit into the evil perpetrated by Mehmed III? Obviously, there is no part in the teachings of Islam – Quran and Hadith – where fratricide is permissible. There are other examples of turpitude and debauchery that affirm those who were at the helm of supposed 'Islamic' affairs, were not Islamic in deed or practice. If there ever was any spirituality historically, the spiritual essence was definitely lost at that point.

Religion, in this case Islam, was used as a tool for exerting power. However, such excesses are not exclusive to Islam. Within Christendom for example, the Romans literally hijacked Jesus for their agenda. The core message of Jesus was manipulated to suit socio-political objectives. Their machinations had many manifestations, which included the creation of their Bible and religion – Christianity, and the eventual Europeanization of Jesus. The literal whitewashing of history caused some people to believe Jesus was European. Due to whitewashing, there are Christians who really did not know that Jesus was from the Middle East. Jesus was deliberately Europeanized by the Europeans (Romans) for their socio-political objectives.

Arabism can be contextualized from this premise. As a result, there are people, especially critics, who fixate on Arabs, rather than the actual message of Islam. With such preconceived notions, which are largely influenced by a fixation on Arabism, the core message of Islam is misconstrued and completely misunderstood. For example, there are people who would want the message in their local language, dialect and intonation. Given permission for such petty-mindedness, the nitpicking would be endless. There is no pleasing everyone, and those who dutifully refuse to be pleased, will never be pleased. For analytical purposes, if the fixation on Arabs, Arabic and Arabism is overlooked and the message of Islam is scrutinized without intellectual encumbrances, the essentiality of the message will be deciphered.

Primarily, the actual message of Islam is the propagation of the "Submission". Submit to what exactly, one may ask? Submit to the reality that you are a creation, and you did not create yourself, and cannot create yourself. In essence, The Creator is establishing a connection with His creation. This consistent message can be understood in any language and in any part of the world. Furthermore, the message is reminding mankind as a creation to be cognizant of the Creator and other co-creations, most especially, not engaging in the worship of any form of creation created by The Creator.

The message of "Submission" is as old as time, but the problem is, mankind got fixated on petty issues like the ethnicity and tribe of the messengers, rather than the actual message. As a microcosmic example, whoever brought the message of submission to the Yoruba nation in modern-day West Africa, may have informed a set of people about the existence of a Creator, and emphasized that the proper thing to do is to worship that Creator. That message would have been delivered in the Yoruba language. However, at some point, the purity of that message of submission to a Creator may have been diluted or adulterated to include worshipping co-creations or the manifestations of co-creations. This scenario highlights how ancestral worship was established; which is at the core of African religions and spirituality. The foregoing process of deviation is typical, and underpins why The Creator kept sending reminders, so humans do not go astray. For centuries, mankind had been contending with forefatherism and ancestral worship issues, and the message of Islam actually came to dispel such ideologies of worshipping autochthonous deities and the deification of fellow creations.

Essentially, the message of "Submit" may have been said for thousands or millions of years in various languages to all forms of people via different races. Nonetheless, what is of utmost importance is the message and not exactly the ethnic characteristics or geographical origin of the messenger. During Prophet Muhammad's era of Islam (Submission to The Creator), his message was nothing different to whichever messengers or prophets that came before him proclaimed, in their respective languages – dialects. However, the unique difference is that Prophet Muhammad ﷺ was conveying the message in Arabic, but the message remains the same. Islam (Submission) is not a new religion started by Prophet Muhammad ﷺ, but a continuation of a divine religious instruction – the undeviating message of Submission.

Fundamentally, the Prophet propagated Islam and nothing else, especially not Arabism. The lives of Prophet Muhammad ﷺand the companions reveal a cosmopolitan society and special multiculturalism among Muslims; making it virtually impossible to promote an Arab oriented agenda, at the expense of Islam. It is vital to emphasize that there were a lot of non-Arabs who were also companions. The companions of the Prophet came from different parts of the globe: those of Sub-Saharan African descent, or Afro-Arabs, or dark-skinned (Black) include, Sumayyah bint Khabbat, Salim Mawla ibn Abu Hudhayfa, Umm Ayman, Usama ibn Zayd, Ayman ibn Ubayd, Mihja' bin Salih, Julaybib, Sa'ad Al-Aswad As-Sulami, Ammar bin Yasir, Bilal Ibn Rabah and his siblings Khalid and Ghufairah, and Muhammad ibn Muslamah – who earned the sobriquet "Knight of the Prophet". The Persians include Salman al-Farsi, Fayruz al-Daylami and Munabbih ibn Kamil. The Romans include Suhayb al-Rumi and Zunairah al-Rumiya. The Jews include Abdullah ibn Salam, Safiyya bint Huyayy and Rayhana bint Zayd. The Assyrians include Khabbab ibn al-Aratt and Addas, and many others.

Evidently, a rich diversity was existent amongst the Muslims of the prophet's era, and the Prophet's message of equality was openly emulated and judiciously implemented. Historically, some of the prominent figures that made immense contributions to the propagation of Islam were not Arabs. The diversity of the companions and generations afterwards surely assisted in propagating the universal message of the oneness of God. If the message was not compatible with other regions of the world, the spread of Islam would have been impossible to propagate and could not have spread outside the boundaries of the Arabian Peninsula. The permeation of Islam through many borders buttresses the universality of the message. Also, it is important to note that Islam does not permit forced conversion; because this action contradicts a core fundament in the acceptance of Islam – the conviction.

Prophet Muhammad 🕌 did not promote Arabism and his priority was always Islam. From an historical perspective, when Islam was revived under Prophet Muhammad 🕌, the first group of people who challenged the Prophet were Arabs, particularly his tribe – the Quraysh. The arrogant Arabs completely rejected the message of the oneness of God. It is instructive to emphasize the preaching of God's oneness by the Prophet, was identified as a growing movement that would upset the applecart and cause adverse socioeconomic effects. Makkah was quite literally a mecca that attracted visitors interested in the gods – at least 360 gods and goddesses that the Arabs worshipped. Up until that point, Makkah earned constant revenues from travellers and traders who made offerings to autochthonous Arab deities. Obviously, the advent of the man named Muhammad, and his teachings could not have been palatable to the ruling elite. From their perspective, this man claiming divine Prophethood was challenging their economic interests; by advocating for the eradication of their income-generating gods and promoting the worship of One God. The hope and confidence the message of Islam was giving to the masses and slaves – about equality of all human beings – meant only one thing: revolution and challenging the status quo. The next obvious move for the scheming Arabs was to crush this man and his new followers. And they did plot to kill the Prophet at any given opportunity. Following failed assassination plots and coercive measures, they resorted to bribing. The ruling elite literally offered Prophet Muhammad 🕌 the keys to the city and power – rulership. The authority was granted on the proviso that he let them maintain their idolatry practices – worshipping of their numerous gods. But, because the Prophet's mission was divine and not personal, neither was the mission Arab or Middle Eastern-oriented, the Prophet rejected the offer and asked them to repent from worshipping their gods and stick to the worship of the one true God: The Creator. Based on these foregoing contextualities, had the mission of the Prophet been for an Arab cause, then there would not have been clashes over the proscription of autochthonous deities. Furthermore, Prophet Muhammad ﷺ would not have rejected their material offers and rulership, which was conditioned on accommodating their deities. The Prophet refused to compromise and endured many hardships until victory eventually came. Logically, it makes no sense at all for Prophet Muhammad ﷺ to go through constant affliction when there was a convenient option of simply compromising on the Submission message and accommodating the autochthonous Arab deities. Fundamentally, there is no difference between the autochthonous deities of the Arabs and the deities exclusive to all world cultures. Initially, the Arabs perceived Islam as a foreign religious tradition that was alien to the cultural traditions inherited from their ancestors. Islam was rejected primarily because the religion invalidates all forms of deities and deification. Essentially, Arabism is different from Islam. Arabism should not be promoted nor condoned because such practices are reminiscent of the days of *jahiliyyah* – age of ignorance. Arabs with Arabism tendencies must realise, Arabs became prominent because of Islam and not vice versa. Arabs were not an advanced nation until the revivification of Islam in Arabia. Interestingly, the Quran explicitly states the desert Arabs will be worst in disbelief:

> *The Arabs of the desert are the worst in Unbelief and hypocrisy, and most fitted to be in ignorance of the command which Allah hath sent down to His Messenger: But Allah is All-knowing, All-Wise.* – Quran 9:97

Based on the foregoing verse, Arabs are not given a special station. Arabs are as susceptible to temptations and sin like everyone, and as such, will pay for the consequences of their actions. For example, during the time of the Prophet, there were those who preferred the practice of slavery continued and there are those who may still feel that way currently. Also, there were racists during the time of The Prophet – which he confronted, and there are still racists now. This emphasizes that being Arab is vastly different from being Muslim – practicing Islam. In this regard, being Arab is not a criterion for salvation, because only piety will save anyone on the day of reckoning. The farewell sermon of Prophet Muhammad ﷺ was explicit on the matter of racial equality and is probably an aspect of the message of Islam Arab imperialists and supremacists do not like to be reminded about and admonished.

In essence, the Prophet is categorically stating that everyone is equal, and mentioning Arabs specifically, is an eternal admonition. Arabs not accepting this message of the Prophet wholeheartedly, is the major reason some of them are still racist towards non-Arabs, especially the darker skinned – colourism. The exemplary life of Prophet Muhammad ﷺ and the admonition of Arabs is testament that Islam is not an Arab religion. Due to this fact, it is a misnomer to label Islam "Arab Religion". The "Arab Religion" label is nonfactual, specifically because the Arabs had their autochthonous religion before Islam re-emerged in their land over fourteen centuries ago. Furthermore, from a cultural perspective, almost all world cultures have their respective autochthonous religion, and the Arabs were no exception.

Arab imperialists existed historically and probably still do contemporarily, if not in practice, they exist ideologically. The inherent challenge the promoters of the Arabism cause must have had was that Islam was established in Arab lands after its revival under Prophet Muhammad ﷺ, so that reality could not be denied or erased from their history. However, what the promoters of Arab ideology and imperialism did was use Islam to promote their Arabism agenda, even though their actions were not in concordance with the teachings of Islam. Overall, those who subscribe to Arabism and related ideological concepts must sincerely ask themselves if they are genuine followers of Islam – Muslims, or are Muslims, because Prophet Muhammad ﷺ happened to be from Arabia and was an Arab.

Culture versus Conviction

Conviction is paramount in the acceptance of Islam. Therefore, those who assume Islam is an "Arab religion" are usually disappointed when they mix amongst Arabs in their communities or live in Arab countries, and discover their practices are not particularly Islamic.

Furthermore, this misassumption extends to South-East Asia and other communities that often usually portray their societies as "Islamic". I have long learnt that stark difference between theory and fiction, and I daresay that cultural orientation is not the ideal way to Islam.

As a similitude, imagine someone happens to learn of the existence of the Yoruba Religion – an autochthonous religion of the Yoruba people of modern-day West Africa. Following the discovery, the person embarks on a journey to Yorubaland in modern-day Nigeria and decides to mingle with the indigenous people to better understand the Yoruba religion. In such a hypothetical scenario, the tourist may be expectant of a fulfilling spiritual excursion. However, such a person would be resoundingly disappointed or shocked. To begin with, the Yoruba religion is not prevalent and widely practiced among the Yoruba people. Also, among those who may claim to practice the Yoruba religion, there is a spectrum of practices, syncretization and incongruity, that may likely confuse the enquirer. Furthermore, contemporary Yorubas practice other religions and some practice no religion. In this regard, the cultural approach of indigenous interaction or societal immersion is not the ideal way of understanding any religion.

From an Islamic viewpoint, Islam is not an ethnic-oriented religion, so the scrutiny of Islam through Arabism or Arab culturalism, is not the ideal way to understand the essence of Islam. In certain situations, Arabs and Islam could be in sharp conflict. There have been many disappointments about the unislamic activities of supposed Muslims in this context. Muslims must realise that their association with Islam is not a bragging right, neither is it a carte blanche to misbehave or feel a false sense of superiority. Muslims are not immune from damnation. Becoming Muslim involves constant striving and hoping for the ultimate Mercy of Allah. Interestingly, I have come across Westerners who accepted Islam and many of them may have been deterred by the activities of supposed Muslims, usually born into Muslim families and communities. However, they were sensible enough to see the religion holistically, and not through the prism of culture or the constriction of Muslim provincialism.

Conversely, there are those who criticise Islam because of their experience with Arabs or Asians. For example, I know someone who lived in some Arab countries and stated the Arabs are as corrupt as the people in some other countries. Based on such a premise, I wondered if the person was expecting to see saints during their stay in Arab lands. These are unrealistic standards, because those who identify with Islam are probably involved in every crime that exists on the planet. The crux of that example is to establish that such mindsets exist, and those in this category may probably explore presumptive regions, based on their biases and false attribution of religiosity, with the expectation of encountering saints in human form. The reality, however, is that those encountered are most likely not the epitome of religiosity or righteousness, and their being Muslim may be culturally-oriented. In view of this, the wiser option is to analyse the religion through its tenets and not its adherents, as the adherents may be bad representatives of the religion – if not the worst of representatives.

As a similitude, if a male student is studying to become an engineer, the primary sources of knowledge should be available engineering manuals and not the behaviour of the engineers encountered whilst on campus.

In a scenario where a trainee engineer fails the exam to become a qualified engineer, and when interrogated about the reason for failure; the excuse given by the trainee engineer is that he spent his time observing engineers, rather than studying engineering manuals. This is an untenable excuse and the basis for a well-deserved failure.

Based on the cited similitude, when such situations arise, it is wiser to concentrate on the scripture and not the supposed adherents of any scripture. More importantly, the reality of the situation is that, when the time comes and people are faced with a personalised examination, they will not be questioned about the actions of others, but, about their own actions. Every human being, without exception, will face a personalised examination and not the examination of others; in fact, other examinations would be the least of their concerns. The above cited similitudes explicate the downside of analysing Islam through a cultural prism. Also, this flawed approach to religion underscores the pitfalls of accepting Islam culturally, rather than intellectually – a process of rationalism to the point of attaining conviction.

Superiority Delusion Syndrome

In Islam, there is no religious superiority or religious subservience. Prophet Muhammad's last sermon was explicit about equality and the non-superiority of the Arab to non-Arabs. I will cite an analogy to buttress the issue.

The Cantabrigian Analogy: A Cantabrigian from the town of Cambridgeshire also happens to be a student at the University of Cambridge. This particular male student is known for constantly boasting about his Cambridge heritage and often informs others at any given opportunity that "my ancestors own this land" and states that "in fact my direct great-great-great- grandfather single-handedly donated the land University of Cambridge was built". The student was really obsessed about his ancestry.

This student's patrimonial obsession, combined with his arrogance and self-delusion, makes him neglect studying the course material provided by the University of Cambridge. Following this tactless decision, the student fails his examinations resoundingly.

Based on the cited scenario of the bragging student, imagine there is another student who also attends the University of Cambridge. However, this particular student decides to withdraw from the university, because of the student rodomontading about his ancestors owning the land that the University of Cambridge was built on. Effectively, the other student deliberately abandoned university and the opportunity to become a graduate, because of some deluded fellow that brags about his ancestry.

The latter scenario typifies the problem of missing the crux of the message and a fixation on the mundane. The lesson is to not let the delusion of others affect our decisions, and ultimate success. On the other hand, the former scenario is the similitude of a deluded Arab thinking his lineage makes him special or superior and decides not to abide by the guidance of Islam yet expects to succeed. Evidently, there are some people who may feel that because of their Arab heritage, they are somewhat superior to non-Arabs. Prophet Muhammad ﷺ being Arab, does not actually make Arabs better than anyone who is non-Arab. From a spiritual position, if any Arab suffers from the superiority delusion syndrome, then they have an overly complex problem. Apart from the fact that such a provincial position is antithetical to the teachings of Prophet Muhammad ﷺ, as emphatically stated in his last sermon, it is a position that is contradictory to Islam. Furthermore, the superiority delusion syndrome can be appreciated as a divine test and burden of responsibility for Arabs; because they happen to share the same ethnicity or geographical location with Prophet Muhammad ﷺ.

Instructively, the arrogance that is sometimes attributed to Arabs is potentially possible by any ethnic group that happens to be in a similar situation.

Essentially, any supposed arrogance or superiority that Arabs are sometimes accused of exhibiting can potentially befall any ethnic group with the same privilege of geographical proximity to the Prophet. Furthermore, Arabs can be analysed from a microcosmic prism; as a reflection of any nation, society, community, ethnicity, tribe or clan that may have been tested with such a prophetic affiliation. Exhibiting arrogance and superiority because a prophet comes from your region, are misplaced attitudes that can lead to damnation. Surely, when the appointed time comes, everyone will meet their Creator and shall explain the source of their supposed superiority. Such actions are nothing but misplaced pride and baseless arrogance.

CONSEQUENTIALISM

Consequentialism in this context is predicated on the concept of rejection. There are people who reject, just for the sake of rejection, and not for any cogent reason. Rejection just for the sake of rejection is not tenable; because it is not a conclusive position, neither does it proffer a viable alternative. For instance, being anti-God or anti-Religion is not a perspicacious position, as it does not address the matter to a logical conclusion. Those who reject arbitrarily need proper introspection to ascertain their actual driving force – motivity and motivation. Rejection is a prerogative, but it comes with concomitant consequences. The ultimate consequentiality is what happens after the point of death – the hereafter.

> *And if they reject you, (it is not something new, because) those before them have (also) rejected (messengers). Their messengers came to them with clear proofs and with scriptures and with the enlightening book.* –Quran 35:25

Rejection is not a new position, as there have been rejectors of yore.

Indeed, there is no compulsion in the acceptance of religion, and those that reject are well within their rights to do so. Nonetheless, everyone must be cognizant of the reality that for every decision, there are consequences.

From a spiritual viewpoint, the acceptance of truth may not entirely be up to anyone. Some people may actually be overwhelmed with irrefutable evidence as salient as accepting the shinning of the sun but would still not accept Islam. The Quran uses analogical scenarios and instances of rejection by habitual rejectors:

> *Even if We had sent them the angels, made the dead speak to them, and assembled before their own eyes every sign ˹they demanded˺, they still would not have believed—unless Allah so willed. But most of them are ignorant ˹of this˺.*
> – Quran 6:111

> *And [even] if We opened to them a gate from the heaven and they continued therein to ascend,*
> *They would say, "Our eyes have only been dazzled. Rather, we are a people affected by magic."*
> – Quran 15:14-15

> *The Hour has drawn near and the moon was split ˹in two˺.*
> *Yet, whenever they see a sign, they turn away, saying, "Same old magic!"*
> – Quran 54:1-2

The foregoing verses are revealing and ruminative. The first two groups of cited verses (Quran 6:111and (Quran 15:14-15) are similitudes based on potential rejections; because Allah The Creator, knows what is in their hearts and minds. The next cited verses (Quran 54:1-2) give an insight into people rejecting what they physically witnessed.

The moon-splitting miracle by Prophet Muhammad ﷺ is a typical example of witnessing a miracle and choosing rejection. Whilst there is documented evidence about the moon split miracle, including accounts of the Hindu King from Malabar who accepted Islam after witnessing the phenomenon in India, the primary focus is on the polytheists who requested and witnessed the moon split miracle by the Prophet. The realities of that point in history reveal that the Prophet was inundated with criticisms from those opposed to the message of Islam. So, it was the norm for the refuters to challenge verses of the Quran, usually as the verses were revealed. However, it is instructive to note that when Surah Qamar was revealed and the aspect about the moon split was mentioned, nobody – especially the usual suspects – challenged the Quran verse (Quran 54:1). The reason for the incontrovertible stance was because the moon split miracle was witnessed by a broad-spectrum of disparate people, including believers and non-believers, friends and foes, supporters and traducers. Specifically, the habitual rejectors that were among the witnesses, branded the miracle "magic". This is profound evidence of blatant rejection. Whether historically or contemporarily, those genuinely seeking the truth do not require much convincing. Typically, it is those who are insincere that would often conjure excuses, despite witnessing evidence, like miracles. Physically witnessing a miracle and not believing it may possibly be down to the spiritual. Habitual rejection presents another dimension to the "seeing is believing" argument, because some of the miraculous feats – especially those documented – that occurred throughout history, were witnessed by certain people, yet that did not make them believe or rescind on their rejection of the truth.

Essentially, the rejection of Allah or Islam does not mean instant punishment or something terrible will occur to such people – in this life. So, lightning is not going to strike anyone – like in the movies – for rejecting God or Islam.

In fact, people who reject the truth or disbelieve, may actually live excellent lives, from a materialism viewpoint, even though there may be a degree of spiritual hollowness. In this world, Allah in His infinite mercy will continue to sustain all His creation, including those who reject amongst mankind. It is the hereafter that the matter gets complicated. Those who believe there is no hereafter, technically have nothing to worry about. However, those who believe in the existence of the hereafter should prepare for the meeting with their Creator accordingly and should not be carried away by the trifling distractions of this ephemeral world.

And be not like those who forgot Allah, so He made them forget themselves. Those are the defiantly disobedient. – Quran 59:19

The above-noted verse (Quran 59:19) is worth pondering over, for many reasons. Sometimes you wonder why some people are averse to God, religion and related matters. The basis of personal rejection is self-inflicted. If a human being decides to abandon reason and primarily relies on conjecturization and assumptions about the basis of existence in an evidently created world, then an intellectual misadventure is guaranteed. Mankind's intellectual capabilities are meant to culminate in the realisation of the Creator's existence. Denying the existence of The Creator is tantamount to denying your own existence as a creation.

Man, a creation confined within another creation, who was once a drop of semen developed into a being with reasoning faculties, and suddenly decides he knows more than The Creator. Often, those in this self-delusional category of rejection, look upon those who believe in The Creator and have accepted the truth with disdain and assume them foolish. This arrogant behaviour is prevalent in society; those who reject the truth mock those who have chosen to follow the truth from their Creator.

The predicament of the arrogant is succinctly captured in the Quran:

And when it is said to them, "Believe as the people have believed," they say, "Should we believe as the foolish have believed?" Unquestionably, it is they who are the foolish, but they know [it] not. – Quran 2:13

Evidently, pride, egocentrism and narcissism play detrimental roles in the rejection of truth. In a Hadith, it states that nobody with even a small amount of pride will enter paradise:

Narrated Abdullah ibn Mas'ud: the Messenger of Allah 鹵, observed: He who has in his heart the weight of a mustard seed of pride shall not enter Paradise. A person (amongst his hearers) said: Verily a person loves that his dress should be fine, and his shoes should be fine. He (the Holy Prophet) remarked: Verily, Allah is Graceful and He loves Grace. Pride is disdaining the truth (out of self-conceit) and contempt for the people. – Sahih Muslim 91 a, Book 1, Hadith 171

In another Hadith, Prophet Muhammad 鹵 stated that everybody has the opportunity to enter paradise, except those who reject the offer:

Narrated Abu Huraira: The Messenger of Allah 鹵 said, "Everyone from my nation will enter Paradise but those who refuse." They said, "O Messenger of Allah, who will refuse?" The Prophet said, "Whoever obeys me enters Paradise, and whoever disobeys me has refused." – Sahih al-Bukhari 7280

Also worthy of consideration are the prejudices some human beings have adopted; which are mainly based on their respective societies. For some people, their aversion to Islam is based on geographical or ethnographical considerations. For example, if Prophet Muhammad 鹵 was from the West, they will be accepting of him and his message. In the same vein, if the Western world were predominantly Muslims, some people, especially those influenced by the West, would not have any problems at all with Islam. Society and the views of members of society is what some people live and die for – societal worship, nonetheless. People need to consider if they are accepting Islam because of others or for the salvation of their own souls. Societal pressure plays a key role on people's decisions, religion inclusive.

Notably, a prominent reason why some people who accept Islam in the Western world do not openly declare their faith or religiosity is because not everyone has the fortitude to deal with societal and familial pressure. Indeed, Allah knows what is in the hearts of His creation and is aware of those who truly submit (accept) and those who reject. From an historical perspective, the Jews and Christians that were aware of a coming prophet, but rejected that expected prophet – Prophet Muhammad ﷺ, for petty unjustifiable reasons, are no different from later generations who reject Islam because of their disdain for Arabs and the Asian region.

Historically, every prophet sent by God faced rejection and those who reject usually try to justify their rejection with the flimsiest of excuses, and often resort to the characteristic ad hominem deflection. Resistance to change is as old as humankind. Once people are set in their ways or are comfortable in a system, they have created for themselves and become accustomed, any suggested alternative, even if individually and societally beneficial, is customarily resisted – especially by the affluent members of society. The Quran mentions this pattern of rejection:

> *And We did not send into a city any warner except that its affluent said,*
> *"Indeed we, in that with which you were sent, are disbelievers."*
> – Quran 34:34

Mankind's Accountability

I want to be free! This is the mantra of those who do not want to be accountable. At the heart of man's quest for total freedom, however elusive, is the escapism of reality. Even from a sociological prism, there is no such thing as absolute freedom; there are laws that act as checks and balances against human excesses in any society. A main reason why some human beings challenge the existence of a God is because of accountability. Man wants to be free to do anything and everything without consequences. The acceptance of divine truth and choosing to be religious is just a level of consciousness; an awareness that all actions have consequences – total accountability. In sooth, it is very possible to be religious and enlightened and cool. Life should not be viewed parochially – as black and white. An explication of the choices available to mankind would be illustrated with the following game of probabilities.

Game of Probabilities: Consider two groups: Group A and Group B. The Group A position is that there is a Creator and an afterlife for the accountability of all human actions. The actions of human beings while on earth, will determine whether their ultimate end will be paradise or perdition.

The Group B position is that the entire afterlife story is balderdash and there is no accountability to any Creator. There is no repercussion or recompense for human actions on earth because heaven or hell does not make any sense and simply does not exist – it is just a figment of imagination for religious people. You live and you die, and it all ends after death!

Based on the respective positions of each group, Group A and B could either be wrong or right but cannot both be right and wrong. One of the groups must be either right or wrong. With the premise established, the probabilities are as follows: Probability 1: Group B is right, and Group A is wrong. Probability 2: Group A is right, and Group B is wrong.

Probability 1: If Group B is right, and Group A is wrong. In such a scenario, the worst that could happen to Group A is nothing! Since there is no afterlife and accountability or judgement, it all ends after death.

So, both Group A and B are safe, technically. Group A does not lose anything whatsoever in such a scenario.

Probability 2: If Group A is right, Group B is wrong. In this scenario, Group B is definitely at a disadvantage. Since the position of Group A is that there is a Creator and an afterlife for the accountability of all human actions on earth. In such a scenario, quite possibly, all that Group B would wish for is to return to the world to rectify things. Unfortunately, there is no coming back from the afterlife because death is the point of no return.

Based on an analysis of the probabilities of both groups, the safer and wiser option is incontrovertibly Group A.

In view of the possible outcomes regarding the game of probabilities, I must emphasize that, I deliberately avoid discussing hell from a judgemental position, because I am not The Judge. Furthermore, it is important to categorically state that nobody owns heaven or hell, and only The Creator can determine everyone's fate. I am only trying and hoping. However, in hypothetical terms, I stand a better chance in the afterlife than anyone who does not believe there is even an afterlife but ends up in the afterlife. Also, in futuristic retrospect, if I decided to believe in an afterlife, I would have lost nothing living my life as I did, regardless of my choice. However, those who dismissed the possibility of an afterlife, have all to lose. In this regard, it is safe to conclude that extreme positions are generally unwise.

And this worldly life is not but diversion and amusement. And indeed, the home of the Hereafter - that is the [eternal] life, if only they knew. – Quran 29:64

The reality of our world is that if certain people are giving a million years to live or the opportunity to live for eternity, they will reject Allah, Islam and the Prophet for as long as they are given permission to exist on earth. This is a plausible explanation for eternal consequences. Accordingly, a reality check on the supposed freedom some people often proclaim actually has its limits.

By human standards, among co-creations, there are rules and regulations influenced by boundaries. In relation to a creator, there must also be boundaries for the creation, even though some choose to be in denial of this existential reality. For example, no human being can abruptly decide to exit earth and go and live on Mars. Nobody will wake up one morning and say: I am tired of living on earth, so I am going to Saturn! In this regard, man must accept that freedom is not absolute and for every action, there are consequences. Accountability is inevitable. Centuries ago, some people would have ridiculed the idea of mankind being accountable for all their actions on earth, but technology has revised that perception.

So have they not traveled through the earth and have hearts by which to reason and ears by which to hear? For indeed, it is not eyes that are blinded, but blinded are the hearts which are within the breasts. – Quran 22:46

POSTFACE

A rational approach to God and religion is possible; if vital facts are considered and certain misconceptions are discounted. From a scientism viewpoint, amongst many other unverifiable claims, nobody in history has been able to logically prove the nonexistence of God, and all attempts to do so, have generally been based on personal desires and conjectural propositions. A position derived from personal sentiments is not a scientific fact. The reality of the world we live in is that everyone is free to claim their disbelief in God and reject religion. Nobody can be forced to believe in anything. The Quran clearly states that there is no compulsion in religion, and that is the default position of Islam, anything else is an aberration.

> *Let there be no compulsion in religion, for the truth stands out clearly from falsehood. So whoever renounces false gods and believes in Allah has certainly grasped the firmest, unfailing hand-hold. And Allah is All-Hearing, All-Knowing.* – Quran 2:256

Essentially, Islam is not by force. However, if anyone decides to follow any religion, there must be certainty that adequate research has been done before a choice is made, if any choice is made at all. Admittedly, everyone's journey to spiritual awareness is personal and I can only share personal experiences or advice based on other people's experiences. If anyone sincerely wants a relationship with The Creator, I am certain, The Most Merciful is open to all His Creation, especially the sincere, however mysterious it may seem. I am of the opinion that if any creation sincerely calls upon The Creator without any intermediaries – mentioning any name or preconceived notions of a deity, and genuinely requests guidance, such a person will be guided. In view of this, whoever wants to identify The Creator is better off doing some research, rather than taking a leap of faith – blind faith.

Religion can be considered a medium meant to be utilised by the creation to communicate with The Creator. Religion is also meant to be a guide and criterion about life generally. There are many religions, but not all religions in existence fulfil certain procedural criteria, from a divinity viewpoint. Anyone genuinely seeking answers to the reason for their existence and trying to identify the Creator can establish a mode of communication. However, the lifelong challenge is to determine which of these various religions, is the one accepted religion - the right path and preferred mode of communication. Those interested in this quest for truth must undertake such a mission using God-given senses and other resources at their disposal.

Personally, I have taken such a journey. And from experience, I have more regard for people who undertake the intellectual journey and discover God and His religion, than people who just happened to be born into a family with Islamic ties. The former tends to appreciate their discovery of truth and the latter tend to take their position for granted. Furthermore, in taking such a journey, one crucial lesson I gained is never to judge any religion based on just its adherents, for me that is too myopic, and is not a cogent basis of assessment. Rather, I have learnt to assess a religion based on its tenets and conceptualization of God, particularly via previously stipulated criteria: The God Test. If anyone believes that a spiritual connection with God can be attained without the medium of religion – then Godspeed and happy peregrination. However, my experience with the world of spiritualism presents other complications. For instance, those who claim to be spiritual but not religious – spirituality claimants – have taken a problematic stance. Self-ascribed spirituality is determined by personal parameters and guided by the dictates of self-indulgent spiritualism. Such a paradigm can be likened to a self-taught medical practitioner, because at some point, unethical practices will come to fore. Some human endeavours permit autodidacticism; however, in matters of spiritualism, it is rather complicated, because at a certain level, self-delusion takes over. Spiritualism without guidance would probably manifest as deluded egoism: such as self-worship or transmutation into an object of worship – becoming a 'god' or demigod. Misguided spiritualism could have disastrous consequences and in some cases manifest as mysticism, superstition or outright evil. For instance, some of those claiming to be spiritual can be led to believe having a bath or general cleanliness is no longer necessary, or that paedophilia and necrophilia are acceptable practices. There will be no drawn lines or boundaries if there are no cautionary measures or guidance on spiritualism – anything goes. The rules governing permissibility and the criterion for right or wrong are necessary in the realm of spiritualism.

In matters of spiritualism, religious instruction can help in distinguishing between dark forces that tend to destroy and promote evil, and the forces of righteousness that tend to promote good and ultimately saves.

Islam proposes an equipoised combination of religion and spiritualism for a fulfilling life and afterlife.

Based on my personal edification, religious conviction can be attained through intellectualism – rationalism. Furthermore, I appreciate religion as a medium to communicate with an incomparable higher-being, on the proviso of the acceptance of, or the conviction in the existence of such a higher-being. Man is one of many creations and started as a single pair.

Extrapolating on the premise of human beings emanating from Adam and Eve, mankind was originally one family, but have over a long period of time manifested as a global entity, with various skin tones, cultures, languages, tribes, ethos, etc. Humankind's cultural diversity is meant to be a source of mutual identification, respect and peaceful coexistence. This confirms that cultural diversity is divinely inspired and deliberate, unlike religious plurality – which was founded on human endeavour and driven by parochial objectives. Man-made religions and traditions are the substratum of religious multiplicity.

The consequent prevalence of such religious practices made it normality, and not too many people are concerned about the origins or why mankind ended up with so many religions.

For those genuinely interested in religion, though without compulsion, my candid advice is to embark on research. Also, of critical importance is a dedicated endeavour to understand the foundations and fundamentals, particularly the claims associated with the revered figure and scriptures of the religion. I posit that it is generally wiser to avoid religions that promote exclusion rather than inclusion, from a global perspective – universality. By exclusion, I mean the religions that are geographically-limited or ethnocentrically-oriented. As a typical example, the Shinto religion originates from modern-day Japan and is part of the family of East Asian religions, and like almost all world religions, is autochthonous – limited by ethnocentrism and based on local traditions. These regional religions are usually founded on forefatherism or ancestral worship and often lack unique scriptures. Based on this premise, as someone from modern-day West Africa, I am primarily excluded for ethnographical considerations. Note: the Shinto religion is symbolic, and its paradigm is applicable to almost all religions in the world.

In view of existing ethnographical factors, religious pluralism is a contemporary reality. Generally, religions can exist to submit to other beings or creations, and not necessarily about submitting to The Creator. In fact, anyone can start a religion, give it any name and would still get followers. This emphasizes why The Creator has to send reminders and some forms of criteria. It is why certain tests are necessary, so people are not misled. Historically, researchers of world religions have already done some of the precursory work, and some of us have not only tapped into that wealth of knowledge but carried on contemporarily. Emphatically, a 'my religion is better than yours' attitude should not be the approach, rather empathy towards those who are yet to discover or embark on the peregrination of truth.

Howbeit, I am of the strong opinion that people are free to believe whatever they want to believe and are well within their rights to do so. One can only suggest, because ultimately salvation is beyond the purview of the creation. On salvation, there may or may not be various paths to attain the Mercy of Allah – The Most Merciful; that is a matter ultimately up to Allah. However, as for attaining the ultimate mercy of The Creator, primarily through religion, I am certain there can only be one path. Fundamentally, the proviso of "no compulsion in religion" is sacrosanct. Ideally, the matter of religion should be primarily for those interested in religion, which includes those interested in undergoing the intellectual and academic rigours of determining the origins of religion, and possibly unravelling the first religion – The Primal Religion

Mankind was [of] one religion [before their deviation]; then Allah sent the prophets as bringers of good tidings and warners and sent down with them the Scripture in truth to judge between the people concerning that in which they differed. And none differed over it [i.e., the Scripture] except those who were given it - after the clear proofs came to them - out of jealous animosity among themselves. And Allah guided those who believed to the truth concerning that over which they had differed, by His permission. And Allah guides whom He wills to a straight path. – Quran 2:213

"Convey from me, even a single verse." – Prophet Muhammad ﷺ

NOTES

Online Resources

All Uniform Resource Locator - URL links were working as at the time of cited online access. In the event that the URL links are unavailable or broken, the resource may still be accessible via a specific search on the cited website or a general search on any good search engine, or a web archive site.

Scriptural quotations are accessible via the following URL links:

Bible: www.biblehub.com

Quran: www.quran.com

Hadith: www.abuaminaelias.com, www.sunnah.com

REFERENCES

[1]Descartes, R. *Discourse on method and Meditations on First Philosophy*. 4th ed. Translated by Cress, D.A. Indianapolis: Hackett Publishing Company, Inc., 1998. Pg 18

[2] Achenbach, J. *Carl Sagan denied being an atheist. So what did he believe? [Part 1]*. Jul. 10, 2014. The Washington Post. Accessed Dec. 25, 2020 https://www.washingtonpost.com/news/achenblog/wp/2014/07/10/carl-sagan-denied-being-an-atheist-so-what-did-he-believe-part-1/

[3] "Deity." *vocabulary.com*. Retrieved Dec. 25, 2020, from https://www.vocabulary.com/dictionary/deity

[4] NASA. *How Old Is the Sun*. Accessed Dec. 25, 2020 https://spaceplace.nasa.gov/sun-age/en/

[5] National Geographic Society. *Biodiversity*. Accessed Dec. 25, 2020 https://www.nationalgeographic.org/encyclopedia/biodiversity/

[6]Clegg, B. 20 amazing facts about the human body. The Guardian, Jan 01, 2013. Accessed Dec. 25, 2020 https://www.theguardian.com/science/2013/jan/27/20-human-body-facts-science

[7] Fine, G. and Irwin, T. *Aristotle selections*. Chicago, Hackett Publishing Company, Inc., 1927. Pg 177

[8] Lanza, R. *Does The Soul Exist? Evidence Says 'Yes'*. Psychology Today, Dec 21, 2011. Accessed Dec. 25, 2020 https://www.psychologytoday.com/us/blog/biocentrism/201112/does-the-soul-exist-evidence-says-yes

[9] Hameroff, S. and Penrose, R. *Orchestrated reduction of quantum coherence in brain microtubules: A model for consciousness*. Mathematics and Computers in Simulation, Volume 40, Issues 3–4, 1996, Pages 453-480. Accessed Dec. 25, 2020 https://www.sciencedirect.com/science/article/pii/0378475496804769

[10] "Is There Life After Death?" *Through the Wormhole*. Season 2, Episode 1, Science Channel, June 08, 2011

[11] Sky News, *Death by Pokémon Go? Game caused up to $7.3bn damage, claim researchers*. Nov. 27, 2017. Accessed Dec. 25, 2020 https://news.sky.com/story/death-by-pokemon-go-game-caused-up-to-7-3bn-damage-claim-researchers-11146310

[12] Baudrillard, J. *Simulacra and simulation*. Ann Arbor, University of Michigan Press, 1994.

[13] *Philip K. Dick Theorizes The Matrix in 1977, Declares That We Live in "A Computer-Programmed Reality"*. Feb 03, 2014. Accessed Dec. 25, 2020https://www.openculture.com/2014/02/philip-k-dick-theorizes-the-matrix-in-1977-declares-that-we-live-in-a-computer-programmed-reality.html

[14] Powell, C.S *Elon Musk says we may live in a simulation. Here's how we might tell if he's right*. The Big Questions, NBC News MACH Oct. 02, 2018. Accessed Dec. 25, 2020 https://www.nbcnews.com/mach/science/what-simulation-hypothesis-why-some-think-life-simulated-reality-ncna913926

[15] Bostrom, N. *Are You Living In A Computer Simulation?* Philosophical Quarterly, Vol. 53, No. 211 (2003): pp. 243-255. Accessed Dec. 25, 2020 https://www.simulation-argument.com/simulation.html

[16] Darwin Correspondence Project, "Letter no. 12041," Accessed Dec. 25, 2020 https://www.darwinproject.ac.uk/letter/DCP-LETT-12041.xml

[17] "Religion." *The American Heritage Dictionary of the English Language*. Retrieved Dec. 25, 2020, from https://ahdictionary.com/word/search.html?q=Religion

[18] "Religion." *Merriam-Webster.com*. Retrieved Dec. 25, 2020, from https://www.merriam-webster.com/dictionary/religion

[19] "Religion." *dictionary.cambridge.org*. Retrieved Dec. 25, 2020, from https://dictionary.cambridge.org/dictionary/english/religion

[20] Lynn Margulis. *New World Encyclopedia*. Aug. 05, 2015. Accessed Dec. 25, 2020 https://www.newworldencyclopedia.org/p/index.php?title=Lynn_Margulis&oldid=1013530

[21] Grovier, K. *Is football the universal religion?* BBC Culture, Jul. 13, 2018. Accessed Dec. 25, 2020 https://www.bbc.com/culture/article/20180713-is-football-the-universal-religion

[22] "Fan." etymonline.com. Retrieved Dec. 25, 2020, fromhttps://www.etymonline.com/word/fan

[23] Grierson, J. *UK Home Office bans 1,200 fans from going to Russia for World Cup*. Jun. 13, 2018. The Guardian. Accessed Dec. 25, 2020

https://www.theguardian.com/uk-news/2018/jun/13/uk-home-office-bans-1200-fans-from-going-to-russia-for-world-cup

[24] BBC News *Brazil referee decapitated after stabbing player.* Jul. 07, 2013. Accessed Dec. 25, 2020 https://www.bbc.co.uk/news/world-latin-america-23215676

[25] Cross, G. *Hellenization of Christianity.* The American Journal of Theology, Vol. 20, No. 4(1916): pp 606-609. Accessed Dec. 25, 2020

http://www.jstor.org/stable/3155556

[26] Guirand, F. and Graves, R. *The Larousse Encyclopedia of Mythology.* United Kingdom, Barnes & Noble, Incorporated. 1994. pp 54-55

[27] Dionysius. *The Mystical Woman and the Cities of the Nations.* London, William Macintosh, 24, Paternoster Row. (1867): pp 22-23

[28] La Châtre, M. *Nouveau Dictionnaire Universel* (New Universal Dictionary) Vol. 2. 1870. Pg 1467

[29] Caithness, M. S. *Old truths in a new light, or, An earnest endeavour to reconcile material science with spiritual science, and with scripture.* 1876. London: Chapman and Hall. Pg 382

[30] Bonwick, J. *Egyptian Belief and Modern Thought.* United Kingdom: K. Paul & Company. 1878. Pg 396

[31] Weigall, A.E. P. B. *The Paganism In Our Christianity.* New York: G. P. Putnam's sons (1928): pp 197-198

[32] Jung, C. G. *Psychology and Religion.* United Kingdom: Yale University Press. 1969. Pg 113

[33] Buzzard, A. and Hunting, C. F. *The Doctrine of the Trinity: Christianity's Self-inflicted Wound.* United States: International Scholars Publications. 1998. Pg XII

[34] Buzzard, A. and Hunting, C. F. *The Doctrine of the Trinity: Christianity's Self-inflicted Wound.* United States: International Scholars Publications. 1998. Pg 5

[35] *The Encyclopedia Americana.* Vol.3. United States, Grolier, 1985. Pg 700

[36] "Jew." etymonline.com. Retrieved Dec. 25, 2020, fromhttps://www.etymonline.com/word/Jew

[37] *Revealed: The world's 20 most expensive buildings.* Jul 27, 2016. The Telegraph. Accessed Dec. 25, 2020 https://www.telegraph.co.uk/travel/lists/the-worlds-most-expensive-buildings/masjid-al-haram-mecca-saudi-arabia/

[38]Ibn Ishaq, M., Ibn Hisham, A. *The Life of Muhammad: A Translation of Ishaq's Sirat Rasul Allah*, by A. Guillaume. Pakistan: Oxford University Press (1982): pp 85-86

[39] Ibn Ishaq, M., Ibn Hisham, A. *The Life of Muhammad: A Translation of Ishaq's Sirat Rasul Allah*, by A. Guillaume. Pakistan: Oxford University Press (1982). Pg 86

[40]*Malcolm X Pleased By Whites' Attitude On Trip to Mecca.* May 08, 1964. The New York Times. Accessed Dec. 25, 2020

https://www.nytimes.com/1964/05/08/archives/malcolm-x-pleased-by-whites-attitude-on-trip-to-mecca.html

[41]*Water Footprint.* Arjen Hoekstra & Water Footprint Network. 2017. Accessed Dec. 25, 2020 https://waterfootprint.org/en/resources/interactive-tools/product-gallery/

[42]*Words of Justice: The Writing on the Walls.* Harvard Law Today. Jul 01, 2012. https://today.law.harvard.edu/words-of-justice-the-writing-on-the-walls/

[43]Hart, M. H., *The 100: A Ranking of the Most Influential Persons in History.* United Kingdom: Carol Publishing Group. 1978.

[44]Michener, J.A.*Islam: The Misunderstood Religion.* Reader's Digest. May 1955. Pg 67

[45] Watt, W M. *Muhammad at Mecca.* Oxford: Clarendon Press, 1953.

[46] Besant, A. *The Life and Teachings of Muhammad.* Adyar Pamphlets, No.162. 1932

[47]Veccia Vaglieri, L. *An interpretation of Islam.* India: American Fazl Mosque.1957. Pg 28

[48]*Young India.* India, Navajivan Publishing House, 1981. Pg 304

[49] O'Leary, D. L. Islam at the cross roads: a brief survey of the present position and problems of the world of Islam. United Kingdom: K. Paul, Trench, Trubner & Company, Limited. 1923. Pg 8

[50]Wells, H. G. The Outline of History. United Kingdom: Macmillan. 1925. Pg 275

[51]Irving, W. 1783-1859. *Life of Mahomet.* London: J. M. Dent & Sons, Ltd., 1920. Pg 232

[52]Dods, M. *Mohammed, Buddha, and Christ: four lectures on natural and revealed religion.* London: Hodder and Stoughton. (1905): pp 17-18

[53] Carlyle, T., MacMechan, A. *On heroes, hero-worship, and the heroic in history.* Boston: Ginn & Co. 1901 Pg 50

[54] Lane-Poole, S. *The speeches & table-talk of the prophet Mohammad.* London: Macmillan & Co. (1882): pp xlvi – xlvii

[55] Smith, R. Bosworth (Reginald Bosworth). Mohammed and Mohammedanism: lectures delivered at the Royal Institution of Great Britain in February and March 1874. London: Smith, Elder, & Co. 1874

[56] de Lamartine, A. *History of Turkey.* Translated from French. D. Appleton & Co. New York: 1855

[57] Britannica, The Editors of Encyclopaedia. "Pharaoh". *Encyclopedia Britannica.* Aug. 20, 2020, Accessed Dec. 25, 2020 https://www.britannica.com/topic/pharaoh

[58] Hoare, C. *Egypt bombshell: How body of ancient pharaoh was discovered 'intact' by archaeologists.* The DailyExpress. Jul.29. 2019. Accessed Dec. 25, 2020 https://www.express.co.uk/news/world/1158280/egypt-pharaoh-body-ramses-II-intact-valley-kings-tony-robinson-channel-5-spt

[59] American Society of Plastic Surgeons. *Americans Spent More than $16.5 Billion on Cosmetic Plastic Surgery in 2018.* Apr. 18, 2019. Accessed Dec. 25, 2020 https://www.plasticsurgery.org/news/press-releases/americans-spent-more-than-16-billion-on-cosmetic-plastic-surgery-in-2018

[60] *A Meeting with the Universe: Science Discoveries from the Space Program.* United States, National Aeronautics and Space Administration. 1981. Pg 70

[61] Zampa, M. *65% of Earth Is Unexplored.* Sentient Media. May. 18, 2018. Accessed Dec. 25, 2020 https://sentientmedia.org/earth-is-unexplored/

[62] Nuwer, R. *Anthropology: The sad truth about uncontacted tribes.* BBC Future. Aug. 04, 2014. Accessed Dec. 25, 2020 https://www.bbc.com/future/article/20140804-sad-truth-of-uncontacted-tribes

[63] Nuwer, R. *The last unmapped places on Earth.* BBC Future. Nov. 28, 2014. Accessed Dec. 25, 2020 https://www.bbc.com/future/article/20140804-sad-truth-of-uncontacted-tribes

[64] *NASA Sees Fields of Green Spring up in Saudi Arabia.* NASA Earth. Mar. 29, 2012. Accessed Dec. 25, 2020 https://www.nasa.gov/topics/earth/features/saudi-green.html

[65] Gardner, F. *Tusk clue to Saudi desert's green past.* BBC News. Accessed Dec. 25, 2020

https://www.bbc.co.uk/news/world-middle-east-26841410

66 Gholipour, B. *Dogs can't speak human. Here's the tech that could change that.* NBC News MACH Jan. 11, 2018. Accessed Dec. 25, 2020

https://www.nbcnews.com/mach/science/dogs-can-t-speak-human-here-s-tech-could-change-ncna836811

67 *Your Dog Has Something To Tell You.* BowLingual website Accessed Dec. 25, 2020

https://bowlingual-translator.com/

68 *Samsung to Showcase Three Creative Lab Projects for the First Time, at CES 2016.* Samsung Newsroom. Dec. 30, 2015. Accessed Dec. 25, 2020

https://news.samsung.com/global/samsung-to-showcase-three-creative-lab-projects-for-the-first-time-at-ces-2016

69 *WELT Smart Belt.* Amazon. Accessed Dec. 25, 2020

https://www.amazon.co.uk/WELT-Compatible-Bluetooth-Healthcare-Measurement/dp/B078W52ZGN

70 *WELT Smart Belt Pro Wins CES 2020 Innovation Award.* Business Wire. Dec.19, 2019. Accessed Dec. 25, 2020

https://www.businesswire.com/news/home/20191230005107/en/WELT-Smart-Belt-Pro-Wins-CES-2020-Innovation-Award

71 Lipka, M. and Hackett, C. *Why Muslims are the world's fastest-growing religious group.* Pew Research Center. Apr. 06, 2017. Accessed Dec. 25, 2020

https://www.pewresearch.org/fact-tank/2017/04/06/why-muslims-are-the-worlds-fastest-growing-religious-group/

BIBLIOGRAPHY

1. Hisham, -K., & Faris, N. A. (1952). *The book of idols: Being a translation from the Arabic of the Kitab al-Asnam.* Princeton, New Jersey.

2. Kirkbride, D. *"Ancient Arabian Ancestor Idols."* Archaeology, Vol. 22, No. 2, 1969, pp. 116 –121. JSTOR, www.jstor.org/stable/41667956. Accessed 8 July 2020

3. Maurice, T. (1819). *The history of Hindostan: its arts, and its sciences, as connected with the history of the other great empires of Asia, during the most ancient periods of the world: with numerous illustrative engravings* (The second edition). Printed by W. Bulmer and W. Nicol.

4. Hitti, Philip K. 1973. *Capital cities of Arab Islam.* Minneapolis: University of Minnesota Press.

5. Ibn Ishāq, M., Ibn Hishām, A. (1982). *The Life of Muhammad: A Translation of Ishāq's Sīrat Rasūl Allāh*, A. Guillaume. Oxford University Press.

6. Sagan, C. (1977). *The dragons of Eden: Speculations on the evolution of human intelligence.* Estados Unidos: Random House.

7. Hastings, James; Selbie, John Alexander, Gray, Louis H. (Louis Hebert), *Encyclopedia of Religion and Ethics.* 1908-1926. Vol. 1-13

8. Deedat, A. (1981). *What is His Name?* IPCI, Durban South Africa

9. Nigel, D. *Human Sacrifice in History and Today* (1981)

10. "Diana." Britannica, The Editors of Encyclopaedia. Encyclopedia Britannica, May 20, 2020. Accessed Dec. 25, 2020https://www.britannica.com/topic/Diana-Roman-religion

11. Lewis, A.H. *Paganism Surviving in Christianity.* United Kingdom, G. P. Putnam's sons, 1892.

12. Adam. & Tschan, F. J. (1959). *History of the archbishops of Hamburg-Bremen.* New York: Columbia University Press.

13. McKenzie, J. L. (1995). *The Dictionary Of The Bible.* Ireland: Touchstone

14. J. Olumide Lucas, *The Religion of the Yoruba*, Lagos, C.M.S. Bookshop,1948

15. *Muhammad, Encyclopaedia of Seerah*. United Kingdom, Muslim Schools Trust, 1981. Pg 186

16. Ibn Khaldun. 1370. *The Muqaddimah, An Introduction to History*. 2005 Edition Translated by Rosenthal, F. Bolingen Series, Pinceton and Oxford, Princeton University Press

17. Adrian, T. and Shin, H.S. 2009. *The Shadow Banking System: Implications for Financial Regulation,* Federal Reserve Bank of New York Staff Report no. 382

18. Bentham, J, 1787. *Defence of Usury*. Published by the Library of Alexandria

19. Fisher, Irving. 1936. *100% Money Plan*

20. Alexis, J. 2013. *Christianity and Rabbinic Judaism: A History of Conflict Between Christianity and Rabbinic Judaism from the Early Church to Our Modern Time*. Nashville, Tennessee, U.S, WestBow Press

21. Fenton, Roger. 1611. *A treatise of Usurie*

22. Marx, Karl. 1843. *On The Jewish Question*

23. Weber, Max. 1905 *Protestant Ethic and the Spirit of Capitalism*

24. Durkheim, Émile. 1915. *The Elementary Forms of the Religious Life*

25. Kant, Immanuel. 1797. *The Metaphysics of Morals*

26. Durant, W. 1954. *The Story of Civilization Part 1: Our Oriental Heritage*

27. Smith, A, 1759. *Theory of Moral Sentiments*, London, A. Miller

28. Smith, A, 1776. *An Inquiry into the Nature and Causes of the Wealth of Nations,* 1904, London, Methuen & Co Ltd.

29. Emerson, R.W. *The Hundred Greatest Men: Portraits of the One Hundred Greatest Men of History Reproduced from Fine and Rare Steel Engravings*. UK, Sampson Low, Marston, Searle, and Rivington, 1879

30. Locke, John. *A letter concerning toleration* [by J. Locke, tr. by W. Popple.]. United Kingdom, Churchill, 1689.

31. Browne, R.W. *The Nicomachean Ethics of Aristotle*. United Kingdom, Bell & Daldy, 1889

32. Del Mar, A. *The Worship of Augustus Caesar.* United States, Cambridge Encyclopedia Company, 1900

33. "emperor worship." *A Dictionary of the Bible.* Ed. W. R. F. Browning. Oxford Biblical Studies Online. 25-Dec-2020. http://www.oxfordbiblicalstudies.com/article/opr/t94/e602

34. "Anu". Britannica, The Editors of Encyclopedia. *Encyclopedia Britannica,* 18 Apr. 2020, https://www.britannica.com/topic/Anu. Accessed Dec. 25, 2020

35. Armstrong, K. *The First Christian: Saint Paul's Impact on Christianity.* United Kingdom, Pan, 1983

36. Armstrong, K. *Muhammad: Prophet for Our Time.* United Kingdom, HarperCollins Publishers, 2009

37. Sand, S. *The Invention of the Jewish People.* United Kingdom, Verso, 2010

38. Maccoby, H. *The Mythmaker: Paul and the Invention of Christianity.* United States, Barnes & Noble, 1998

39. Wilson, B. *How Jesus Became Christian.* United Kingdom, Orion, 2011

40. Aslan, R. Zealot: *The Life and Times of Jesus of Nazareth.* United Kingdom, Saqi, 2013.

41. X, Malcolm. *The Autobiography of Malcolm X.* United States, Random House Publishing Group, 2007

42. Ali, Muhammad, and Ali, Hana Yasmeen. *The Soul Of A Butterfly.* United Kingdom, Transworld, 2015.

APPENDICES

Appendix 1

CORSU CRITERIA FORM	
Creator	
Origin	
Reverence	
Scripture	
Universality	
NOTES	

Appendix 2*

CORSU CRITERIA FORM	
Shinto	
Creator	None specified
Origin	Japan
Reverence	Kami
Scripture	Various texts – Kojiki and Nihongi
Universality	Not applicable
NOTES	
Shinto religion originates from modern-day Japan and is part of the family of East Asian religions. Due to its autochthonous orientation, it is not universally applicable.	

* Sample CORSU Criteria Form. The form can be used to assess any religion in the world. The rudiments of CORSU are in Chapter 11, and the ultimate objective is to determine the universal applicability of any world religion.

Appendix 3

Alphabetical List of Some World Religions

Agnosticism, Atheism, Bahá'í, Bon, Buddhism, Cao Dai, Christianity, Confucianism, Druze, Eckankar, Falun Gong, Gnosticism, Hare Krishna, Hinduism, Islam, Jainism, Jehovah's Witnesses, Judaism, Mormonism, Rastafarianism, Satanism, Scientology, Seventh-Day Adventism, Shinto, Sikhism, Spiritualism, Taoism, Theosophy, Wicca, Yoruba Religion and Zoroastrianism.

Printed in Great Britain
by Amazon